D0238611

Books are to be returned on or before
the last date below.

-8 DEC 2004

Commerce and Mass Culture Series

EDITED BY JUSTIN WYATT

Sure Seaters: The Emergence of Art House Cinema

BARBARA WILINSKY

Walter Wanger, Hollywood Independent

MATTHEW BERNSTEIN

Hollywood Goes Shopping

DAVID DESSER AND GARTH S. JOWETT, EDITORS

Screen Style: Fashion and Femininity in 1930s Hollywood

SARAH BERRY

Active Radio: Pacifica's Brash Experiment

JEFF LAND

Sure Seaters

The Emergence
of Art House Cinema

BARBARA WILINSKY

Commerce and Mass Culture Series

University of Minnesota Press
Minneapolis • London

The University of Minnesota Press gratefully acknowledges permission to reprint the following. Portions of this manuscript originally appeared in "A Thinly Disguised Art Veneer Covering a Filthy Sex Picture: Discourses on Art Houses in the 1950s," *Film History* 8 (1996): 143-58; reprinted with permission of John Libbey and Co., Ltd. An earlier version of chapter 5 originally appeared as "Demitasse Intermissions and Lobbies Hung with Paintings: The Techniques of Running an Art House," *Spectator* 18 (spring/summer 1998): 36-46; reprinted by permission of the University of Southern California.

Published by the University of Minnesota Press
111 Third Avenue South, Suite 290
Minneapolis, MN 55401-2520
http://www.upress.umn.edu

Library of Congress Cataloging-in-Publication Data

Wilinsky, Barbara.
  Sure seaters : the emergence of art house cinema / Barbara Wilinsky.
    p. cm. — (Commerce and mass culture series)
  Includes bibliographical references (p.   ) and index.
    ISBN 0-8166-3562-5 (alk. paper) — ISBN 0-8166-3563-3 (pbk. : alk. paper)
    1. Motion picture theaters—United States. 2. Experimental
  films—United States. 3. Foreign films—United States.   I. Title.   II. Series.
    PN1993.5.U6 W496 2001
    791.43'0973—dc21

                                                    00-010166

Printed in the United States of America on acid-free paper

The University of Minnesota is an equal-opportunity educator and employer.

11 10 09 08 07 06 05 04 03 02 01   10 9 8 7 6 5 4 3 2 1

For my parents

Contents

Acknowledgments

The phenomenon of the art house movement's growing popularity in the late 1940s raises many questions about why people go to see motion pictures. Several years ago, as an aspiring entertainment publicist, I was part of the system that encouraged film and theater attendance in New York City. I was consistently interested in what made people attend certain movies or pay a good deal of money to see a Broadway show. And although I had not planned this course of study, when I entered graduate school I quickly became interested in the whys behind film-going: why certain films are popular with audiences at certain times, why film exhibitors try to attract audiences in certain ways, and why people go to movie theaters. These are the questions that this study of art film exhibition has allowed me to explore.

Over the course of this project there were many people who helped me shape the questions to better understand the why of art film–going, people who showed me ways to answer those questions, and people who reminded me that sometimes you should just stop asking questions and go see a movie. Tom Gunning, Chuck Kleinhans, and Jim Schwoch guided this project at its beginning, and I am indebted to them for their direction and thoughtful feedback. I am especially grateful for Tom Gunning's friendship and generosity. Other people who (with or without their knowledge) provided insight, ideas, and encouragement include Tim Anderson, Amy Beer, John Belton, Matthew Bernstein, Karla Berry, Mike Budd, Jack Ellis, Karla Fuller, Barbara Goffman, Douglas Gomery, Julie Lindstrom, Debbie and Rich Neves, Pat Phalen, Julie Sandor, Eric Schaefer, Dan Streible, Alison Trope, Mark Williams, Mimi White, and all my colleagues in the Department of Media Arts at the University of Arizona.

People at the archives at which I worked, such as Robert Haller at Anthology Film Archives, Charles Silver at the Museum of Modern Art, and the entire staff at the Theatre Historical Society were incredibly helpful and patient. And, of course, I thank the art film exhibitors who took the time to share their memories and insights with me: Elmer Balaban of H & E Balaban Theatres, Richard Brandt of the Trans-Lux Corporation, Richard Stern, who now runs the Wilmette Theatre in a suburb outside Chicago, and particularly Charles Teitel, who ran the World Playhouse in Chicago. These art film exhibitors were responsible for exhibiting (and in some cases distributing) many innovative and exciting films during the post–World War II art house movement. I hope that their dedication to cinema and their interest in fostering a community around film-going will be appreciated and respected by anyone reading this work.

Justin Wyatt has gone above and beyond the call of duty as editor, colleague, and friend. Justin's steady enthusiasm for the project turned my concerns to excitement as he offered clear and insightful suggestions to expand my vision. This project has benefited from his involvement in countless ways. Moreover, Justin's good humor and supportive nature made revisions (virtually) painless. Similarly, Jennifer Moore at the University of Minnesota Press was enthusiastic and reliably helpful throughout. My thanks to Jennifer and to everyone at the University of Minnesota Press for their assistance.

Finally, I must thank my family. My sister offered her understanding as a writer and has been a wonderful friend. My brother and sister-in-law and their children offered me a necessary refuge from my world whenever possible. And I owe more than words can say to my husband, Sanford Selznick, who knew just when to motivate and when to entertain. His work ethic is an inspiration, and his support, humor, generosity, patience, and caring carried me through.

Although my parents still may not know all that they do to help, their encouragement and emotional support mean more to me than I can ever say. For giving me faith in myself, I dedicate this book to my parents.

The Image of Culture:
Art Houses and Film Exhibition

> The sure-seater has a subtle snob appeal that helps at the box office. You go into a theater that has a few tasteful paintings in the lobby and a maid serves you a demitasse of coffee. You've just paid top admission prices, but the coffee creates a pleasant aura. Then you're shown to a comfortable seat in a well mannered audience.
>
> The show lasts two hours; there is no Class C horror or murder mishmash to pad out a double feature program. You see a picture that assumes you have average intelligence and it's such a refreshing switch that you are flattered to be among such perceptive folks who are sharing the experience.[1]

As this quote from 1952 suggests, *sure seaters* was a nickname given to art film theaters. Initially, the nickname meant that patrons attending these theaters were sure to find seats. By the end of the 1940s, however, the meaning of *sure seaters* had changed. People referred to art film theaters as exhibition sites that were sure to fill all their seats. This change in conception of the art film theater undoubtedly relates to the atmosphere described in the opening quotation. Art film theaters were most often small theaters in urban areas or university towns that screened "offbeat" films such as independent Hollywood, foreign language, and documentary films. These theaters featured art galleries in the lobbies, served coffee, and offered specialized and "intelligent" films to a discriminating audience that paid high admission prices for such distinctions. And many of the people attending art houses did want distinction from their filmgoing experiences. These audiences searched for films and theater environments different than those offered at mainstream film theaters. Sure seaters offered such a difference, and in exchange art cinema became a considerable force within the film industry. According to the *Film Daily Year Book,* an industry reference guide, the number of first-run art houses in the United States increased from approximately 80 in 1950 to 450 in 1963.[2]

These years after World War II, in which art cinema developed, were important for the United States film industry. Film attendance declined, and United States courts, in the *Paramount* decision, ordered the film studios to separate from their theater chains. Changes such as these, along with social, economic, and cultural shifts in the United States, created a sense of uncertainty within the film industry. All factions of the film industry, from independent film producers to mainstream theater operators, faced these changes as they attempted to attract audiences and earn profits. At the same time, transformations within society resulted in changing reasons for movie going for many people. The interaction of social factors such as the cold war, the growing and conflicted youth culture, and the rising popularity of television with the shifting economics of U.S. society impacted the shape and meaning of filmgoing and art film–going.

Both Pierre Bourdieu and Herbert Gans offered an understanding of the relationship between socioeconomic class and culture.[3] Their examinations asked us to consider both how concepts of art and high culture operate in societies and the role of cultural hierarchies in determining how people use culture. Much of the existing historical research that has examined the connections between class, culture, and leisure importantly has focused on the development of the cultural hierarchy in the United States in the nineteenth century and at the beginning of the twentieth century, examining how cultural hierarchies developed and shifted through these turbulent times.[4] Other research, such as that of Andrew Ross in *No Respect: Intellectuals and Popular Culture* and Joan Shelley Rubin in *The Making of Middlebrow Culture,* has considered these issues in more recent times, including the years following World War II.[5] Jackson Lears, as well as scholars like David Riesman and C. Wright Mills, have focused on the particular role of culture in postwar United States society.[6] Lears examined how the belief that economic discrepancies were disappearing in the United States led to a growing emphasis on taste and culture at that time. This increased concern with issues of taste resulted in changes in the country's cultural hierarchy in which mass culture became a common object of disapproval, as illustrated in the work of cultural critics such as Dwight Macdonald and even some popular periodicals such as *Harper's* and *Life*.[7] John Belton's research on wide-screen cinema built on these ideas to illustrate how this shifting relationship between economics and culture influenced films and filmgoing. Through the promotion of wide-screen cinema, Belton explained, the motion picture industry attempted to offer people a way to differentiate themselves from others in the middle-class film audience.

Like wide-screen cinema, art cinema can be seen as an alternative that allowed art film–goers to distinguish themselves from "ordinary" filmgoers. Art houses offered an image of a more intellectual filmgoing experience. Attached to this image were notions of high culture, art, and prestige. Industrial reports on art houses support the idea that art house operators attempted to offer patrons a sense of prestige and status by promoting art houses as sites of intellectual, artistic, and high culture leisure.

Rising up as a new, emergent culture in reaction to changes in social values, cultural hierarchies, and industrial systems, art cinema shaped itself as an alternative to dominant culture. In his essay "Base and Superstructure in Marxist Cultural Theory," Raymond Williams defined alternative culture as "that of someone who simply finds a different way to live and wishes to be left alone with it."[8] With this as a working definition of alternative culture, we must wonder at the ability of a mass commercial culture, such as art cinema, to be "left alone." When profits rely on attracting as many people as possible, can an industry afford to remain alternative, or does it feel the need to become part of the mainstream in order to maximize profits? Although art film audiences might be interested in keeping art cinema alternative and exclusive, operators of the industry might constantly seek to expand their audiences. Despite the apparent contradiction, would industry participants attempt to "sell" the exclusivity of alternative culture to as large an audience as possible? Furthermore, how would the dominant culture, recognizing the potential profit from an alternative culture, try to integrate it into the mainstream?[9]

Exploring the emergence of art film theaters in the immediate postwar period, this study unravels the relationship between an alternative and a dominant culture. By focusing on the theaters that presented art films to audiences, we can demystify the art cinema as an alternative culture seen, at various times, as more artistic, realistic, and personal than mainstream cinema. Art cinema has certainly offered viewers some exceptional films and unique and exciting places in which to see these films. However, we must also remember that art cinema worked to create its image of difference for particular (and, oftentimes, financial) reasons. Operating within the cap-italist commercial film industry, art cinema is in constant negotiation with the mainstream cinema, a process that has ultimately shaped both cultures.

In the United States, movies considered art films tend to come from outside the mainstream film industry to satisfy the significant segment of the audience wanting more adult, intelligent films than those produced by Hollywood. By the late 1940s, an "independent" industry rose up to serve this market, and it created a space for itself alongside the conventional film industry. Films like *The Bicycle Thief* (Vittorio De Sica, 1948), *The Red Shoes* (Michael Powell and Emeric Pressburger, 1948), *Wild Strawberries* (Ingmar Bergman, 1957), *And God Created Woman* (Roger Vadim, 1956), *8½* (Federico Fellini, 1963), and many others illustrated the potential of "alterna-tive" films. Even Hollywood funneled some of its more mature films through art cinema channels (for example, *A Raisin in the Sun* [Daniel Petrie, 1961] played in many art houses in the South).[10] By the mid- to late 1950s, Hollywood discovered this potentially successful market and usurped it as its own, producing adult films such as *The Man with the Golden Arm* (Otto Preminger, 1955), *Paths of Glory* (Stanley Kubrick, 1957), and *The Defiant Ones* (Stanley Kramer, 1958) for intelligent audiences. The major studios eventually "commercialized" art cinema and produced "art films" that might appeal to the mass audience. By the 1960s and 1970s many of the themes and techniques of the art films of the 1940s and 1950s were taken up in making mainstream films.

Recently, major film companies have associated themselves with art films. Films such as *Life Is Beautiful* (an Italian film distributed in the United States by Miramax in 1997), *The Full Monty* (produced in the United Kingdom and distributed in the United States by 20th Century-Fox in 1997), and *Eyes Wide Shut* (co-produced by companies in the United States and the United Kingdom and distributed in the United States by Warner Bros. in 1999) might be considered art films that mainstream Hollywood distributors marketed to the mass audience. Much is also made of Hollywood studios' buying out independent film producers and distrib-utors.[11] For example, Miramax Films, one of the largest U.S. independent film distributors, is now a subsidiary of Disney Interfinance Corporation. It appears as though many art films (or seemingly independent films) are actually connected to Hollywood studios. Current periodicals run articles about Hollywood's attempts to exploit the art film niche.[12] The studios probably are interested in expanding the audience for art films—and this perhaps makes these films less alternative according to Williams's defini-tion. However, we must wonder whether this is really any different from what the "independent" art cinema industry wanted, but did not have the resources to achieve. In other words, was the art film industry ever interested in being an alternative culture that was "left alone," or was it simply interested in its *image* of exclusivity? Did art house operators, perhaps, exploit the appeal of being part of an alternative culture detached from concerns about the mass audience, yet market this distinction to as many people as possible? Since at least the 1940s, art cinema has balanced its desire for difference and its desire for maximum profits. The motivations behind and the impact of this balancing act are revealed when we look at the relationship between postwar art houses and the mainstream film industry.

In addition to influencing the practices of the mainstream industry, art cinema, as an alternative culture, also affected how people think about film. Art cinema both emerged from and impacted the changing conceptions about the value of film as an art form, the cultural role of motion pictures, and the legitimacy of film censorship. In 1952, a case concerning the exhibition of the Italian film *The Miracle* resulted in the Supreme Court's determining that "it cannot be doubted that motion pictures are a significant medium for the communication of ideas."[13] This decision began a chain of court rulings throughout the 1950s and 1960s that extended protection under the first and fourteenth amendments of the Constitution to films and reversed the 1915 court decision that deemed motion pictures "a business pure and simple, originated and conducted for profit."[14] The 1950s court decisions, which elevated motion pictures to a form of art, reflected larger social changes in the values ascribed to film. In 1955 *Newsweek* commented on the shifting role of filmgoing in U.S. culture, running an article entitled "How Do You See the Movies? As Entertainment and Offensive at Times or as Candid Art?"[15] Although the study of movies in college classrooms is commonplace today, in the 1940s this type of serious consideration of film was quite rare. Art cinema influenced audiences' understandings of what cinema should and could be. The image of prestige and culture associated with films by the art cinema industry, particularly art film theaters, helped elevate cinema to the level of an art form and encouraged people to think of film as something more than "mere" entertainment. Thomas Elsaesser discussed the impact that art cinema had on the academic study of motion pictures as well as its effect on U.S. filmmakers such as Martin Scorsese and Woody Allen. He wrote, "Without the European art and auteur cinema, film studies might never have found a home in American universities."[16] Another example of the way art cinema was seen to influence people's perceptions of filmgoing is illustrated in a 1966 article from New York's *World Journal Tribune* in which Edward Schuman, an executive with a New York theater circuit, commented on the new type of filmgoing. Schuman said: "It's different from the days when movies were popular family entertainment—the relaxing kind of pleasant thing that TV does today.... With more intellectually significant films today—the foreign imports and the serious Hollywood pictures—we get an audience that deliberately goes to the movies. It's like the Broadway theater. They go on time. They like a small place that has no popcorn and no kids."[17] Therefore, to understand how and why art film theaters positioned themselves within the cultural hierarchy is also to (begin to) understand how and why motion pictures came to be studied in college courses, freed from some elements of censorship, and considered one of the most influential art forms of the 1900s.

As the previous discussion illustrates, art films and art houses brought together industrial, socioeconomic, and cultural factors in different ways at various moments. We must remember that the meaning of the term *art cinema,* or the terms *art house* and *art film,* are not static, but change over time. To allow for a careful historicization of art cinema and to avoid generalizations, I concentrate on the postwar years of the 1940s. In its focus on the late 1940s, this study considers both the origins of the postwar art house and the emergence of the images and reputations that established the position of art film theaters in society. At this time, the meaning of the term *art house* and the practices associated with this type of film theater were taking shape; the focus and strategies of the art house movement were being determined. I end the study around 1950, when both the industry and the audiences seemed to understand what to expect from an art film theater. In 1950, the *Film Daily Year Book* began to list the first-run art houses in the United States. The attention to art houses within this industry reference guide indicates both that art houses were considered a significant element of the industry and that people were able to understand the term *art house* well enough to recognize which theaters belonged in this category. Jim Lane's recent essay on the Brattle Theatre in Cambridge, Massachusetts, which began showing foreign films in 1953, indicates that the Brattle's operators and its patrons had preconceived notions of what did and did not work when running an art house. The theater operators immediately advertised in the Harvard University newspaper, drew attention to the film directors in theater promotion, and used quotes from influential critics in advertisements.[18] These strategies, which seemed obvious to the Brattle's managers, became associated with art houses during the late 1940s. I focus on understanding how and why such techniques became mainstays of the art house.

Centering on the immediate postwar years also allows me to move away from the static notion of art cinema that privileges particular filmic texts as defining art cinema.[19] Most of the studies of the postwar art house movement, while significantly clarifying the qualities of art films, have actually focused on a certain canon of films (including films by directors such as Akira Kurosawa, Ingmar Bergman, and Michelangelo Antonioni). The independent or classic (though perhaps mainstream) U.S. films (by directors such as Orson Welles and Charlie Chaplin) or the films made in foreign countries or by foreign filmmakers (films by directors such as Vittorio De Sica, Carol Reed, and Marcel Pagnol) that dominated most commercial art houses immediately after World War II are often left unconsidered. However, these are the films that set the stage for later art films and prepared audiences for things to come. Richard Schickel recalled his art film–going at the University of Wisconsin, Madison: "Italian neorealism and the Ealing comedies from Britain had already opened our eyes to the alternative cinemas of other nations. And now here came Akira Kurosawa and Ingmar Bergman and the beginnings of the French New Wave. Not to mention Brigitte Bardot."[20] Furthermore, the films were often analyzed outside of their industrial and social context. Some scholars, such as Mike Budd, Peter Lev, Stephen Neale, and John Twomey, have expanded the notion of art cinema to include the industrial relationship between art films and the commercial market.[21] However, these studies still focused on the films—their production and their aesthetics—without considering how these films gain meaning from their exhibition context.

Our notion of cinema studies expanded as researchers such as Douglas Gomery, John Belton, and Gregory Waller began to examine the spaces in which films are seen. This analysis of art film theaters draws on and contributes to such research, focusing on only some of the possible avenues of consideration made available through exhibition studies. For example, I do not highlight the important geographic differences within the art house movement. Although art houses are discussed in this project as a particularly U.S. phenomenon, they did not have the same impact or role in different parts of the United States. However, because of the limited research that exists on art houses, I have found it more difficult to narrow the geographic location than the time period. Therefore, this study is not expressly limited geographically, though at points I consider the differences that existed in the art house movement in different locations.

Although there is no methodological concentration on any particular location, there is, due to the availability of material, an actual emphasis (particularly in the last chapter) on New York City and Chicago. This focus on two major metropolitan areas, perhaps motivated by the pragmatic accessibility of information on art houses from these areas, actually provides a rich background for the art film movement. Although New York cannot be seen as a model for the way the art house movement played out across the country, the important role that this city played in the development of art houses, as will be discussed, makes it quite difficult to think about art houses (particularly in the early postwar period) without considering New York City. The pattern of seemingly easy acceptance of art houses in New York is tempered here with examples from Chicago. As a major metropolitan area, Chicago was an ideal center for art house activity. However, Chicago also displayed signs of midwestern attitudes that rejected art films and art houses as overly cerebral and pretentious. Chicago illustrates the ambiguous position of art cinema, and that city's art houses provide examples of how these theaters worked to establish and maintain their place within a complex industrial, economic, and social context. However, although the information gathered on these two cities provides different perspectives and somewhat varied understandings of the art house movement in the United States, it should not be forgotten that the development of a more regional and geographic understanding of the art house movement would be an interesting and fruitful continuation of this project.

Within this study, I rely on various types of sources, most notably periodicals and interviews. I found writings about art houses from the postwar period in film industry trade papers (including *Variety, Motion Picture Herald,* and *The Hollywood Reporter*) and popular periodicals (such as *The New York Times, Life, Harper's, The Saturday Evening Post, Newsweek,* and *Time*). In addition to examining publications from the time under consideration, I also conducted interviews with film exhibitors who ran art houses following World War II. The art house operators interviewed include three men who ran prominent Chicago art houses. Richard Stern's family operated the Cinema Theatre, which began exhibiting British films in the early 1930s, making it the first theater in Chicago dedicated to foreign films. Stern now runs the Wilmette Theatre in Wilmette, Illinois (a northern suburb of Chicago), which screens predominantly art films. Charles Teitel and his father ran the World Playhouse, the first theater in Chicago to regularly screen foreign-language films. Teitel and his father also distributed art films in the midwest region. And Elmer Balaban and his brother Harry were the two youngest brothers of the family made famous by the Balaban and Katz theater chain. They ran H & E Balaban Theaters, a comparatively smaller midwest theater chain that included two Chicago art houses: the Surf Theatre, specializing in small British films, and the Esquire Theatre, offering a mix of foreign, independent, and "sophisticated" Hollywood subrun films. Adding to these perspectives was

Richard Brandt, currently chairman of the board of the Trans-Lux Corporation. Brandt joined Trans-Lux after World War II and was involved in the company's conversion of its chain of newsreel theaters to art film theaters.

Although this project examines how art houses provided less powerful film industry insiders with a market niche, speaking to these art house operators (and, in some cases, distributors as well) made it very clear that they were dedicated to promoting film as an art form and providing audiences with high-quality entertainment. Business motivations existed, but these certainly did not preclude (or precede) the sincere commitment of art house operators, as well as other art film industry participants, to art house culture. Additionally, these interviews provided me with a sense of the tight community that evolved around the art film industry. All of the interviewees were acquainted with (and probably had done business with) one another. The small size of the art film industry and the warmth with which the interviewees spoke of the art film culture suggests the bond formed by their participation in this unconventional and marginalized community. Both Charles Teitel and Richard Brandt recalled their experiences fighting censor boards to allow the screening of "unconventional" films. Elmer Balaban clearly displayed his love of the films he exhibited in his art houses, speaking of the films as if he had just seen them. And Richard Stern, still an art film exhibitor, expressed his satisfaction at providing his community with a chance to see nonmainstream films. So, although I discuss the business and marketing aspects of the art film industry, I do not want to lose sight of the service these exhibitors have provided. They have offered screening space for some very original and beautiful movies and a place for intellectual and cultural conversation. Their work has furthered the acceptance of the serious and critical examination of films, making this book possible.

Periodicals and interviews provide valuable information; however, they also present certain complications for researchers. It must be remembered that publications often reflect certain biases, whether a tendency to support certain industrial factions or to appeal to certain socioeconomic groups. I have attempted to account for such inevitabilities either by finding supporting material for information that possibly reflects such biases or by considering the information as a possible indication of a publication's economic and industrial interests. Other problems arise when relying on interviews about events fifty years in the past. I have certainly attempted to find material to verify what was remembered by the film exhibitors. As with my use of periodicals, though, when information could not be supported by other sources, I have considered the information as a memory and noted the significance of an event's being recalled in such a way.

The following chapters explore the issues of industry, socioeconomics, and culture raised in the previous pages. Questions of alternative versus mass culture, industry versus art, and actual conditions versus image are raised through consideration of how art houses attempted to find their place in the U.S. leisure culture. Beginning with an examination of the concept of art cinema in the industrial and economic context of the late 1940s, the first chapter asks the basic question "What is an art film?" Noting the ambiguity of the idea of both the art film and the foreign film, this chapter illustrates the importance of looking beyond the films to understand art cinema and paves the way for the following consideration of art film theaters as important forces for defining art cinema. Taking up the development of art cinema in the United States, the next chapter considers the context for the rise of art houses following World War II, looking at the mainstream film industry in the postwar United States and the historical predecessors of art film theaters (including the little cinemas of the 1920s and the later newsreel and upscale subrun theaters). Examining issues such as the changes in the postwar film industry and the worsening economic conditions for independent exhibitors, the third chapter discusses why art houses began to increase in number in this postwar period. The fourth chapter considers the influence of sociocultural factors on the shape and scope of art houses in the United States at this time, including the appeals of art, prestige, and culture as popular marketing tools for art house audiences. The ways these appeals were used to create an image of exclusivity and high culture for audiences is examined in the fifth chapter. There the actual techniques involved with running an art house are considered for their ability to build a certain environment for art film–goers.

It is this theater atmosphere—growing out of social, cultural, economic, and industrial forces in the postwar United States—that distinguished art houses and helped define art cinema as an alternative culture. Examining art film theaters as they existed at the time of their emergence as part of a unified cultural movement allows us to understand the relationship between alternative film cultures and dominant Hollywood cinema. Furthermore, art house culture reflected the business and economic interests of film industry participants and the desires and aspirations of potential audience members. To understand postwar culture and the role of leisure in U.S. society, requires an examination of art film theaters as both places of film exhibition and sites shaped by the country's social, economic, and cultural hierarchies. The unification of these different levels of study will ultimately provide us with a greater understanding of art cinema's role in society, the film industry, and the U.S. leisure culture both in the past and today.

1

Reading for Maximum Ambiguity:
A Consideration of the Art Film

In 1949 Otis L. Guernsey Jr., wrote, "At the moment Art seems to be any-thing a lot or a little esoteric, particularly foreign language films, quaint British comedies or American pictures that are old enough to have acquired the respectable green mould of antiquity."[1] In 1952 film distributor Joseph Burstyn said, "I hate the expression 'art film.' ... There are only two kinds, good films and bad films."[2] In 1984 Mike Budd spoke of "Art cinema, [as] a mode of discourse which differentiates itself in limited modernist direc-tions from the dominant mode of classical narrative, but which neverthe-less is produced and consumed largely *within* the commodity relations of advanced capitalist societies."[3] And in 1993 Peter Lev wrote, "At the risk of tautology, one could say that art films are what is shown in art theatres."[4] These very different conceptualizations of the art film and art cinema illus-trate that despite variations in definitions, and whether or not independ-ent film distributor Joseph Burstyn liked it, a category of motion pictures called art films exists, if nothing else as a discursive category. However, these disparate views on the art film also require us to question how cate-gories of cinema (such as classical Hollywood cinema, exploitation films, and art films) are created and why. These classifications, used by acade-mics, industry insiders, and audiences, are interesting in that they provide information about the type of film under discussion and also suggest an entire context of production and reception. For example, describing a film as a classical Hollywood movie not only provides information about the film's textual properties, but also allows presumptions about the film's production, distribution, and exhibition. Formal and industrial issues, therefore, tie into the categorization of films. To understand the role of art film theaters in U.S. society, therefore, we must also understand the category of film around which these theaters formed. Therefore, we begin with the question What is an art film?

The reconceptualization of cinema and categories of films by academics in scholarly writing and the creation of terms applied to films "after the fact" (such as *classical Hollywood cinema* and *film noir*) require that we distinguish between the meanings of these terms as theoretical constructs and as pragmatic industrial commodities embedded within particular historical contexts. The term *art film* is such a concept. It can be broken down in terms of both academic and industrially applied meanings. It is tempting to discuss the art film as if it is a static concept with a fixed meaning. Certain films by certain directors that display certain qualities are called art films. However, an examination of notions of the art film in the late 1940s indicates the different ways these films operated within the film industry and had meaning for industry insiders and filmgoers. It becomes apparent that the term *art film* as a practical and commercial concept within the film industry was (and undoubtedly still is) ambiguous and flexible. In art cinema, as in classical Hollywood cinema, the cinematic texts—the art films—not only influence, but also develop out of particular industrial and social relations. In other words, the art film as filmic text does not solely determine the functions, uses, and meanings of art cinema or how art films are produced. Rather, a synergetic relationship exists in which the industrial complex of art cinema, as well as its aesthetics, functions, uses, and meanings, contributes to the creation of art films.

Within the United States motion picture industry, dominated by Hollywood studios, the art film industry defined its films against classical Hollywood product and potentially offered alternatives to mainstream film institutions through production companies, distribution firms, exhibition sites, and film societies. However, the terms of differentiation between mainstream and art cinemas were quite unstable, since the commercial art film industry walked a thin line to provide filmgoers with products different from Hollywood films, yet not so different that they alienated potential audience members. Art films, and the discourse surrounding art films, focused on high culture and intellectual engagement to reflect shifts in

U.S. taste cultures and class hierarchies (discussed in greater detail in chapter 4). However, the ambiguities and instabilities found within the categorization of art films necessitated the support of an entire art cinema industry including institutions such as art film distributors, theaters, and film societies to set boundaries around art films and provide them with the desired meanings and values in the postwar U.S. film market. Therefore, beginning with a consideration of the art film allows us to tease out some of the complex issues relating to the role of art cinema and how art theaters helped to shape this role. Furthermore, this discussion demonstrates how the complications and ambiguities inherent in the attempt to define and categorize the art film suggest the important functions that art film theaters played in shaping the parameters for and the uses of art cinema.

Most discussions of art cinema have tended to focus on the cinematic texts. For example, in one of the most thorough analyses of art films, David Bordwell considered the formal elements (such as editing, mise-en-scène, and narrative) that unite art films as a "mode of film practice" falling somewhere between classical Hollywood cinema (with its subordination of all filmic elements to the narrative and the logical exposition of this narrative) and modernism (distinguished by a "radical" split between narrative structure and cinematic style).[5] Later work by scholars such as Steven Neale, Mike Budd, and Peter Lev moved away from the idea of the primacy of the text in defining art cinema. Neale wrote that "art cinema is by no means simply a question of films with particular textual characteristics."[6] This work draws out the importance of the web of institutional relations that produce art films. Budd explained that, "art cinema is not just a type of film, but a set of institutions, an alternative apparatus within the commercial cinema."[7]

Like classical Hollywood cinema, then, the art film can also be considered in terms of both its textual properties and its industrial context. The intricacies of this multidimensional position complicate the possibility of finding a simple answer to the question What is an art film? As I outlined at the opening of this chapter, Otis Guernsey Jr., Joseph Burstyn, Mike Budd, and Peter Lev presented four very different conceptions of the art film. An examination of two other definitions of the art film indicates the questions that emerge from such attempts at categorization. Writing about art houses in 1956, John Twomey offered a list of the types of films played in art houses (and films that could therefore be considered art films). He wrote that art film theaters exhibited "films from other countries, reissues of old-time Hollywood 'classics,' documentaries, and independently made films on offbeat themes."[8] Although Twomey pointed out that the majority of foreign films imported into the United States actually played in foreign-language neighborhood theaters (or ethnic theaters) and not in art houses, he did not examine how a foreign film was selected to play at one or the other of these types of theaters. Therefore, we must still ask What makes a foreign film an art film? Also, Which films rank as Hollywood "classics," and What is an "offbeat theme?"

In 1993, Peter Lev offered a more theoretical yet equally ambiguous definition of the art film, writing that "the term 'art film' refers specifically to feature films made in the post–World War II period (and continuing to the present) which display new ideas of form and content and which are aimed at a high culture audience."[9] Questions emerge regarding Lev's definition and its relation to Twomey's categorization. The most ambiguous elements of Lev's definition are the "new ideas of form and content" and the "high culture audience," which could mean different things to different people. Additionally, although Lev placed art films in a particular time period (films produced after World War II), Twomey did not. Is *The Cabinet of Dr. Caligari*, produced in 1919 but still shown in art cinemas today, an art film (as Budd suggested)? What about reissues of classic Hollywood films (included in Twomey's categorization, but not in Lev's)? Is *Singin' in the Rain* today considered an art film? Would the answer to this question depend on whether this classic Hollywood film displayed new ideas of form and content? What are new ideas of form and content?

Singling out the work of Twomey and Lev is not at all meant to suggest the particular inadequacies of their definitions, but rather to show how even the most thorough and useful definitions of art films are still incomplete. Clearly a discussion of art films requires a great deal more qualification and explanation than can be offered in one or two sentences. Undoubtedly, questions and complications would emerge from any attempt to define the art film. However, whatever the problems with a simple definition of the term *art film*, it cannot be denied that the term has meaning for many people. As Lev explained, some of the difficulties in defining the art film come perhaps from attempts to discuss the category synchronically—that is, atemporally, without considering changes in the meaning of the term *art film* over time.[10] A diachronic view, which Lev proposed, considers the art film historically. This historical contextualization of the art film allows an understanding of what *art film* meant at a specific point in time (and perhaps accounts for some of the differences found in the conceptualizations by Guernsey, Burstyn, Twomey, Budd, and Lev).

The consideration of the art film proposed here, like the rest of this project, avoids ahistorical arguments by focusing specifically on the immediate postwar period and examining what the category of art film included at that time. Additionally, I consider how people *of the time* made use of art film–going in their cultural lives, as well as how these people thought and talked about art films (how art films were defined discursively). For example, to understand what an art film was in the late 1940s, it seems important to know that Universal Pictures, which had both a general release distribution system and a special art film unit, was so uncertain as to how to release British films that it set up a theater in New York to test screen the films for an audience. Audience reaction then helped Universal determine which films could be distributed as general releases and which needed to be marketed as art films.[11] Our difficulties in defining the art film seem less surprising when we learn that even film distributors did not know exactly which films were art films. The financial and industrial decisions that went into defining the art film, then, were clearly more ambiguous than is suggested by the unchanging and concrete conceptions of the art film put forth by more theoretical, academic work.

Despite the contradictions in attempts to fix the boundaries of the art film, one characteristic generally agreed upon is that art films *are not* mainstream Hollywood films. In fact, it often seems that art films are not defined by their thematic and formalistic similarities, but rather by their differences from Hollywood films. As Bordwell wrote, "The art cinema defines itself explicitly against the classical narrative mode and especially against the cause-effect linkage of events."[12] Here Bordwell, known for his careful and sophisticated analysis of classical Hollywood cinema,[13] considered the manner in which art films differ textually from mainstream (classical Hollywood) films. Therefore, crucial to this examination of art films is an understanding of these films as alternatives to mainstream Hollywood cinema—not just in terms of their formal and thematic differences, but also in terms of their potentially alternative systems of production, distribution, and exhibition in the United States. An examination of the art cinema as "counterprogramming" to Hollywood films[14] encourages a questioning of how and why art cinema functions in the United States.

Toward this end of considering art cinema as "alternative"—which, as discussed above, involved not just being a separate culture, but also wanting to be separate—the following discussion examines three spheres of definition and differentiation for art films (particularly in the late 1940s): the form and content of art films, the national and industrial origins of the films, and art cinema's role within the commercial film industry. To illustrate these different spheres, I draw examples from three main film texts: *Open City, Lost Boundaries,* and *Tight Little Island.*

Open City, directed by Roberto Rossellini and released in the United States in 1946, is a well-known Italian neorealist film. One of the most popular art films of the postwar period, this foreign-language film even found success in mainstream theaters and is often credited with beginning the art film boom.[15] Set in Rome, *Open City* deals with the activities of a few members of the Italian Resistance and those who try to help (or hinder) them. Shot on location in war-torn Italy, just after the Nazis pulled out of Rome, the filmmaker frequently used natural lighting and location sets to give the film a feeling of authenticity. Some of the circumstances in the film even incorporated real events from the lives of people involved with the production.[16] After the war, a returning American GI brought *Open City* into the United States and arranged the film's distribution with independent foreign film distributors Arthur Mayer and Joseph Burstyn.[17] *Open City* went on to enjoy critical and (relative) commercial success, reportedly grossing approximately $1 million in the United States within a year of its release.[18]

Lost Boundaries, produced by Louis de Rochemont (who created and produced the "March of Time" newsreels), contributed to the "social problem" film cycle of the postwar period in the United States. Although perhaps not strictly considered an art film, *Lost Boundaries* was singled out by critics for its differences from mainstream cinema and for its artistic form. As an independently produced and distributed feature film, *Lost Boundaries* was expected to do well with the "better class of theatregoers,"[19] and it was therefore distributed to art houses. *Lost Boundaries* tells the true story of a light-skinned African-American doctor and his wife (played by white actors Mel Ferrer and Beatrice Person) who pass as white in a small New England community. The first half of the film explains why the couple decides to pass as white, and the second half examines what happens when the truth is revealed after twenty years, not only to the community, but also to the couple's children, who were unaware of their heritage. Shot on location in Maine and New Hampshire with few artificial sets, the filmmaker employed a number of local residents in small parts (the pastor of de Rochemont's church played the significant role of the pastor in the film). Although, as will be discussed below, de Rochemont began working with MGM on *Lost Boundaries,* he ended up producing it independently for approximately $500,000 and releasing the film through the independent distributor Film Classics.[20]

Finally, Alexander Mackendrick directed the British film *Tight Little Island* (originally *Whiskey Galore!* in England) for Michael Balcon's Ealing

Studios in 1949. This film exemplifies a very popular genre of art film, the droll British comedy, and illustrates the role of the English-language foreign film in United States art cinema. *Tight Little Island* also shows how a film representing another culture—Ealing Studios dedicated itself to representing British culture on-screen—could prove popular with U.S. audiences (the film had a run of twenty-six weeks in one New York City art house).[21] Shot on location on a Hebrides island in Scotland, the comedy focuses on the community of a small island whose whiskey supply is cut off during World War II. Desperate for whiskey, the lifeblood of the island's inhabitants, the community learns that a nearby ship is about to sink with fifty thousand cases of whiskey onboard. Members of the community work together to steal and hide the whiskey despite the efforts of the local home guard officer (who takes it upon himself to prevent the theft of the ship's cargo, even if it is about to sink). *Tight Little Island* (like all of Ealing's films at this time) was released by J. Arthur Rank and distributed to art houses in the United States by Universal Pictures-International.

These brief synopses open the door for a consideration of these films as art films, a consideration that includes a closer examination not only of the films' textual properties, but also of the films' commercial and industrial contexts. This analysis of the art film begins with a consideration of the form and content of art films. Looking at the style of these films allows us to see how they were, and were believed to be, different from Hollywood films. Next I explore how the national and industrial origins of films impacted their role in art cinema. As discussed, foreign films were strongly associated with art cinema, but, as we shall see, different nationalities played different roles in the art film industry. Similarly, modes of production and distribution of films (independently produced and distributed films, reissues of classic films, films with connections to major studios) affected not only films' textual properties, but also how they were thought about in the art cinema field. Finally, I look at the relationship between art films and commercialism. Examining the place of art films in the commercial sphere of the film industry allows a greater understanding of how art films were viewed in terms of their commercial potential, yet also separated from the "commercial" Hollywood industry. A consideration of all these elements—form/content, national and industrial origins, and the art films' role in the commercial industry—highlights a major tension within art cinema: the tension between the art and the business of the U.S. film industry.

The Form/Content of Art Films

As mentioned earlier, the form and content of art films tend to dominate discussions of art cinema. The more recent work on art films has generally focused on the unique form and themes that group art films together and allow their distinction from classical Hollywood cinema. Mainstream cinema, for example, subordinates all formal elements to narrative; it is marked by the foregrounding of one or two heroes psychologically motivated to achieve very specific and clear goals. Additionally, a chain of cause and effect dominates the narrative of the classical film, which allows the viewer to clearly follow the story and character motivation.[22]

Art films, on the other hand, are seen to be more loosely structured, working against the primacy of cause and effect in Hollywood films.[23] These films foreground the artistry of the auteur (the director conceived as author) and navigate between the subjectivity of the auteur and an aesthetic of realism, resulting in ambiguous causal linkages and motivations. Bordwell, discussing how these films embrace ambiguity, suggested, "When in doubt read for maximum ambiguity."[24] Comprehending the complexities of these films requires more participatory modes of viewing than Hollywood films. This fact, of course, does not deny that audience members "make meaning" from Hollywood films; however, the extent to which this meaning is guided by the filmmakers is considered variable. Consequently, art films develop a different relationship with audiences than do classical films. Robert Self has compared an art film to a puzzle that the viewer must solve: "The art cinema positions the spectator as a game-player for whom meaning is not given but half perceived and half created."[25]

It should be made clear that much of the contemporary theorization of art films is based on a later period of art films than is under consideration here. For example, Bordwell considered films such as *Wild Strawberries* (Ingmar Bergman, 1957), *Jules and Jim* (François Truffaut, 1961) and *8½* (Federico Fellini, 1963), whereas Pamela Falkenberg compared Jean-Luc Godard's 1959 *À bout de souffle* and Jim McBride's 1983 United States remake of the film *Breathless*.[26] Clearly the same theoretical statements about art films are more difficult to attach to the major art films of the late 1940s (such as Italian neorealist films and droll British comedies), though they certainly apply in some ways. Critics like André Bazin have noted the increased ambiguity found in Italian neorealist films. Through the use of deep focus and the long shot, neorealist films give the viewer more freedom to determine where to look within a frame. According to Charles Barr, even *Tight Little Island* does not emphasize the main point of the scene through camera work and editing. Noting the scene in which the town's postmaster blackmails a British officer into helping to steal the whiskey, Barr noted that audience members work to follow the film: "[The viewer] has to comprehend ... a continuous interplay of motives and perceptions, and the process—because of the amount that is left unsaid and unsignposted—is an active one akin to that which faces the characters themselves."[27] The lack of "signposting" often found in classical-style films, the use of editing, camera positioning, or camera movement to highlight the important elements of the scene, makes the experience of watching this film a more active one for audiences, Barr argued; audience members must work to keep up and figure out what is happening in such films.

Although the art films of the post–World War period may be considered more participatory, an association with "realism" most strongly assured a film screen time in an art film theater. The term *realism* means various things when applied to art films. Though the meaning of the term *realism* is ambiguous, it is always meant to imply something different from mainstream cinema's illusion of reality. The confusion about the "realistic" nature of film undoubtedly reflects the various theoretical and cultural uses of the term and the misinterpretations of these applications. Realism, for example, has frequently been associated with naturalism in drama (in the work of Henrik Ibsen, August Strindberg, and Emile Zola), acting (Konstantin Stanislavsky's "method" acting), and art (particularly in France in the mid-1800s). Forms of realism have been defined as the tendency to deal seriously with the problems of the lower social classes, whereas naturalism has been seen as displaying an interest in social reform.[28] Linda Nochlin has explained that the realist movement in French art in the 1800s was based on the "aim to give a truthful, objective, and impartial representation of the real world, based on meticulous observation of contemporary life."[29] Realists, according to Nochlin, emphasized "the low, the humble and the commonplace, the socially dispossessed or marginal."[30] *Open City, Lost Boundaries,* and *Tight Little Island* were all labeled "realistic" in some way.

Artistic and literary definitions of realism like those above most closely fit the Italian neorealist film movement. *Open City* (see Figure 1), shot on location with few artificial sets, little artificial light, and no sound equipment, and using improvisation of some dialogue for spontaneity as well as vernacular language, focuses on the problems of the lower social classes— the marginal, those who do not have enough food and who live in groups in small apartments, those who storm a bakery for bread. Despite its tight story structure and melodramatic moments, *Open City,* like most Italian neorealist films, also attempts to present an "objective" view of the world by observation of contemporary life. The film's form demonstrates an interest in objectivity, and the film's content deals with issues pertinent to Italians in the 1940s. Bazin wrote that a Rossellini film "lays siege to its object from outside. I do not mean without understanding and feeling— but that this exterior approach offers us an essential ethical and metaphysical aspect of our relations with the world."[31]

The scene in which Pina, the fiancée of Francesco, a Resistance fighter, returns home to find Manfredi, a hunted Resistance fighter, waiting for her fiancé illustrates the objectivity of style connecting this film with realism. In this scene, and the film in general, the filmmaker uses some classical Hollywood techniques in editing and camera positioning; however, the grunginess of the apartment building and the rooms as well as the unglamorous view of Pina and her life suggest the messiness of ordinary life, which is not sanitized for the camera. As Pina leaves the frame to get the key to her fiancé's room, the camera waits in the dreary hallway with Manfredi. A static, high-angle, medium-long shot allows us to experience the surroundings. The space and time of the scene are not fragmented through editing. And we, the viewers, do not see from Manfredi's point of view; we do not cut

Figure 1. Film still from *Open City*.
Image courtesy of the Museum of Modern Art Film Stills Archive.

into a close-up as he looks around, nor do we follow Pina inside to get the key, but we wait with Manfredi in the hallway. The film, as Bazin said, "lays siege to its object from outside." And here the object is Manfredi, whom we grow to understand from seeing him within these everyday surroundings.

The film's reviews in 1946 duly noted the unusual style of *Open City*, frequently comparing the film to a documentary. Writing for *The New York Times*, Bosley Crowther noted that *Open City* "has the wind-blown look of a film shot from actualities with the camera providentially on the scene."[32] Manny Farber, reviewing the film for *The New Republic* wrote, "'Open City' shocks you because of its excessively realistic look.... This has an appearance of actuality that you used to get in old time newsreels."[33] And *Life* magazine observed that *Open City* has an "earthy verisimilitude which will make many American audiences think of it as a documentary film rather than as a plain melodrama."[34] Clearly, *Open City*'s neorealist style distinguished it from mainstream films. This difference surprised and engaged many reviewers and allowed them to focus on this point of distinction as artistic, (successfully) encouraging audiences to see this important film.

Neorealism was not the only definition of *realism* that was applied to art

Figure 2. Film still from *Whiskey Galore!* / *Tight Little Island* (U.S. title).
Image courtesy of the Museum of Modern Art Film Stills Archive.

films in the 1940s. At times *realism* was used to refer to the use of location shooting. An article in the *Christian Science Monitor,* for example, proclaiming "British Film Goal: Realism," described the beauty of the English countryside and said it was ideal for outdoor and location shooting.[35] *Tight Little Island* (see Figure 2), for example, includes many picturesque images from the Hebrides islands in Scotland. Shot on location (as reviews noted), the film opens with images of the seashore, the horizon, people working on the shore, dogs on the beach, children playing in a cozy island village, images of houses with hills in the background. These striking images, shown while a narrator sets up the story, gives the film the feel of a travelogue introducing viewers to a real (rather than fictional) island community.

Other times, the application of the term *realism* to art films suggests that these films deal with issues and problems of the "real" world, as opposed to the escapist fare of Hollywood films. *Lost Boundaries* (see Figure 3), shot on location, based on a true story, and using local residents in small roles, begins with a narrator introducing the story as a "drama of real life." However, unlike *Open City*, which has qualities that liken it to newsreel footage shot by a camera capturing events as they unfold, *Lost Boundaries*

Figure 3. Film still from *Lost Boundaries.*
Image courtesy of the Museum of Modern Art Film Stills Archive.

feels more like a restaging of events for the newsreel cameras (in keeping with the style of the "March of Time" newsreels also produced by de Rochemont). The "sanitary realism,"[36] or what Bosley Crowther called the "re-enactment style"[37] of *Lost Boundaries,* comes across in moments like the one in which the narrator explains how, twenty years after their arrival, the Carter family fit into the New England community. An off-screen narrator tells us that Dr. Scott Carter is now one of the first citizens of the community as we see an image of him sitting in a living room chair wearing glasses, reading a newspaper, and smoking a pipe. Mrs. Carter, who we are told is now chairman of the town's Red Cross, smiles at her husband as she knits. Both parents look over to the piano, where "young Howard Carter," a college student and "promising musician and composer," sits and plays. Finally, we are introduced to Shelly Carter, well-liked despite not being "the most beautiful young lady" in town, sitting in front of the fireplace roasting marshmallows.

These scenes come across as recreated images of typical family behavior staged to work with the narration, not as the spontaneous unfolding of action before a documentary camera or even as the illusion of reality unfolding that classical Hollywood style offers viewers. Most important, the film, although attempting to restage "reality," features white actors in the roles of the black family members (a point noted only in *Life*'s review of the film). So, although reviews of *Lost Boundaries* connected this film with documentary filmmaking,[38] it certainly offers a different style of documentary than that associated with *Open City.* As *Variety* noted, "De Rochemont has given the production a straight documentary treatment, along March of Time style, with some loss, unfortunately, of three-dimensional quality."[39] Critics praised *Lost Boundaries* for its "realistic" handling of serious issues, for, as *Theater Arts* commented, "pos[ing] more questions than it answers."[40] *Lost Boundaries* was considered by some a "realistic" film because of its presentation of complex issues regarding the problems of African-Americans in the United States. The film does not suggest an easy answer for this black family that feels compelled to pass as white so that the main character can work as a doctor rather than as a train porter or a shoemaker. The film also attempts to present the views of the African-American community on the subject of passing as white rather than limiting the film to the point of view of white society.[41] *The Saturday Review* stated that "'Lost Boundaries' must be admired for its courage. It is another welcome proof of Hollywood's newfound willingness to treat adult subjects in an adult way."[42] Although this review associated *Lost Boundaries* with Hollywood (most probably because of de Rochemont's involvement), as I discuss below, it may have been the film's independent status that allowed its creators to produce a film offering an "adult" approach to the issue of racism.

Central to the depiction of the "real word," therefore, was the focus on mature themes and more complex treatments of stories. The depiction of drug use and torture in *Open City,* the questioning of law and regulations in *Tight Little Island,* and the examination of racism in *Lost Boundaries* helped categorize these films as adult films. Art films were particularly associated with a more forthright and explicit depiction of sexuality than that found in Hollywood films. Neale explained that Europeans considered film an art form and allowed films the same leeway as other artistic endeavors in terms of depicting risqué subject matter. This association of film with the "high arts" allowed European filmmakers to enjoy more freedom than their Hollywood counterparts. Neale wrote, "The consequence was that continental films differed—or were able to differ—from those of Hollywood with respect to representations of sexuality and the cultural status that those representations were able to draw on."[43] Therefore, *Open City*'s depiction of a woman pregnant before her wedding, two young women essentially working as prostitutes to maintain their lifestyle, and a lesbian Nazi did not result in the film's classification as a sordid exploitation film by most mainstream critics and intellectual audiences. Rather, the film was viewed as an adult and realistic view of the lives of Italians under fascist control. In a statement that would be taken out of context in advertisements (see Figure 10), *Life* wrote, "[*Open City*'s] violence and plain sexiness steadily project a feeling of desperate and dangerous struggle which Hollywood seldom approaches."[44]

This focus on realistic (or adult) themes and subjects (including sexuality) reflects the art films' shift from a focus on the mass audience to a concentration on the more selective (and select) adult audience. In 1939 foreign film distributor Joseph Burstyn wrote in *The New York Times,* "The audience for foreign films is still comprised of movie-goers seeking an escape from Hollywood escapism, people interested in unusual stories, mature treatment and realistic performances."[45] These perceptions lasted into the postwar period, as one New York magazine reported that foreign films' "themes and treatment differ, but the one thing they have in common is a basic assumption that the average movie-goer thinks and feels like an adult instead of a child."[46] This tendency toward "adult" treatment at a time when critics, such as *The New York Times*'s Bosley Crowther, accused Hollywood of having "run dry of ideas," encouraged the belief that foreign films were "better" than Hollywood films.[47] U.S. reporters actually asked

British film mogul J. Arthur Rank—in the presence of Motion Picture Association of America President Eric Johnston—why British films were so much better than American films.[48] Art films, therefore, established a particular relationship with their audiences. If not yet puzzles for audiences to decipher (as Self described later art films), the art films of the immediate postwar period did assume a certain level of intelligence and social interest on the part of viewers.

The move away from the mass audience toward a more select audience, impacted the relationship between art films and U.S. censors. Motion pictures in the United States in the late 1940s faced several forms of censorship, including industry-imposed self-censorship in the form of the Production Code Administration, religious censorship through organizations such as the National Legion of Decency, and governmental censorship on the federal, state, and local levels. Art films, with their more "sophisticated" and "cosmopolitan" subject matter, were believed to break away from the standards of decency imposed by U.S. censorship and offered viewers a more honest depiction of the world than was possible for mainstream films. However, some forms of censorship constrained art films and their potential for difference.

To avoid national governmental censorship, the Motion Picture Association of America (MPAA) established the Production Code Administration (PCA) in 1934 as a self-regulatory body to enforce a set of rules of moral acceptability in motion pictures.[49] Although in 1942 the MPAA eliminated fines and penalties against theaters that screened films without Production Code certificates of approval, the member companies (many of which owned large theater circuits) "pledged to maintain in their theaters moral and policy standards as exemplified in the Production Code and accompanying regulations."[50] Even theater owners not affiliated with the MPAA still used the PCA certificate of approval as a criterion for exhibition and refused to show films without the certificate.

The Production Code's strict moral standards left little room for art films, which distinguished themselves by their alternative style and partiality for mature themes. Some distributors of foreign and independent films chose to avoid the PCA completely, aware that the "realism" in their films—here suggesting possibly risqué content—would result in refusal to issue the certificate of approval. Richard Brandt, who was involved with distributing imported films for Trans-Lux, said that Trans-Lux did not submit these films to the PCA, explaining that Trans-Lux simply "felt it was unnecessary."[51] As a result, the tendency of many foreign films, and some independent films, to attempt a depiction of the "real world" severely limited their potential exhibition sites by disqualifying them from exhibition in theaters that required the PCA certificate of approval.

Realism and its focus on "honest" expressions of sexuality also incited moralistic condemnation from the Catholic Church's National Legion of Decency (founded in 1934), which rated films according to their acceptability (completely unacceptable films received a rating of "C" for "condemned").[52] Many theater owners paid careful attention to the ratings films received from the Legion of Decency and refused to show films condemned by the Legion (presumably to protect their images and avoid protests). As with the PCA, some film distributors avoided pre-screening their films for the Legion.[53] *Open City* was not screened for the Legion of Decency because the film's distributor was planning for it to play only art houses, "where an opinion about its morality was unimportant."[54]

Federal censorship focused on imported films. Before being admitted into the country, motion pictures were inspected by customs for any objectionable material. If a film was found unacceptable, depending on the extent of the objections, the government either required that cuts be made before the film was allowed into the United States or the film was returned to its country of origin without the option of having cuts made. For example, the U.S. government kept the French film *Le Diable au corps* out of the country for over a year on the grounds of obscenity before a censored version of the film was allowed into the United States in 1948.[55]

More common was regulation by state and local censor boards, which took active roles in determining which films could be screened commercially within their jurisdictions. A *Time* article reported in 1949 that "seven states and 50 cities in the U.S. still put up with official movie censors."[56] Films, whether art films or mainstream features, had to be screened for these government censor boards in order to receive a license for commercial exhibition. Without this license, the films could only be screened for private film societies and clubs. Herman Weinberg, who subtitled foreign films for U.S. release, explained that he subtitled films with the state and local censors in mind: "Sometimes I have utilized a dash instead of a word, leaving it to the audience to supply mentally the obvious word, which could not be translated. Probably the most widely viewed in this direction was in *Open City* where I turned *Ma che* ... into — em!"[57] Foreign film distributor and art house operator Charles Teitel said that Chicago's local censor board was particularly suspicious of foreign-language films and sometimes brought in linguists (usually priests) to determine what was actually being said in a foreign tongue.[58] Teitel recalled that the Chicago censor board was also very particular about obscenity: "They called everything obscene. That was their favorite word. Obscenity was a very big thing."[59] Though not submitted for screening before the Legion of Decency, *Open City* made changes for the New York state censors for commercial exhibition in the important New York market. The New York state censors told *Open City*'s distributors to eliminate the word *slut* from a subtitle and to cut a vial clearly marked "cocaine" and some of the more graphic torture scenes, the reasons for the eliminations being that the scenes were "indecent" and "inhuman" and "[tend] to incite to crime."[60]

In addition to the official censorship, implicit political and moral censorship—particularly after the Hollywood Ten were accused of Communist affiliations, blacklisted from the industry, and then jailed for contempt of Congress—generated concerns about charges of Communism and immorality. That political charges were used against films can be seen in the case of the Polish documentary *On Polish Land*. In 1949 the Maryland censorship board refused to license the film because the board did not "believe that it presents a true picture of present day Poland." Rather, the board held that the documentary "appears to be Communist propaganda."[61] Italian neorealist films were considered examples of immorality on the screen simply because of the known fact that many of the filmmakers were leftists or even Communists.[62] *Open City* even presents a Communist hero who dies an honorable death and is mourned by a priest. In February 1951, seventy members of the Knights of Columbus went to a theater in Queens, New York, demanding that a showing of *The Bicycle Thief* be canceled because the film "glorifies a thief."[63] Clearly, politics and issues of morality became a focus of concern that also influenced the boundaries of films with commercial aspirations.

Defined against Hollywood films, then, the form and content of art films distinguished them as more formally ambiguous and "realistic" and thematically mature. However, although these films pushed at the limits of moral acceptability, distributors' desires for commercial exhibition limited the risks these films could take—how far across the mainstream boundaries they could venture. For example, though it is not clear why the distributor changed the name of *Whiskey Galore!* to *Tight Little Island* for U.S. distribution, it undoubtedly related to questions of U.S. acceptance of a film title featuring the word "whiskey."[64] And, although *Open City* displays many stylistic differences from classical Hollywood films, it is considered the most narratively focused of Rossellini's neorealist films. With a focused story line and moments of high drama, the film clearly has a few main characters whose goals motivate the story. Of course, *Open*

City, unlike most Hollywood films, also illustrates how social and political context shapes its characters, but the mainstream elements of *Open City* cannot be ignored. It is hardly surprising, then, that *Open City* was such a commercial success in the United States, as it was the perfect film to introduce U.S. audiences to neorealist techniques, for the film was different from Hollywood films, but not too different. Therefore, the extent to which art films—as opposed to purely modernist cinema or avant-garde/experimental films, which mainly played for private film societies—could offer an alternative to Hollywood cinema was limited both by censorship and economic interests.

Art Films' National/Industrial Origins

In addition to form and content, art films can be distinguished from mainstream films by their origin both in terms of their country of production (frequently outside the United States) and the mode of operation dominating their production (usually not Hollywood studio production). For the most part, mainstream films in the United States in the late 1940s came from Hollywood studios or independent producers with major Hollywood distribution deals. Art films, on the other hand, often came from outside the Hollywood industry. The makers of art films, generally supposed to be independent foreign filmmakers or small U.S. producers working outside the Hollywood system, were seen as having greater artistic control over their work.

Although the origin of production seems the most straightforward method of distinguishing art cinema from mainstream cinema, this is the category in which one sees the most complications and confusion in the postwar era. Divisions existed *within* the types of films broadly categorized as art films (foreign films, independent films, documentaries, and reissues) that impacted their position in the U.S. film market. As Richard deCordova explained in his study of Chicago art theaters, "Not all films imported were exploited as art films, and even among the art films there are some important distinctions to be drawn."[65] Differences existed among these films that led some to be considered art films and others not.

Independent Films and Reissues

Independent productions included different types of films geared toward different sites of distribution, ranging from mainstream theaters to art houses to exploitation theaters specializing in the exhibition of films violating the Production Code rules (particularly in their use of language and their depiction of sex and violence). *Lost Boundaries* is an example of an independent production categorized by some exhibitors and audiences as an art film. Produced by Louis de Rochemont and directed by Alfred Werker, *Lost Boundaries* began as an MGM production based on a *Reader's Digest* true story (which de Rochemont originally suggested to the *Reader's Digest* writer). De Rochemont did not last long as a producer for MGM after the studio canceled the *Lost Boundaries* project. One newspaper report claimed that MGM chose not to pursue *Lost Boundaries* for financial reasons (the budget was too high, and the studio already planned two other films dealing with "Negro questions"), but another article reported that MGM and de Rochemont disagreed over how to "treat the story."[66] Though it is not clear how MGM and de Rochemont differed, it may very well have been over de Rochemont's interest in filming *Lost Boundaries* on location in the style of a restaged newsreel, as discussed earlier. Once MGM abandoned *Lost Boundaries,* de Rochemont got out of his contract and went on to make the film as he wanted. Film Classics, a company that mainly distributed reissues, distributed the film. Although mainstream film theaters exhibited *Lost Boundaries,* it was also considered acceptable for the art film market.

Foreign films also used various modes of production that influenced their art film status. J. Arthur Rank's production policies provide an example of a system that offered some filmmakers more freedom from the studio system. The Rank Organization included various operations, each with different modes of organization and different purposes. These ranged from the Gainsborough Company, a studio directly controlled by Rank, to independent units, such as Michael Powell–Emeric Pressburger's and Ian Dalrymple's units, which purportedly operated "independently" using money supplied by Rank.[67] According to an article in *Harper's,* Rank did not expect the independent units to earns profits; they needed only to break even. The article explained that Rank considered these units "experimental," whereas Gainsborough strove for mass appeal.[68] Certainly these differing attitudes toward the operations encouraged more experimentation among the independent units. Gainsborough's films, on the other hand, would be more likely to rely on familiar conventions expected to attract a mass audience and earn profits. Rank also financed Ealing Studios, which produced *Tight Little Island.* Although Ealing Studios retained creative freedom from Rank, the studio's ability to produce small films reflecting

British culture was at least partly made possible by its association with the larger studio, which provided money and guaranteed distribution for Ealing's films.

Other foreign films released in the United States in the immediate postwar period had similar freedoms from financial concerns, most probably because the films' producers never expected to make much of a profit. *Open City* began production even before Italy's film studios were rebuilt. According to Rossellini, when he shot *Open City* "directors had an entirely free hand; the absence of any organized industry favored the least banal undertakings. The field was wide open for innovation."[69] Freedom from studio structure made the production of *Open City* a difficult and financially unstable venture, but gave Rossellini the freedom to produce the type of film he wanted to create.

Certainly, though, not all independent films of the time were considered art films. Independent productions of B films became particularly important following World War II when, as is discussed in greater detail later, the major studios cut back on in-house production of B films.[70] Similarly, not all reissued Hollywood films were considered art films. Some reissues were general rereleases of "classic" films. However, other rereleases—for example, reissued silent or foreign films—played mainly in art theaters. In 1949 a group of art house operators requested that the major studios rerelease certain films only on a limited basis in order to make them somewhat exclusive and possibly grant them "art film" status.[71] Paramount was the first to respond to the needs of art houses, reissuing film packages on a limited basis, including a double bill of the Marx Brothers' *Animal Crackers* (1930) and *Duck Soup* (1933) and a double bill of the Marlene Dietrich films *Desire* (1936) and *Shanghai Express* (1932).[72] 20th Century-Fox also planned to rerelease a double bill of Will Rogers films for art houses (a move that certainly justifies questioning what was considered an art film).[73]

British Films and Foreign-Language Films

In his essay "Art Cinema as Institution," Neale foregrounded the importance of considering the industrial context of the nations from which art cinema emerges. Neale considered how the film industries in Germany, Italy, and France encouraged filmmakers to produce films that would differentiate national films from Hollywood films, resulting in art cinema. I would add to this argument that we must also consider how audience members in the United States received films coming from different nations.

Foreign films played a particularly large role in postwar art cinema, reportedly accounting for approximately 80 percent of art house product as late as 1958.[74] Discussing the meaning of the term *art film*, art house operator Richard Stern explained, "Years ago we called an art film, to an extent, a film that was from another country."[75] However, as deCordova described, both audiences and U.S. film industry insiders distinguished between British films and foreign-language films. On a very practical and basic level, British films used English dialogue, and, although audiences complained about the lack of stars, the "longhair themes," and the accents in British movies,[76] these films did not require the subtitles or dubbed dialogue that made foreign-language films less appealing to U.S. audiences. British films, therefore, had a greater chance than foreign-language films of playing more mainstream theaters.[77] The close ties between the British and U.S. film industries, discussed in greater detail in chapter 3, further encouraged the mainstream distribution and exhibition of British films in the United States.

The U.S. film industry and U.S. filmgoers also distinguished between different sorts of British films, as evidenced by Rank's U.S. distribution deal with Universal Pictures. Universal released "big Rank films" through its regular channels of distribution and "certain types of J. Arthur Rank pictures" for art theaters.[78] The bigger releases from Rank and other British producers were clearly categorized with Hollywood films. The Motion Picture Association of America's Community Service division even distributed promotional material for *Great Expectations,* an unusual thing for the MPAA to do for a "foreign competitor."[79] The difficulty in drawing distinctions between what would be a "major" release or a "prestige" release from Britain is illustrated by the fact, mentioned earlier, that Universal needed to preview its films to determine which should be marketed as art films and which as "regular" Universal releases.[80] It must be questioned, then, whether British films seen in studio-affiliated theaters and large circuit theaters (such as *Great Expectations,* which played in Radio City Music Hall)[81] should be considered in the same way as smaller British films (such as *Tight Little Island* or *Kind Hearts and Coronets*) or foreign-language films that primarily played in small independent art houses or in theaters of small art house circuits.

Foreign-language films, deCordova noted, "unlike their English counterparts, rarely entered directly into the main lines of American distribution," but rather needed to prove themselves with phenomenally successful art house runs before heading into more mainstream theaters.[82] Although, according to a *Variety* survey, Chicago filmgoers did not think of British films as foreign films, "foreign language product is forced into 'arty' houses or, where most of them are shown, foreign language neighborhood houses."[83] This observation demonstrates not only the complexities of understanding what people in the late 1940s considered a foreign film, but also the difficulties in determining which foreign films were considered art films.

Hollywood's involvement with overseas production following World War II made the category of "foreign film" even more murky. At this time, Hollywood studios and mainstream U.S. independent producers occasionally went overseas to produce English-language films highlighting foreign locales. Many of these films received mainstream distribution, and although they were considered prestige films, they were not necessarily considered art films.[84] An example of such a film is *The Search* (1948), an English-language film produced by MGM with exteriors shot in Germany and interiors in Switzerland. MGM had a difficult time marketing the film, as it attempted to strike a balance between the prestige of foreign films and the prejudice against them.[85] This phenomenon of U.S.-produced foreign films further illustrates the complications involved with using the terms *foreign film* and *art film* interchangeably.

How (and which) foreign films received art film status was at least partly determined by their specific countries of origin. In the immediate postwar period, Italian and French films seemed the most "successful" of the foreign-language films and the most likely to receive art film status. *Open City* helped generate interest in other Italian films. Meanwhile, films from other countries, particularly non-European countries, encountered difficulties in their attempts to be considered anything other than "ethnic films." *The Hollywood Reporter* took note of Azteca, a major distributor of Mexican films in the United States, which wanted to break into the art house circuit then "dominated by the English and European pictures."[86] European film, associated in the United States with high culture and artistry, also profited from the increased interest in European culture on the part of GIs returning from the war. Mexican films did not have these benefits. Azteca created a special division to distribute its more "high budget" films to art film theaters.[87] Apparently, Mexican film distributors had to fight (and shape their marketing strategies) to obtain art film status for their films (signified by exhibition in art film theaters). It can be seen, therefore, that hierarchies among foreign films based on their country of origin and their mode of production impacted the shaping of the category of art cinema. Additionally, these hierarchies generally manifested in the relative ease (or difficulty) with which films got screen time in art film theaters.

The Commercial Sphere

That some film producers and distributors worked to get their films cate-gorized as art films reflects the tension found in art cinema between art and business. Association with art cinema granted films, producers, dis-tributors, and exhibitors prestige and allowed the marketing of this prestige for profit. For example, according to *Variety, Open City* and *Shoeshine* were each expected to earn distributors a net profit of over $200,000, whereas the French film *Panic* was expected to earn approximately $185,000 in net profits.[88] By its fourteenth week playing in one New York art house, the British film *Brief Encounter* netted a total of $105,000 for its distributor.[89] However, despite the obvious commercial interests of art film industry par-ticipants, the making of art cinema is often imagined to be motivated by artistic rather than economic interests. The making of Hollywood films, on the other hand, is considered to be motivated solely by economics. Neale wrote that a basic difference seen between Hollywood films and art cinema is that "the former is the realm of impersonal profit-seeking and entertain-ment, where the latter is the realm of creativity, freedom and meaning."[90]

Certainly an appreciation of the unique and artistic qualities of art cin-ema motivated the association between high art and art films; however, these associations were also foregrounded for economic and sociocultural purposes. People invested in art cinema—from critics to filmgoers to those involved in the film industry—perpetuated this myth of the "noncommer-cial" art cinema. For the most part, periodicals (other than the film indus-try trade journals) mentioned the economics of the art film industry only when budgets were excessively low or grosses very high (as did the press with regard to *Lost Boundaries* and *Open City,* respectively). Focusing on the artistic aspect of art cinema gave critics an important position as arb-iters of taste who were helping filmgoers understand and appreciate these films. Filmgoers, as will be discussed in chapter 4, gained status from their association with high culture. And art film producers, distributors, and exhibitors each reaped economic benefits from appealing to the interests of audiences by distinguishing art films from mainstream films. In a recent interview, art house operator Elmer Balaban mentioned that his art house exhibited a film that did not interest the "commercial houses."[91] Even *Vari-ety* sometimes separated commercial cinema and art cinema, as when it reported that a new Universal Pictures distribution unit would handle "pictures that might die commercially but which would be appreciated by the audiences patronizing the arty theaters."[92]

In "The Production of Belief: Contribution to an Economy of Symbolic Goods," Pierre Bourdieu explained the economic benefits for art industries in "disavowing" economic interests. Giving primacy (at least discursively) to the artistic side of the field, according to Bourdieu, increases the "symbolic capital" and long-term prestige of the art object and leads to greater economic profit over time. Bourdieu wrote: "The opposition between the 'commercial' and the 'non-commercial' reappears everywhere.... Thus the opposition between 'genuine' art and 'commercial' art corresponds to the opposition between ordinary entrepreneurs seeking immediate economic profit and cultural entrepreneurs struggling to accumulate specifically cultural capital, albeit at the cost of temporarily renouncing economic profit."[93] Furthermore, Bourdieu suggested that this reliance on notions of culture and art emerges when dominated producers in an artistic field (such as the participants in the art film industry, subordinated to the mainstream industry) "in order to gain a foothold in the market, have to resort to subversive strategies which will eventually bring them the disavowed profits only if they succeed in overturning the hierarchy of the field without disturbing the principles on which the field is based."[94] Therefore, those involved in the art film industry found a niche within the competitive, Hollywood-dominated U.S. film industry. Promoting ideas of culture, art, and status allowed art cinema participants to increase (in the long run) the symbolic capital of their films and subsequently their economic capital. However, applying Bourdieu's theories to the film industry, it can be seen that the long-term economic benefits of symbolic capital could be reaped only if the art film industry—though finding an untapped niche within the field—did not attempt to alter the basic principle of the U.S. film industry: commercial capitalism.[95] To succeed *within* the commercial film industry as best as possible, it was to the benefit of art film industry participants to support the discursive separation between commercial entertainment and art through a disavowal of economic interests and a focus on artistic excellence.[96]

A consideration of the discourse surrounding art films in the late 1940s reveals the complexities of the role of economics in art cinema. Film industry insiders, for example, kept close tabs on how art films fared at the box office. *Variety* frequently reported on the economic successes of art films, running articles such as "Italo 'Open City' Freak B.O. in U.S.," "Average French or Italian Film Nets Only 20–40 G in U.S. Market," and "'Hamlet,' 'Red Shoes' Big in the Black Belie Yank Antipathy to British Pix."[97] Commercial interests certainly also guided art film industry participants. Pamela Falkenberg has suggested that art cinema's "primal fantasy is to achieve the same profitability as the commercial (Hollywood) cinema without thereby losing its elite position."[98] While perpetuating the mythic separation of art cinema from commercial cinema through her choice of words, Falkenberg foregrounds the commercial motives and desires circulating within the art film industry. Reports on art film distributors in the late 1940s have supported Falkenberg's statements. Many of these distributors aimed not just to supply art houses and other small theaters, but to find films that could break out of limited exhibition and cross over to mainstream theaters. Looking toward the future, foreign film distributor Leon Siritzky commented, "Some day soon, when great French pictures are imported, there will be a greater place for them on the regular American film market."[99] That his films were frequently relegated to art houses in the United States disturbed J. Arthur Rank, whose "intent was not to aim at a small, specialized market but rather to compete with the A films of the major studios."[100] Additionally, *The New York Times*'s profile of distributor Joseph Burstyn emphasized his economic efficacy by reporting that Burstyn "has a passionate affection for the film medium and a philosopher's outlook on life. But he also has a cool, calculating, commercial mind."[101] The commercial interests of the art cinema, then, were never completely disavowed even from within the art film industry itself.

Foreign producers also expressed interests in modifying their films to make them more "commercial." In 1948 *Variety* observed that the "French Too Get That American Idea ($)," reporting that French filmmakers intended to use U.S. and British film stars in their films to increase their international market.[102] And in 1949 *Variety* suggested that reports of the declining quality of foreign films might relate to foreign film producers' attempts to "emulate the b.o. success of Hollywood."[103] Although it is not definite that the use of better-known film actors or the efforts to increase box office potential prevented the creation of "art films," the interest in attracting a larger audience may have decreased the risks filmmakers took related to the form and content of their films. Furthermore, this interest in profits and in U.S. box office success certainly contradicts the traditional image of the creators of art films as artists working against the mainstream Hollywood system. The category of art film may be difficult to maintain in the face of success.

Producers and distributors circumscribed their intended audiences and the scope of distribution for their films partly through their choices about subtitling and dubbing. A dubbed film (frequently considered less artistic) had a greater chance of playing mainstream theaters than a subtitled film. Foreign film distributor Thomas Brandon explained, "Dubbing is urged because the producers and distributors think that by erasing the foreign language and substituting American or English voices a broader market will be achieved in the theaters of the United States."[104] Efforts to make "bilingual" films resulted in the production of two versions of the same film in different languages. RKO financed two versions of a René Clair film: the all-French and subtitled *Silence d'Or* (intended for art houses) and *Man About Town,* another version of the same film that included shots of Maurice Chevalier (the film's star) explaining the story in English. According to Clair, the second version (which he considered the less artistic of the two) was made for "those who don't like to read subtitles."[105] Art houses preferred to exhibit subtitled foreign-language films rather than the dubbed or English-language versions, since the "serious" cinephiles of the art houses preferred to think of themselves, according to Lev, as "cosmopolitan, nonchauvinistic spectator[s] who can empathize with characters from many nations."[106] The production of dubbed films or English-language versions of foreign-made films, therefore, clearly indicated the filmmakers' (or production companies' or distributors') interest in moving out of the art house circuit and expanding the exhibition potential of these films, the desire to break out of the small niche of the art film.

Furthermore, some filmmakers demonstrated their primary interest in profits rather than aesthetics by their willingness to conform to "standards of acceptability." Making cuts for censors helped them obtain more extensive distribution deals and therefore larger audiences. However, these cuts also potentially decreased the films' ability to deal with mature adult themes. Certainly, the many levels of censorship in existence (and the fact that in some cities and states films could not be screened commercially without a permit from censorship boards), made some acquiescence to censors inevitable. The importance of a New York run for an art film made it almost essential that art film producers and distributors adhere to the requirements of the New York state censorship board (such as the eliminations from *Open City*). However, some producers and distributors refused to make certain cuts required by national censors that would have allowed for the possibility of more widespread exhibition, instead choosing to maintain their commitment to their art—or, as discussed earlier, choosing to seek long-term financial benefits by aligning their films with high culture rather than popular culture.

The willingness of some foreign and independent filmmakers to follow the Production Code to get more bookings curtailed the differences between Hollywood films and some foreign and independent films. In 1946 the British Film Producers Association invited Joseph Breen, then head of the PCA, to Britain to "advise them on how they can conform their product to the American code before they begin lensing their films."[107] J. Arthur Rank readily made adjustments to his films to appease the U.S. censors. For example, in 1947 Rank shot a new ending for *Black Narcissus* to placate the Legion of Decency.[108] In 1950, the MPAA established an Advisory Unit for Foreign Films "to make available to foreign film producers the information, knowledge and merchandising experience needed to help them gain increasing audiences for their films in the United States market."[109] Although *The New York Times* reported that Italian filmmakers questioned the gesture, wondering "what changes will be necessary to make [films] 'acceptable,' and will those changes cripple the artistic quality of Italian film,"[110] sessions held by the Advisory Unit reportedly attracted forty-three producers from eighteen countries (more than half from Italy and France).[111] These foreign filmmakers indicated an interest in producing viable films for the mainstream U.S. market. Given these reports, clearly not all foreign and independent films were intended to be, or were received as, art films. Although some of these films were promoted as "regular," mainstream films, others were produced for and enjoyed within the ethnic theater circuit (discussed in chapter 2). Distinctions existed between foreign and independent films, making attempts at simple and unvarying definitions of the art film even more complicated and ambiguous.

Furthermore, the "realistic" and risqué elements of art films, in addition to providing art films with a more high-culture image, also provided critics of art cinema a means by which to question the commercial motivations of the art film industry. People opposed to art cinema—those within Hollywood, censorship groups, and even the art film industry itself—pointed out the financial benefits gained by art film industry insiders who exploited sexual content to attract audiences. In his autobiography, art film distributor and exhibitor Arthur Mayer wrote, "The only sensational successes scored by [partner] Burstyn and myself in the fifteen years in which we were engaged in business were with pictures whose artistic and ideological merits were aided and abetted at the box office by their frank sex content."[112] Similarly, *Variety* reported that, for foreign films, "biological lure is the strongest pulling force outside of the coterie of regular patrons."[113] As *Variety* suggested, imported films that reached beyond the regular art film audiences were believed to do so because of sexual content and exploitative promotion.[114] According to Eric Schaefer, this tendency to associate foreign films with obscenity and perversity is a strategy used by the U.S. industry since at least the 1930s to distinguish between Hollywood films and "other" films. Distinctions made between "the 'good' movies made by

Hollywood and the 'bad' films made by independents and foreigners served to reinforce the organized industry's cultural and economic dominance in the United States."[115] The "clean and moral" image of Hollywood films, Schaefer suggested, opposed the obscene and perverse reputations of foreign films.

That the mainstream U.S. film industry may have used morality to gain advantage over foreign films can be seen in the case of Vittorio de Sica's *The Bicycle Thief.* In 1950 the MPAA refused to give a seal of approval to *The Bicycle Thief* because of two scenes: one in which a young boy goes to urinate and the other a brief scene in a bordello. As Bosley Crowther pointed out in *The New York Times,* other Hollywood films that made use of similar scenes received the certificate.[116] The wide critical praise of *The Bicycle Thief,* along with the general belief in the inoffensive nature of the two scenes in question, led to rumors that the U.S. film industry wanted to discourage filmmaking outside of Hollywood. Joseph Burstyn, the film's distributor, stated that "Hollywood wants to discourage any picture made outside the film capital."[117] Crowther commented that "one is impelled to wonder after a case such as this of *The Bicycle Thief,* whether the only considerations are those of 'purity.' One cannot help but wonder uneasily whether the code has not here been used to support some parochial resentment toward alien and adult artistry."[118] The distributors of *The Bicycle Thief* refused to make the changes, and so limited the exhibition potential of the film (while also gaining publicity for the film and arousing curiosity in filmgoers).

The "sophisticated" and "cosmopolitan" qualities associated with art films, then, had two different effects on the understanding of art films as commercial products. First, by equating art films with high culture and high art, the "realism" and artistry of certain films allowed the disavowal of the economic motivations of art cinema and a separation of these films from the commercial industry. This tactic permitted the association of qualities such as status and prestige with art cinema and encouraged the long-term economic potential of these films. The adult handling of mature themes, however, also opened up room for these films to be attacked as perverse. To promote their own films and further their beliefs, critics from Hollywood and censorship organizations used the sexual openness of the films to both criticize the films and denounce art film industry participants for preying on lewd interests to make money. Art films, therefore, were seen to offer two very different alternatives to Hollywood cinema. On the one hand, art cinema was seen as "noncommercial" and artistically motivated, offering an escape from the brash commercialism of Hollywood. On the other hand, though, critics depicted the art cinema industry as actually more vulgar in its commercialism than Hollywood, willing to take advantage of any sexual angle to attract an audience.

This examination of the double-edged discourses surrounding art films—they were art yet still commodities, alternative yet marketable to a mass audience, different from Hollywood films yet somewhat similar—illustrates the complexity of answering the question What is an art film? The category of art film changes over time and is seriously affected by changes within social, industrial, and cultural contexts. Historicizing the conception of the art film is clearly essential for understanding this, and any, classification of cinema. This approach allows us to think about the art film as a dynamic and shifting concept created with pragmatic functions within the complex (and shifting) financial and industrial systems of the U.S. film industry.

Furthermore, this understanding of the economic goals that motivate art cinema requires a questioning of the characterization of art cinema as alternative to mainstream Hollywood cinema. Art cinema, like mainstream cinema, exists in and supports the commercial film industry and as such does not deviate from Hollywood cinema too drastically in terms of either business operations or stylistics. Art films are produced outside of the Hollywood studio system, but still aim to earn money. Art films push at the boundaries of "acceptable" morality in films, yet retain a level of "decency" that allows for their commercial exhibition. Existing somewhere in between mainstream cinema and experimental, avant-garde, or modernist cinema, art films are different, but not too different. Rather than accepting a static notion of the art film as an abstract concept, we become aware of the instability of the notion of the art film and it becomes clear that the entire art film industry was needed to ground the art film, define the term, and determine the values of the growing art film phenomenon. As the exhibition sites for art films, art houses helped to establish art cinema's image as well as its qualities.

Some scholars suggest that the basic variance that characterizes art films as alternative is not a difference in film form or in mode of production, but relates to the image surrounding the films: the ways in which the films are marketed and consumed. Falkenberg wrote, "The question of the art cinema ... is the question of its status, its difference in status and its status difference."[119] She went on to explain that the only substantial difference between an art film and a classical narrative film is the art film's "consumption by a particular social class as a status distinction."[120] Neale agreed that a level of taste discrimination surrounds art films that does not work to subvert the operations of the dominant film industry, but attempts to allow art cinema participants to find a niche within the film industry.[121] This niche, Budd wrote, is based on "a distinctive commodity fetish—a particularly prestigious, cultured and individualistic one."[122] Issues of class, status, prestige, and culture become important in considering the way that art cinema truly acted (and still acts) as an alternative to the mainstream, Hollywood-dominated film industry.

Although there are certainly very real differences in the form, content, production, and industrial position of art films, there is enough ambiguity about what makes a film an art film to indicate that this "fetish" of culture and art not only is created and found in the films, but is fostered and shaped. Art film theaters helped to create this aura of prestige, and thus the attractions of art films for U.S. audiences and the relationship between art cinema and filmgoers. As Bourdieu wrote, when class is so closely aligned with consumption, "places—galleries, theaters, publishing-houses— make all the difference because these sites designate an audience which ... qualifies the product consumed, helping to give it rarity or vulgarity."[123] Through location, promotion, and theater environment, art houses influenced the type of audiences who viewed art films, the reasons viewers attended the films, and the potential for these films to work as alternatives to the classical Hollywood cinema.

The next chapters consider art cinema as an alternative to Hollywood cinema by looking at the development of U.S. art houses and the ways in which art house operators attempted to attract audiences. How art houses helped to shape and define the values associated with art cinema, providing stability for the ambiguous and ever-changing understanding of the art film is also explored. Returning to Lev's suggestion (quoted at the opening of this chapter) that art films are those screened in art houses, it must be remembered that Lev warned against the tautology that can lead to the presumption that art houses can then be defined as theaters that screen art films.[124] Although, as the discussion of the art film shows, Lev's definition of the art film may be as adequate as any other one-sentence definition, the implied definition of art houses is quite inadequate. Operating an art theater required much more than screening art films. The position of art houses in the overall structure of the U.S. film industry as well as the significance of prestige and status to art cinema must be investigated to consider how and why art house operators mobilized certain concepts of high culture to carve out a niche for themselves, allowing, and perhaps requiring them, to walk the fine line between the art and the business of the competitive U.S. film industry.

2

Around the Corner from the Big Top:
Contextualizing the Postwar Art House

Arties. Longhair theaters. Sure seaters. These are a few of the names the trade journal *Variety* gave to art houses to differentiate them from more mainstream theaters. A central question rarely considered, though, is what actually made a motion picture theater an art house. Attempts to define and classify the art house, like the attempts to define and classify the art film discussed in chapter 1, were complicated. The complexity of figuring out which films were art films frequently fell to film exhibitors who not only chose films for their theaters, but also helped to imbue them with the status of high culture by screening them in a particular context. To move beyond the idea that an art house is simply a theater that shows art films, we must examine the complex industrial pressures that encouraged theater owners to seek out unconventional film products at this time, the reasons art films proved attractive alternatives, the influences that helped shape the form of art film exhibition, and the precedents for art houses. Before turning to discuss art film theaters, therefore, we first must consider the context out of which they emerged.

Mainstream Film Exhibition in the Late 1940s

Art film exhibitors in the postwar period existed within a complex industry that limited the success of any business operating outside of the studio-dominated system. Vertical integration and monopolistic practices on the part of the largest Hollywood studios helped maintain their dominance and keep independent exhibitors, like those running art houses, on the periphery of the film industry. To understand the context out of which art houses emerged, I will briefly sketch the situation of film exhibitors operating within the U.S. film industry of the 1940s.

The Big Five and the Little Three

Operating as an oligopoly, the motion picture industry was controlled by the major film studios, of which there were two tiers: the Big Five (Paramount Pictures, Loew's-MGM, 20th Century-Fox, Warner Bros., and RKO) and the Little Three (United Artists, Universal, and Columbia). The difference between these two groups of studios was that the Big Five were vertically integrated companies involved in all aspects of the film industry—film production, distribution and exhibition—whereas the Little Three produced and distributed films (except for United Artists, which only distributed independently produced films), but did not own major film exhibition chains.[1] Among the major studios, then, film exhibition separated the "big" from the "little" companies. The studios that owned theaters (the Big Five) derived the majority of their profits from film exhibition.[2]

To retain their position of power within the film industry and to control film exhibition, the studios did not have to own the majority of U.S. film theaters; they needed to own only the largest and most prosperous theaters in urban areas. Tino Balio has estimated that in 1945 the Big Five owned only three thousand of the eighteen thousand film theaters in the United States. However, Balio wrote that "this number represented the best first-run houses in the metropolitan areas."[3] The type of theaters owned by the studios is illustrated by Mae D. Huettig's comparison of the seating capacities of U.S. theaters in 1944. Although the average seating capacity for film theaters at this time was 623 seats, the average "deluxe" theater (most of which were owned by the studios) had 1,445 seats.[4] The smaller theaters were owned either by independent circuits (theater chains not affiliated with studios) or independent owners (individuals owning a small number of theaters).

Runs, Zones, and Clearances

The studios' powerful role in film production and distribution allowed them to maintain control over exhibition while owning only select theaters. Certain distribution practices markedly helped the studios dominate film exhibition. For example, the studios organized and regulated the industry by separating geographic regions into zones. Theaters within these zones were assigned to a particular run—first run, second run, third run, and so on—which determined how soon after a film's release a theater had access to a film. A first-run theater screened a film immediately upon its release. Once the film played out its first run, the studio removed the film from distribution in that zone for a set amount of time, known as a clearance. After the clearance time, the film would then be distributed to second-run theaters. Following the second run and another clearance time, the film then went to third-run theaters. This process continued until all interested theaters had played a film. In general, first-run theaters tended to be the larger downtown theaters owned by the studios. In 1944, Huettig determined that the major studios owned 126 of the United States' 163 first-run theaters, leaving only 37 independently owned.[5] The smaller neighborhood theaters (most of which were part of independent circuits or owned by independent theater operators) received films in their subsequent runs ("subruns"). This division of film distribution into a system of runs, zones, and clearances allowed the studios to maintain the larger share of the profits by establishing their own theaters as first-run theaters. These deluxe downtown first-run theaters attracted the largest numbers of viewers and charged the highest admission prices for the privilege of seeing new films.

Additionally, first-run theaters benefited from the promotional campaigns that film distributors launched for a film's opening. The distributors' investment in promotion diminished for the subruns. Therefore, subrun theaters generally had to prepare (and pay for) their own promotional materials or rely on word of mouth from a film's first run. As a result, a film's first run was important for establishing its reputation and determining its future grossing potential in later runs. The system of runs, zones, and clearances also became an effective way for the studios to retain their control over production and distribution as well as exhibition. Many independent producers and distributors found they could not get subrun theaters to exhibit films that did not have first runs. Since the studios determined which films received first runs through their affiliated theaters, the studios could limit the success of independent producers and distributors.

As Huettig wrote: "If most exhibitors book only those picture which receive first-run showings, then control of the first-run theatres is, in effect, control over all the others. Once the independent producers were denied access to the screen, the process of encirclement was complete: The major producers were also the major exhibitors. It was for them to say whose pictures would be shown."[6]

Other Distribution Practices

Additional distribution techniques contributed to the studios' dominance of film exhibition and limited the control of independent exhibitors over the films they rented and how they presented their films. Eventually these industrial practices would encourage exhibitors to seek out alternatives to mainstream Hollywood films, and therefore encourage the growth of the art house movement. Block booking and blind bidding, for example, helped ensure that almost all studio films would be rented by tying exhibitors to films they may not have wanted to rent. Block booking was a practice whereby the studios packaged films together as a unit for the purposes of theatrical rental.[7] The rental package of a grade A film (a high-budget film featuring stars) may have also included a number of grade B films (low-budget films usually without stars). Therefore, to rent the high-profile A film (which had potential to bring the theater profits), exhibitors also had to rent other less-than-promising films.

Blind bidding referred to the practice of requiring exhibitors to rent a film before seeing it and without the studio's providing substantial information about the film. Exhibitors had no way of knowing if the next Humphrey Bogart film or the next Bette Davis film was a particularly good film, but had to rent it before seeing it or risk losing the opportunity to rent it at all. These practices of block booking and blind bidding guaranteed that the studios would rent all their films regardless of quality. Furthermore, Balio noted that the studios did not apply block booking to any of the studio-affiliated theaters. The major studios' exhibitors, therefore, could consistently screen films of their own choosing, whereas independent exhibitors were strong-armed into exhibiting certain (low-quality) films.[8]

The method of determining film rental fees also maximized profits for the major film studios and decreased profits for independent exhibitors. When theater operators screened films that were successful at the box office, they found themselves paying higher distribution fees, thus limiting their profit potential. Film rental costs were usually based on a film's box office gross, with the distributor getting a percentage of this gross. In the

most common percentage rental agreement from the late 1940s (known as
the sliding scale percentage), the percentage collected by the distributor
varied according to the total gross: the higher the gross, the larger the distributor's percentage.[9] Since they had an interest in the film's gross, distributors frequently set minimum admission prices for their films, requiring
that exhibitors agree to charge these prices when showing the films. This
practice often meant that smaller exhibitors operating subrun theaters
could not even attempt to rent some of the "better" films, since they could
not ask their patrons to pay the higher admission prices set by distributors.
Price setting limited the access of smaller exhibitors to the most desirable
films while securing minimum profits for the distributors.

In addition to the controls over film exhibition that grew out of the studios' distribution practices, the major studios also determined the types
of films available to exhibitors. The major studios not only set their own
production schedules, but, through the Production Code Administration
(PCA), also influenced the content of all films intended for mainstream
commercial theaters. Members of the Motion Picture Association of America (MPAA) pledged to exhibit in their affiliated theaters only those films
that upheld the moral standards of the PCA. Therefore, films without the
PCA certificate or films that were not "as pure as films passed by the PCA"
were unlikely to receive screen time in the first-run, studio-affiliated theaters.[10] After noting the importance of a first-run showing for a film, it
becomes clear that although the PCA certificate may not have been a con-
tractual requirement for exhibition, certain systems of distribution and
exhibition certainly made adherence to the code an unspoken necessity for
a film intended for mainstream exhibition.

These practices of the mainstream film studios, which gave them control
over first-run film exhibition and film content, clearly helped to regulate all
of film exhibition and maintain the dominance of the major studios. Following World War II, however, changes within the film industry as well as
shifts in the socioeconomic structure of the United States affected film
exhibition. Importantly, many of the strategies of film distribution and
exhibition discussed in this section, including the system of runs, zones,
and clearances and the practices of block booking, blind bidding, and
price setting, came into question both industrially and legally. Additionally,
declining U.S. film attendance, changes in the foreign markets for films,
and the 1948 Supreme Court ruling requiring that the studios separate from their affiliated theater chains were only a few of the shifts that
destabilized the existing system of film exhibition. The specific effects of
these changes on the development of art cinema will be discussed in

greater detail in the next chapter; however, it must be recognized that unconventional modes of film exhibition developed within, and as a reaction to, this context of the studio-controlled, vertically integrated film industry.

Unconventional Film Exhibition: Models for Art Houses

The idea of providing unique spaces in which to show unconventional films did not originate with the post–World War II art house movement. From the 1920s several different forms of exhibition had been distinguished from mainstream exhibition sites such as the picture palace or the neighborhood theater. The nonmainstream exhibition environments that emerged within the context of the studio-dominated U.S. film industry served as models for the postwar art house movement. Little cinemas, ethnic theaters, newsreel theaters, upscale subrun theaters, and private film venues (such as film societies and museum showings) all influenced the growth and shape of the art house movement. Each of these forms of exhibition demonstrated the potential of art film exhibition and offered ideas about how art houses could operate.

Sanctuaries of the Cinema: Little Cinemas in the 1920s

Demonstrating qualities later integrated into art houses, little cinemas were the most decisive historical precedents to the postwar art film theaters. The little cinemas of the 1920s demonstrated the potential of establishing an alternative art film culture by setting up an entire industrial system around alternative films, distinguishing alternative theaters from mainstream theaters not just by showing different films, but also by establishing unique atmospheres within the theaters and, finally, by differentiating the little cinemas and the films shown in them from the Hollywood film industry on the basis of artistry and culture.

Growing out of several industrial and social factors of their time, two of the main influences on the development of little cinemas in the United States were the legitimate theater's own little theater movement and the French ciné clubs. The U.S.-based little theater/art theater movement promoted unconventional plays that could not find producers for or did not want larger productions. The ciné clubs were French film theaters that screened specialized films and focused on the artistic nature of cinema. These theaters, according to Kristen Thompson, "were typically smaller, depended on regular patrons rather than extensive advertising campaigns and paid less in rentals for films; they also often charged higher admissions than other theaters and attracted an elite audience."[11] The idea of showing alternative productions in small, specialized theaters was picked up by some people involved with the U.S. film industry who searched for a way to separate the "'big appeal' business from [the] 'limited appeal' business" of motion pictures.[12] Beginning around 1926, the year in which Symon Gould began showing art films at the Cameo Theatre in New York City, the little cinema movement spread to several large cities around the country. By 1927, nineteen theaters reportedly operated as little theaters either full time or on a part-time basis.[13] These little cinemas were mainly located in large urban areas; nine of them operated in New York City, two in Washington, D.C., and one each in Los Angeles, Chicago, Cleveland, Baltimore, Boston, Akron, Cambridge, and East Orange (New Jersey).[14]

DEVELOPMENT OF AN INDUSTRY

The growth of these theaters provided outlets for films that might not have found screen time in mainstream theaters. Although picture palaces screened *The Cabinet of Dr. Caligari* (1920) in its first release, the film became a classic when it was made a staple of the little cinemas. Discussing the initial release of *Caligari*, Mike Budd wrote that this film was an "art cinema text without the corresponding institutions of cinema reception— theatre, critical discourse, and a defined, perhaps even self-conscious, audience."[15] Therefore, the little cinema movement demonstrated that certain films found their niche within the industrial organization of art cinema. It was not enough to have alternative films available; an entire system of film production, distribution, and exhibition was necessary to create and support these films.

Little cinemas developed largely as exhibition sites for unconventional European films receiving little screen time at mainstream theaters. Anthony Guzman reported that from 1920 through 1929, at least five hundred features were imported into the United States from Europe. Some of these films were seen only in private trade screenings, and most were not seen outside of little cinemas in the major U.S. cities.[16] The European films available in the United States in the 1920s provided the product for an unconventional film culture like the one found in legitimate theaters and made the programming of little cinemas possible. With the financial success of *Passion (Madame DuBarry)* and the critical success of *The Cabinet of Dr. Caligari* in 1921, the major studios became interested in importing films from Europe. To counter the charge that Hollywood catered to the lowest common denominator, Charles E. McCarthy, advertising manager for Famous Players–Lasky, sent a letter to *The New York Evening Post* highlighting the important role that the major studios played in importing art films. For example, McCarthy noted that Universal Pictures released *The Last Laugh* and Paramount distributed *Dr. Jekyll and Mr. Hyde*.[17] By the end of April 1921, Adolph Zukor alone had imported 129 German features for Famous Players–Lasky to distribute in the United States.[18] In addition to the economic potential demonstrated by foreign films in the United States, the major studios also looked to importing films as a way of increasing friendly relations with countries then beginning to institute quota laws against U.S. films. However, as the economic success of foreign films in the United States fluctuated (and as the influx of foreign films, along with the loosening of the standards that went into choosing films to import, caused some critics to question the quality of foreign films), so too did the involvement of the major studios. The studios turned away from exhibiting European films in their own theaters, though they continued to distribute foreign films as part of distribution deals made with foreign producers.[19] Several independent distributors of foreign and independent United States films also emerged. Art film exhibitor Symon Gould went into film distribution,[20] continuing the strategy of film exhibitors distributing films to help keep their theaters full.

Without encouragement from the major studios, it was difficult to convince nonaffiliated mainstream theaters to exhibit foreign films. Most exhibitors considered the box office potential of foreign films below that of Hollywood product, if only because foreign films featured no recognizable stars to attract audiences. So, as the major studios pulled away from an interest in the exhibition of foreign films in the United States, the little cinemas became increasingly important for foreign film distributors as the primary potential exhibition sites for their films.

Independent exhibitors who developed little cinemas supported the importation of foreign films to encourage competition within the consolidating, vertically integrating U.S. film industry, decrease films' rental fees, and prevent the major studios from holding a near monopoly over film product in the United States.[21] Art film exhibitor Charles Teitel said, "In order for an independent [exhibitor] to play a film that hadn't had too many runs, they had to go to some independents [distributors], and the most independent films they could get were European."[22]

European films were not, however, the only films played at little cinemas. Operators of little cinemas also made efforts to promote independent U.S. cinema, as Michael Mindlin did at his Fifth Avenue Playhouse by sponsoring amateur film contests.[23] U.S. avant-garde films, seemingly distributed by the producers themselves or by amateur film groups, were often paired with European art films in little cinemas.[24] Little cinemas also found loyal audiences for revivals of classic films, and they presented rereleases of films by Charlie Chaplin, D. W. Griffith, and Fatty Arbuckle, as well as older nickelodeon films.[25]

Several types of supporting institutions developed to promote the artistic concerns of the film culture encouraged by little cinemas and art films. Groups and clubs interested in film as an art form grew in the 1920s. The National Board of Review, for example, "sought to encourage the 'Little Photoplay Theater' movement, both as a projection of the Better Films idea and as a means of enlisting the support for the motion picture as a medium of artistic expression."[26] Additionally, other "better films" groups around the country nurtured the appreciation of alternative films.[27] Amateur film groups, of which there were over a hundred in the United States and overseas by 1928,[28] encouraged both the production and the discussion of film as an art form. Journals devoted to the more theoretical and aesthetic study of film, such as the *National Board of Review Magazine* (originally *Exceptional Photoplays*) and *Close Up*, began publishing, advocating the serious discussion of European, avant-garde, and amateur films. And, as Budd noted, journals that previously had not paid much attention to film, such as the *Journal of the American Institute of Architects*, began printing articles about films, and more popular magazines, like *Photoplay*, turned from plot summaries to more complex and thoughtful film reviews.[29] These various institutions and publications helped support the little cinema industries by bolstering the perception of film as high culture. This image was further supported by the spaces in which the films were screened.

THEATER ATMOSPHERE

Little cinemas did not just provide spaces in which to see foreign and other unconventional films, but also offered audiences in the 1920s a different type of filmgoing experience. Writing about little cinemas, Harold Lefkovits noted, "It was the task of the new exhibitors not simply to procure these [unknown] films, but to create a mood for their acceptability."[30] In little cinemas films could be viewed as an art form and film viewers were expected to think about films in a serious way. As Peter DeCherney wrote, "the little cinema movement sought to make film into art and spectators into individuals."[31] In little cinemas, audience members would not be treated as a mass, herded through expansive lobbies as was done in the flagship theaters of the Hollywood studios, the large picture palaces. Rather, little cinemas created atmospheres to attract people who felt "alienated by Hollywood's appeal to the middle class."[32]

Generally small theaters (between approximately two hundred and five hundred seats), little cinemas offered a more intimate setting in which to see films, in contrast to the picture palaces.[33] Serving coffee and cigarettes in the lounge, management encouraged people to congregate at the little cinemas, creating a clublike environment. This notion of intimacy appears to have been quite important for promoting a feeling of exclusivity and belonging among the audiences of little cinemas. *The New York Sunday World* reported one account of the Fifth Avenue Playhouse: "An air of intimacy is fostered among its patrons and the gatherings in the lounge during an evening resemble more a social function than a group of almost total strangers."[34] Some little cinemas also exhibited paintings or sculpture, distributed programs similar to those available at legitimate theaters, and offered patrons the use of card rooms, ping-pong tables, and even small ballrooms.[35] Most little cinemas barred children from regular screenings, reinforcing the impression of these theaters as spaces for intellectual contemplation of the cinema.

Decor also contributed to the "elegance, dignity and charm"[36] of little cinemas. These theaters departed from the grandiose and ornate styles of the picture palaces, tending toward the modern. Writing in *Mayfair,* Julia Older commented on Michael Mindlin's Fifth Avenue Playhouse: "The theatre is tiny and cozy, the seats sufficiently upholstered, but the intimate touch is achieved in the lounge.... The lounge, which was decorated by Mrs. Mindlin ... is a charming entrance room. The high, slim bookcase of California redwood, perhaps the most striking furnishing, has the lines and subtle balance suggestive of the setting in 'The Cabinet of Dr. Caligari.'"[37]

The Film Guild Cinema, operated by Symon Gould, was also noted for its unconventional decor. Designed by Frederick Kiesler and opened in 1929, the Film Guild illustrated an innovative and experimental style of theater presentation (see Figure 4). Located in New York City's Greenwich Village, the Film Guild was promoted as the first space designed solely for the exhibition of films. According to Lisa Phillips:

> Kiesler referred to [the theater] as a "megaphone" design, planned for optimum acoustics and angle of vision. The traditional proscenium was abolished, and not only the floor but the ceiling as well were graded toward the screen, prompting some to compare it to being inside a camera. The

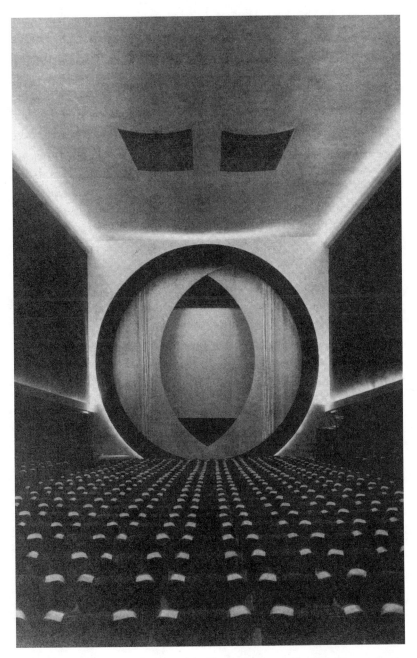

Figure 4. The auditorium of the Film Guild Cinema, New York City.

cinema was equipped with an eye-shaped screen, and a multiple projection system was planned but not realized. The modernistic architecture and decor created a stir: the glistening black exterior was punctuated by heavy white concrete lines; on the inside, black and white tiles covered the walls and the silver and black auditorium was bathed in pink and blue lights. Some found the austere modernism too harsh, bleak and coffinlike; others hailed it as a bold and daring design.[38]

This more modern design not only associated these theaters with the high culture of modernism, but also related to more theoretical interests in film as an art form. Theaters such as the Film Guild attempted to create an ideal environment for film viewing by eliminating distractions for the audience.[39] Writing for *The National Board of Review Magazine,* Seymour Stern explained that, to focus the viewer's attention on the film, the music must be hidden and all decoration must be removed from the auditorium. Stern wrote, "The audience should emerge from the cinema-house with one unified, unadulterated, psychological impression, that of the picture."[40] Therefore, the simple, modern design of a theater like the Film Guild provided what some cinéastes believed to be the proper environment for film viewing, in which all lines directed the eye to the screen, discouraging audience distraction.

Theater atmosphere was augmented by the types of audiences who attended (or who were believed to attend) little cinemas. Little cinemas sought and promoted upper-class and intellectual audiences. An editorial in the *Electrical News Letter* in 1927 noted that at the Fifth Avenue Playhouse "you rub shoulders with most all of the great artists of the country. The '400' also meet there afternoons."[41] The *National Board of Review Magazine* quoted *The Washington Daily*'s comments on the little cinema movement: the "rebels of the movies have simply opened up a simpler, smaller and quieter tent just around the corner from the Big Top. They offer to intelligent, civilized and curious people the new, thoughtful and often thrilling things that some movie-makers are attempting to create in the celluloid medium."[42] Furthermore, keeping the subscription format of the little theaters, some little cinemas required that audience members have a significant amount of disposable income on hand in order to pay in advance for an entire season of films.[43] According to Guzman, the subscription format of these little cinemas led to their nickname of "sure seaters," a pejorative term meaning that the theaters needed to sell films on a subscription basis out of fear that the individual films would not draw audiences;[44] however, it was also an interest in exclusivity that drew some little cinemas to adopt the subscription system. Even little cinemas that did not require subscriptions used admission prices to encourage a more exclusive clientele. In 1927 *Variety* noted that patrons of the Fifth Avenue Playhouse, then charging $1.10 as its top admission price, "have made inquiries why Mindlin doesn't tilt the scale to $1.50 and $2, the idea being for ultra exclusiveness."[45] Clearly, either patrons of the Fifth Avenue Playhouse were willing to pay more money for the little cinema experience or Mindlin wanted the trade to believe that was the case and so reported this story to *Variety*. Either way, little cinemas "cultivated an image of modernity and chicness to become fashionable with the upper class elite."[46]

In addition to appealing to the upper classes, the little cinema movement attracted the intelligentsia. Little cinemas frequently disregarded censorship rules imposed by the mainstream industry by showing, for example, motion pictures featuring Fatty Arbuckle, which most other theaters refused to exhibit following Arbuckle's involvement in a 1921 scandal connecting him to the death of an actress at a Hollywood party.[47] The use of season subscriptions, in addition to limiting the audience, also gave these little cinemas standing as private clubs and exempted them from state and local prior censorship laws.[48] These theaters could then screen foreign films made in countries with different "standards of decency" than the United States. The Photoplay League, for example, restricted screenings to members only (charging a nominal fee of $1 a year for membership) to fulfill its goals to present "films free from censorship."[49] The more sophisticated nature of these foreign films attracted intellectuals who felt confined by the dominant morals of the middle class generally represented in Hollywood motion pictures.[50] Moreover, urban intellectuals appreciated the modernist style and leftist politics apparent in some of the little cinemas' films (such as the German expressionist, Soviet, and avant-garde films).

DIFFERENTIATION FROM THE HOLLYWOOD FILM INDUSTRY

To appeal to the upper class and the intellectual elite, the little cinema movement clearly separated itself from the mainstream Hollywood industry. As Budd wrote, "A rising elite, in this case a progressive fragment of middle and upper class urban professionals, intellectuals and artists, helps define itself and its interest in opposition to the masses of moviegoers by creating institutions of minority film culture."[51] Instead of attempting to compete with mainstream films on Hollywood terms (this strategy, employed in the early 1920s, simply made the European films seem technically and thematically inferior), the art film industry now emphasized the increased artistry of the European, amateur, and avant-garde cinemas.

Promotion of the artistic value of these alternative films is seen in Eric Clarke's call for special theaters to show films "of high artistic merit but of limited appeal."[52] Although these films were not popular with large audiences, Clarke, the general manager of the Eastman Theatre in Rochester, New York, suggested that if a film has "artistic merit it leaves its mark on the box office product of the future."[53] These unique films, then, even though not widely popular with audiences, could increase the artistic standards of all films. The existence of "better films" groups also illustrates how European, amateur, and avant-garde films were set apart from Hollywood films; these films were, after all, "better," and such groups aided their appreciation and acceptance. Finally, magazines like *The National Board of Review Magazine* (and its predecessor, *Exceptional Photoplays*), as Budd stated, offered "a sustained discourse on the aesthetic potential of cinema, an attempt to apply to this new mass medium criteria from older high arts like painting and music."[54] Even the little cinemas themselves were set apart from Hollywood by their focus on the creation of an ideal space for film viewing. Articles written about little cinemas, such as the article written by Seymour Stern discussed earlier, compared them (favorably) to the picture palaces and noted that little cinemas offered a more artistic and fulfilling film-viewing experience. Therefore, we can see that little cinemas and the films they screened were set apart from the mainstream film business by focusing on the artistic and intellectual values of the little cinema movement. However, in the late 1920s, this appeal was not able to sustain an art film movement as a commercial venture.

THE DEMISE OF LITTLE CINEMAS

By 1930 it was clear that the little cinemas would not spread throughout the country in the large numbers originally imagined by exhibitors and distributors of art films. As Guzman wrote, "The close of the decade saw the little theatre movement firmly entrenched in many of the large cities in the United States, but its early promise remained unfulfilled."[55] In 1929, *Theatre Arts Magazine* sounded the death knell for the little cinema movement, commenting, "That [little cinemas'] bright day is done and they are for the dark, within only four years of their inception, is the unhappy comment on an art movement that from the first was characterized not so much by art as by a truly astonishing lack of the simplest foresight, and later by merely bad business methods."[56] The facts of and motivations behind this article have been questioned;[57] however, it certainly appears that by the end of the 1920s, the little cinema movement was diminishing.[58]

Although operators of little cinemas promoted their artistic concerns, it is certain that most people opened little cinemas with hopes of economic success. Little cinemas, however, never became large-profit businesses, but they managed to sustain themselves simply because they ran with relatively lower overheads and were charged low rental fees for films. The pressures of the film business eventually caught up with the little cinema movement. Combined with the economic pressures of the depression and changes in the Soviet and German film industries, the availability of fewer European films in the United States toward the end of the 1920s (as the major studios stopped importing these films) strongly impacted the little cinema movement.

Furthermore, as the decade progressed, the support of the little cinemas' audiences decreased. Many filmgoers, fascinated with the newer sound films, lost interest in foreign films.[59] Reacting to the rise of sound films, little cinemas actually became known as the last bastion for the silent film, frequently reviving classic silent films—if only to keep their screens filled during a time of decreased European importing.[60]

Additionally, although art films intrigued the intellectuals, the upper classes grew more interested in enjoying the amusements of the more exclusive theaters. As Guzman suggests, the different interests of the specialized audiences of little cinemas seemed to result in a lack of focus on the part of operators of little cinemas.[61] Michael Mindlin, a driving force in the little cinema movement, began plans for more luxurious theaters. In 1929, the *Newark News* reported Mindlin's plans to build a new theater in Newark, New Jersey, that would feature a tea room with a dance floor, a ping-pong room with a gallery seating a hundred people, a billiard room, a bridge room, and a speaker-phone room in which people could record their own voices. The *Newark News* also reported that a decision had not yet been made as to what types of films would be exhibited at this new theater, which seemed to be more of a center of entertainment than a little cinema dedicated to film as an art form.[62]

With the major studios more or less removed from the importing, distributing, and exhibiting of foreign films in any significant way and audiences losing interest, exhibitors came to rely more on ethnic audiences, the very audiences that little cinemas seemed to have ignored when establishing their public reputation.[63] The breakdown of the little cinema audience resulted from business practices as well as social and economic conditions in the United States in the late 1920s. The strategies of the little cinema movement, adopted and transformed, would find greater success in the industrial, economic, and social context of the United States after World War II.

Other Possibilities: Beyond the Little Cinemas

Other forms of exhibition also offered ideas and inspiration for the post-war art house movement. For example, ethnic theaters, newsreel theaters, upscale subrun theaters, and private venues of film exhibition all provided models for ways of balancing alternative yet marketable filmic experiences. These forms of exhibition offered art house operators ideas about ways of developing a specialized film culture, the types of audiences they might attract, and ways of appealing to these audiences.

ETHNIC THEATERS

As the little cinema movement disintegrated, ethnic audiences became increasingly important to foreign film distributors. Ethnic theaters were mainly located in ethnic neighborhoods in urban areas and showed foreign-language films to people who spoke the languages of the films screened. It is estimated that in the 1930s there were approximately five hundred theaters in the United States catering to ethnic audiences.[64] Screening films in native tongues for audiences speaking foreign languages, these theaters illustrated the potential (if limited) of foreign-language films in the United States and also kept the lines of distribution open between the United States and Europe.

However, as Douglas Gomery noted, "Case after case seems to indicate that it was just not possible to establish a foreign language theater outside a teeming ethnic neighborhood."[65] Moreover, once the United States entered World War II, it seemed possible for all theaters to make money showing Hollywood films. Therefore, many of these ethnic theaters switched over, becoming subrun mainstream theaters.[66] While illustrating the potential for foreign-language film exhibition, ethnic theaters were not art houses. Since ethnic theaters operated mainly as neighborhood theaters at which people could see foreign-language films, art houses clearly had to do more than just screen similar films to gain the desired status. To be defined differently than ethnic theaters, art houses offered more than foreign films; they created a unique environment for viewing films.

UPSCALE THEATERS

Although the breakdown of the little cinema movement led to the increased exhibition of foreign-language films for ethnic audiences, the theatrical environment of the little cinemas was carried on in a somewhat more mainstream mode of exhibition: the upscale, subrun theater catering to a high-class audience. Discussing the newly opened Punch and Judy film theater in Chicago, a 1930 article in the *Exhibitors Herald-World* described the theater as an offshoot of the little cinemas, but different in that it intended to "follow a policy of presenting American-made pictures of the type regarded as appealing to the so called 'discriminating' portion of the citizenry."[67] With a focus on creating a distinctive filmgoing experience for the upper classes, not on offering artistic and high-culture films, the Punch and Judy maintained some elements of the environment of the little cinemas (it had an art exhibit in the lobby and served coffee); however, it did not show "art films."

Chicago's Esquire Theatre (which would later be classified as an art house) also represented the upscale, subrun theater. Opened in 1938, the Esquire, as *Variety* noted, was "a class nabe with the ultimate in deluxe service."[68] Unlike many theaters in the 1930s, the Esquire showed not double features, but single features paired with sixty minutes of shorts, dubbed the "Esquire Hour."[69] Like the little cinemas, the Esquire emphasized its decor as a means of differentiation from the mainstream. The Esquire was considered a prime example of modern architecture in upscale film theaters. Named after *Esquire* magazine, "the Esquire was meant to be a departure from the grandiose, Spanish, Mediterranean, and Far Eastern palaces usually associated with Balaban and Katz. Because the site was in the Gold Coast area, a sophisticated and modern approach was to be used."[70] Joseph Ducibella of Society Designs, a Chicago design firm, explained that the Esquire's more modern style was intended to appeal to this upscale Gold Coast audience: "Just as early nickelodeons and 1920s movie palaces, the Esquire represents a statement, art moderne, of excitement and purpose wherein 'the show begins at the curb line.'"[71]

These "high-class" exhibition sites continued to be developed throughout the 1940s. Walter Reade opened the Park Avenue in 1946 as a theater for which the upper classes could purchase yearly subscriptions so they did not have to stand in line to buy tickets. The lowest subscription cost was $62.40 for a seat at the 7 P.M. show once a week. A seat at the 9 P.M. show cost $93.60. Since the Park Avenue did two changeovers a week, as *The New Yorker* observed, the highest possible amount one could spend on a subscription was $187.20.[72] This policy was short-lived, and Universal Pictures soon leased the Park Avenue, turning it into a showcase for the British films of J. Arthur Rank that the company distributed in the United States. Therefore, although the "prestige" theaters illustrated the upscale audience's interest in seeing films in a unique space, apparently the audience also wanted something other than mainstream films to go along with this special exhibition experience. Art houses would offer them these unconventional films.

NEWSREEL THEATERS

Newsreel theaters also demonstrated audiences' interest in a different type of filmgoing experience combined with a different type of film product. Mainly located in New York City, newsreel theaters were small theaters screening programs of newsreels and shorts. As Christine Grenz explained in her account of the Trans-Lux Corporation, which ran a chain of newsreel theaters, Trans-Lux opened its first newsreel theater in Manhattan in 1931, "offering to the public current popular fare of celebrities, ceremonies, and, of course, a good share of tantalizing catastrophes."[73] At that time, Trans-Lux planned to open a chain of newsreel theaters around the country, "some with only 100 seats and others with 200."[74] Newsreel theaters, then, illustrated to future art house operators the potential of specialized screenings in small theaters.[75]

In addition to differentiating its product, the Trans-Lux newsreel chain also focused on its environment, attempting to attract upscale audiences interested in world events. Trans-Lux theaters offered patrons larger seats with more leg room and wider aisles. These theaters were built and decorated in the modern art deco style; what *The New York Times* referred to as "an ultra modern design" (see Figure 5).[76] As Gomery wrote, "A Trans-Lux Theatre was meant to symbolize the modern and attract a higher class of trade."[77] Like the upscale subrun theaters, Trans-Lux theaters also catered to high-class audiences.

Interestingly, many newsreel theaters eventually switched to an art house policy. Richard Brandt, who was involved in switching the Trans-Lux newsreel theaters to art houses, explained the reason for the change in policy: "The motivation for that change was quite obvious in that newsreel theaters were the only way that people could see what was going on in the world prior to television. Once television came in and became popular ... there was no reason to go to a newsreel theater except maybe to see some shorts that went along with ... the news. So what do you do if you have a theater that has newsreels and is no longer attracting people? You look for something else. And this was the something else: the art film."[78] Therefore, newsreel theaters like those in the Trans-Lux chain aimed to exhibit a different kind of filmic product, and their success illustrated the potential of product differentiation for a select audience. Later, for Trans-Lux as well as

Figure 5. Trans-Lux Thearte, Eighty-fifth Street and Madison Avenue, New York City.
Reprinted courtesy of the Trans-Lux Corporation.

other newsreel theaters, the art house policy replaced the newsreel policy as the method of differentiation from the mainstream.

PRIVATE VENUES

Finally, the growing number of private exhibition venues also helped to illustrate the viability of art film theaters. These venues, such as film societies, amateur film clubs, museum series, and college courses, focused on the "intellectuals" interested in film. In the 1920s, avant-garde filmmakers developed amateur film clubs to foster "artistic" filmmaking. As discussed earlier, the Amateur Cinema League had local clubs all over the United States and even helped to distribute amateur films.[79] Documentary filmmakers were also involved in the amateur film movement. In addition to film clubs, in the 1930s colleges and museums began the serious study of film. For example, New York City's Museum of Modern Art began its film library in 1935, and the New School for Social Research, also in New York, offered a course in documentary film in 1938.[80]

Film societies also fostered the study of film. As early as 1934, the Film and Photo League presented a series of film screenings for the subscription cost of $2.[81] Film societies became particularly popular following World War II, with *Variety* estimating in 1949 that approximately five thousand private and semiprivate film clubs operated in the United States.[82] Some of the more offbeat film groups specialized in independent and avant-garde films. Art in Cinema offered a series of independent films in San Francisco between 1947 and the early 1950s.[83] In New York, Cinema 16 was established as a private film society in 1948, with a membership fee of $10 and an emphasis on avant-garde and documentary films.[84] Cinema 16 not only exhibited films, but the organization also provided information on the films it screened in the form of program notes, presented filmmaking awards, organized college courses, and distributed independent, avant-garde, and documentary films.[85]

Amos Vogel, the driving force behind Cinema 16, and his wife Marcia had begun an early version of Cinema 16 in New York in 1946. Vogel had rented out the Provincetown Playhouse, a theater seating two hundred people, and sold single admissions to the program, which attracted so many viewers that he repeated it one night a week for sixteen nights with two shows each night.[86] In 1948 Cinema 16 was reorganized into a private, nonprofit educational film society due to the erratic nature of single admissions and the desire to avoid censorship laws. The membership system of a film society eased tensions about admissions, since members paid their dues in one lump sum, whether they attended the programs or not.[87] Clearly, this admissions policy differed from that of the commercial art houses, which needed to attract audiences to every program to make money.

The administrators of Cinema 16 also had more freedom when choosing their programs—in part due to Cinema 16's exemption from censorship laws, its reliance on membership dues instead of single admissions, and its nonprofit status (and the resulting reduced pressure to make money). Vogel exercised this freedom by programming films, both nonfiction/documentary films (for example, ethnographic and scientific films) and avant-garde films, that he believed would educate and disturb viewers.[88]

With approximately two hundred members, Cinema 16 began screenings as a private film society in 1948 at the Fifth Avenue Playhouse.[89] In 1949, with nine hundred members, Cinema 16 moved its screenings to the Central Needle Trades High School auditorium, which seated sixteen hundred people.[90] By 1953, Cinema 16 had five thousand members who attended monthly Wednesday-evening screenings (with the same program offered twice each night).[91] Others, known as "Sunday brunch" members, viewed the programs late Sunday mornings at the Beekman Theatre (then a new and fashionable art house).[92] In later seasons Cinema 16 also rented the Murray Hill and Paris Theatres for Sunday screenings.[93] Occasional Tuesday-night screenings also helped to accommodate the growing membership,[94] which Vogel estimated to have reached as many as seven thousand people one season.[95]

The growth of private groups illustrated the increased intellectual interest in film. Art house operators undoubtedly recognized the potential audiences for unique films. Furthermore, organizations like Cinema 16 showed people's willingness to pay a bit more money for the opportunity to see such films. Venues such as little cinemas, newsreel theaters, and film societies both demonstrated and cultivated the potential audiences for specialized films screened in unique atmospheres.

These nonmainstream exhibition sites also laid the groundwork for the growing association between cinema, art, and high culture. Art house operators used and transformed the ideas and the frameworks established by these models to find a space for themselves within the competitive market of film exhibition in the late 1940s. Although some other forms of non-mainstream exhibition, particularly the little cinemas, did not last long, the art houses of the 1940s spread in relatively large numbers throughout the country. Art cinema, no longer strictly marginalized, carved out a space within the shifting mainstream industry. Operating in the cracks of the conventional film industry, art houses found large, diverse audiences and gained national publicity by developing a filmgoing experience that was both popular with specialized audiences of the time and economically feasible for the exhibitors.

3

Limited Audience Appeal:
Shaping the Art House Industry

"Vog Plans to Import 20 French Features"; "Influx of British Films Shifting More U.S. Theatres to Foreign Policy"; "Big N.Y. Play for Foreign Pix"; "Sir-itzky to Import 15 Annually from France"; "3 Out of 4 New B'way Pictures British"; "B'way Gets 6 New Films; 5 European." As this list of articles featured in the trade press suggests, the increasing number of foreign films imported into and exhibited in the United States generated interest within the film community.[1] Following World War II, some films that would surely be considered "art films" (such as *Open City* and *Brief Encounter*) actually appeared in many U.S. theaters, including large studio-affiliated houses. After acknowledging the accomplishments of such films, including their artistic style and content and their abilities to address adult audiences, questions emerge from the ambiguities of art films playing in mainstream theaters, such as Why did art films become more popular in U.S. film theaters after World War II? Why did the motion picture industry turn to new sources of product then? And if more "conventional" theaters were screening art films, what qualities did a theater actually need to possess to be labeled an art house?

The opening of new theaters and the conversion of older theaters to art film policies interested both the trade and popular press during this postwar period. Trans-Lux's 1948 announcement that it would convert its newsreel theaters to feature film theaters emphasizing foreign films rated a page-one headline in *The Hollywood Reporter*.[2] Major periodicals reported when the French film production company, Pathé, Inc., opened the Paris Theatre in New York City with an eye toward building "as many as twelve other small, fancy houses in U.S. cities."[3]

The Paris Theatre, located at what Douglas Gomery called "the posh corner where Fifth Avenue meets Central Park,"[4] opened on September 13, 1948, with a "gala event" featuring Pathé's *Symphonie Pastorale*, directed by Jean Delannoy. The program for the opening festivities declared Pathé's intention: "The Paris will bring to its screen the most noteworthy films made abroad, combining the artistry and talent of leading Continental writers, directors and artists" in the theater's attempt to "bring a touch of France and its culture to the heart of New York."[5] To bring this "continental" culture to the United States, Pathé invested in fine decor. The chrome and glass marquee alone cost $300,000.[6] Pathé also installed 571 natural birch seats[7] and served "Nescafé, Nestea and Maggi Bouillon" in the lounge.[8] Pathé created this atmosphere of elegance and refinement as the exhibition site for its films that had not met with much financial success in the United States since the end of World War II. Put more bluntly, Louis Metayer, Pathé's head of U.S. distribution, said, "We make more profits in Colombia than we do in the United States."[9]

Interestingly, Pathé's attempts to restore the position of French films in the United States involved the opening of a foreign film theater with hopes that exposure at the Paris would encourage other exhibitors to rent French films. Mainstream theaters willing to show art films tended to be small subrun theaters that generally had access to Hollywood films only after their first and second runs in other theaters. These smaller theaters found they could make more money showing art films either full or part time than they could showing subruns.[10] Often independently owned, subrun theaters required a great deal of product to accommodate at least three complete changeovers of two films per week.[11] These smaller theaters also operated on a very low budget and attracted an audience looking for low-priced entertainment. Toward the end of World War II, while the first-run theaters reached their highest attendance ever, the lower-admission subrun neighborhood houses had a business drop-off of 10 to 30 percent—even within major cities.[12] As the decade progressed, the entire industry suffered from an economic downturn, putting even more pressure on the smaller theaters. Some exhibitors turned to art films either exclusively or simply as occasional screen-time fillers.

Art houses, generally small theaters located in urban areas, were not necessarily the outlets desired by foreign film producers, but grew out of certain conditions in U.S. society and the film industry that encouraged some film exhibitors to seek alternatives to exhibition of conventional films. The force of industrial and social shifts for exhibitors was so powerful that, according to one report, between 1950 and 1952 the number of art theaters doubled to 470.[13] An additional 1,500 theaters, though not exclusively art houses, had some policy of booking "art" pictures.[14] An understanding of why art films became attractive alternatives for smaller theaters requires consideration of the small film exhibitor's position within the U.S. film industry.

The Search for Product:
The Postwar Film Industry and the Small Exhibitor

Even the brief discussion of the little cinema movement in chapter 2 illustrates that the Hollywood industry played an important role in creating an environment in which the little cinemas could grow (for example, by importing foreign films). If art theaters were indeed sites of alternative culture, they were certainly shaped by that to which they provided an alternative: the major Hollywood film industry. U.S. motion picture theaters reached their peak of attendance in 1946. When the decline began in 1947, film executives, though recognizing that profits were still higher than in the prewar years, seemed anxious to find ways to battle the downturn. The decrease in attendance (greater than the actual decrease in profits) had many causes from within and effects on the film industry that both directly and indirectly shaped the plight of the smaller film exhibitors and art house owners. However, it was the decreased production of Hollywood films and the increased rental costs for these films, caused by the rise in production costs, the antitrust actions against the film industry, and the constricting European export market, that most heavily impacted the independent film exhibitors. Each of these factors strongly and negatively affected the smaller exhibitors' abilities to fill their screen time with Hollywood films, requiring them to seek out alternative products for their theaters.

Increasing Production Budgets

The general rise in costs for goods and services after World War II inflated production budgets and caused producers to limit the number of films made. With films costing more, the studios produced fewer films. As Albert Warner, vice president of Warner Bros., wrote in 1947, the studios were "cutting down on quantity so as to increase quality."[15] The major studios also chose to produce fewer low-budget films. In a society offering people a greater variety of leisure alternatives, the major studios chose to focus on high-quality films to appeal to audiences. B films, frequently a staple of the smaller independent theaters, became less important to the major studios, and in the late 1940s they grappled with consideration of the extent to which to produce these "lowbrow" films. As early as 1946, Herbert J. Yates, president of Republic Pictures, saw B films on their way out of favor with the film industry.[16] Joseph Schenck suggested that the poor quality of B films might even keep audiences away from theaters.[17] Studios making fewer films could not meet the demands of theaters offering frequent changeovers and double features. Additionally, with fewer films available for rental, the studios could raise film rental costs, knowing that theater operators who wanted to show Hollywood films would pay the higher prices.

Antitrust Actions

Traditionally, film history marks the 1948 *Paramount* decision in which the Supreme Court ruled for the divestiture of theaters by the studios as the motivation for a remarkable number of changes within the film industry. The government's suits against the major and minor studios, which began in 1938, stalled repeatedly as the studios appealed court rulings and made deals with the government.[18] It was not until after World War II, and the expiration of a 1940 consent decree, that the government began another serious consideration of the monopolistic practices of the film industry, leading to the 1948 ruling for total divestiture.[19] Conditions in the 1940s leading up to this ruling and the actual divestiture caused confusion within the industry throughout the 1950s that affected production schedules, fueled the already existing animosity between the studios and unaffiliated theaters, and decreased profits for independent exhibitors. For example, one decision pending appeal at the time would have forced the studios to sell any theaters of which they owned a share of less than 95 percent. With the possibility that this ruling would go into effect, studios attempted to purchase complete control of any theaters they owned jointly with other companies. This large outlay of cash further reduced already limited film budgets and production schedules within the studios.[20] The following discussion draws on a detailed study of the trade papers to reveal the complexity and confusion of the times.

The entire system of runs, zones, and clearances (which was very important to subrun theaters) came into question; one of the major issues of the antitrust actions was the length of clearances between runs.[21] The length of runs became a factor that fluctuated with the supply of product. *Variety* seemed almost randomly to report both the increased length of runs and their decrease at various points throughout the late 1940s (and even within the same month).[22] Whether runs were getting longer or shorter for the first-run theaters, the results seemed to be the same for the smaller independent subrun theaters: they needed more inexpensive product than was available. If the first-run theaters held films over for longer runs, the subrun theaters needed films with which to fill time until they could get the newer films. Additionally, when the subrun theaters received films, they had played longer at the first-run theaters, and many people had already seen them at these sites. Therefore, the subrun theaters needed even more films for more changeovers in order to attract audiences. On the other hand, shorter runs meant that the first-run theaters required more film product, creating a seller's market that drove up film rental prices. As we can see, changes in run lengths affected small exhibitors by increasing a need for more films and driving up the rental prices of mainstream films. The shifting and unclear conditions created by the breakdown of the system of runs, zones, and clearances encouraged subrun theaters to seek inexpensive alternatives to Hollywood films, such as foreign films, to fill their screen time.

Even before the 1948 consent decree, accepted rulings already eliminated blind bidding and limited block booking.[23] The restrictions on block booking directly influenced the practices of the film industry and eventually helped create space for the art film movement. The proposed elimination of block booking meant the studios could no longer depend on selling all of their films.[24] Although the 1940 consent decree limited block booking to packages of five films, later court decisions required the major studios to sell each film separately. This led to a complete reconceptualization of the relationship between the producers/distributors and the exhibitors, who now had to rent each film based on its own individual merits.[25] Furthermore, the courts proposed a means of selling these individual films that would attempt to ensure that all theaters had equal access to all films: competitive bidding (or auction selling). The competitive bidding system required producers to accept bids for films from every theater in a zone during the appropriate run of a film. In other words, to determine which theaters would screen a film in its second run, a studio had to accept bids from all the second-run theaters in a zone that wanted to bid and then accept the best proposals. Contrary to the wishes of the exhibitors, the courts planned to permit studios to set minimum bids. Additionally, although studios were originally exempted from the process of competitive bidding when planning to exhibit the films in their own theaters, it was later decided that the major studios would need to request bids from all theaters even before renting films to their own affiliates.[26]

Intended to help independent exhibitors by attempting to offer them opportunities to at least bid for top films, in practice competitive bidding actually forced independents to bid against larger theater chains with more resources with which to acquire the same films. Competing for top-quality films required independent exhibitors to raise their admission prices at a time of fluctuating attendance.[27] Smaller exhibitors also could not afford to appeal the decisions if they felt the studios rejected their bids unfairly.[28] According to the Motion Picture Theatre Owners of America (MPTOA), a trade organization for independent theater owners, competitive bidding only worked to drive up prices and squeeze out the independent exhibitors.[29] A survey done by MPTOA found, in fact, that exhibitors were "almost unanimous in their opposition to auction selling."[30] The introduction of competitive bidding seemed only to hurt the independent exhibitors, wiping out any amicable relationships they may have previously established with distributors and driving up the prices for film rentals.

A review of the trade papers from the late 1940s indicates that perhaps the most notable outcome of the antitrust suits against the film industry and the proposed competitive bidding was the general confusion and turmoil they provoked. As *Variety* reported in 1947, the feuds resulting from competitive bidding led to such unpredictable sales that at times some studios even sold films away from their affiliated theaters.[31] *Motion Picture Herald* acknowledged the confusion caused by the antitrust actions and their resulting appeals, running a "Decree Appeal Boxscore" that charted the issues involved in the court cases, the position of the Department of Justice on each of the issues, and which of the Big Five and Little Three studios planned to appeal which decisions.[32] Uncertainty dominated as the studios and the exhibitors struggled to keep up with the latest court rulings, unsure of what was considered legal film rental practices and even more unclear as to what would be considered legal in the days and years to come.

The stress resulting from these changes (and proposed changes) in the film industry upset the already tenuous relationship between film producers/distributors and exhibitors. During the late 1940s, with tensions high, distributors and exhibitors exchanged accusations of responsibility for the falling box office grosses.[33] According to exhibitors, producers artificially created a seller's market by holding back films from release[34] and by failing to make enough prints of existing films to meet exhibitors' demands.[35] Exhibitors also complained about the low quality of films[36] and the lack of assistance from the studios in promoting films.[37] The studios had their own complaints about exhibitors. Major distributors charged that exhibitors worked in collusion when bidding on films[38] and cheated distributors out of their rightful percentages of box office grosses.[39] "Lazy" showmanship on the part of exhibitors was also pointed to as the cause for decreased attendance.[40] Even *Variety* could not help but express disgust at the constant bickering between the two camps, referring to a squabble in 1948 as "another round of exhib and distrib perennial feuding."[41]

Industrial factors such as the tense relationship between exhibitors and distributors, as well as the changes in film rental policies and increased production costs, acted against the small film exhibitors. With the film industry as a whole becoming more complex and economically insecure, film rental prices for Hollywood films increased, and it became more difficult for smaller exhibitors to gain access to these films.

The Constricting Export Market

Restrictions on U.S. films in international markets also contributed to the studios' decreased production output and the increased pressure on the owners of small independent theaters.[42] In the aftermath of World War II, the European countries attempted to rebuild their economies. Many nations found that money spent on importing U.S. films could be better spent on other goods. As Thomas Guback wrote, "European nations ... could not afford the luxury of importing American films when essential commodities were needed."[43] Limiting the presence of U.S. films in Europe also allowed these countries to revive their own national film industries.[44] According to Robert Sklar, the presence of the U.S. film industry abroad "conflicted with the other countries' desire to nurture their own national film production, and in the precarious economic conditions of immediate postwar years the extraction of huge profits by Hollywood was among the factors threatening several nations with financial calamity."[45] To protect their economies and their film industries, various European nations, such as Britain, France, and Italy, considered quota laws and taxes to limit the presence of the U.S. film industry.

Britain took the most drastic step in 1948, establishing a 75 percent customs duty on imported U.S. films.[46] Later that year, the British and U.S. film industries established the Anglo-U.S. Film Pact, which eradicated the tax, but limited the amount of money U.S. companies could take out of Britain to $17 million. Additional funds could be taken out of Britain in proportion to the amount of money British films earned in U.S. theaters.[47] In the late 1940s, Britain also established a quota rule requiring that 45 percent of films screened in British theaters be of British origin. Other countries, such as France and Italy, established their own quota rules and monetary withdrawal limits, imposing what Hollywood considered "restrictive actions of government or territorial monopolistic industry practices [to] prevent or handicap free licensing of American films."[48]

Although the Motion Picture Export Association (MPEA), established in 1945, worked to eliminate and avoid further trade restrictions, the Hollywood industry turned to the domestic market to make up for its foreign market losses. *Business Week* reported that quota laws abroad led producers to raise film rental prices in the domestic market and to cut back on advertising and promotion spending.[49] Undoubtedly, the fear of impending losses also contributed to the studios' decreased production budgets and further encouraged the reduction in film production.

The results of changes in the postwar industry, such as the declining film export market, strongly influenced exhibitors, and smaller independent subrun theaters were particularly affected. The increased costs of studio film rentals (necessitating increased admission prices), tension between the major distributors and exhibitors, and the decrease in the amount of film product from the studios (especially less expensive B films) all motivated exhibitors to search outside of the mainstream industry to fill their screen time. As film exhibitor/distributor Arthur Mayer noted when he switched his theater from screening B action/horror films to screening foreign films, Hollywood had been turning to "action pictures studded with big names and bigger expense which are rarely available for a non-circuit-owned independent theatre like the Rialto."[50] The same industrial shifts leading exhibitors away from the major studios also made alternative product available for their theaters.

Finding the Product: Alternatives

As conventional Hollywood films grew increasingly difficult to book and increasingly expensive to rent, alternative films such as independent U.S. films, classic reissues, and foreign films became more accessible, making them popular with smaller theater operators. As discussed in chapter 1, these types of films, which were, in some cases, truly alternative to mainstream films in terms of form and content, would also become associated with the art film. Theaters looking to promote the artistic nature of film often found themselves exhibiting such films. However, the increased availability of reissues and the increased production and distribution of independent and foreign films made it practical for a large number of theaters, not just art houses, to fill their screen time with nonmainstream films.

Independent U.S. Films

Toward the end of World War II, the number of independent producers rose significantly. Tino Balio has noted that, although there were only fifty independent production companies in 1945, there were over a hundred by 1950.[51] Most of these companies, however, involved people operating within the sphere of mainstream Hollywood filmmaking. As in other realms of mass culture (such as theater and radio), producers, directors, and stars broke away from the studios to benefit from tax law loopholes allowing them to earn more money if they operated as independent business owners rather than employees.[52] The studios helped support this move to independent production by distributing films from major Hollywood players and sometimes even assisting with financing. For example, Burgess Meredith and Paulette Goddard (then married to each other) produced *Diary of a Chambermaid*, directed by Jean Renoir; United Artists distributed the film. Frank Capra, William Wyler, and George Stevens formed Liberty Films in 1946. This company, which lasted only a couple of years before it was sold to Paramount, allowed these prominent directors to produce their own films, but major studios such as RKO (*It's a Wonderful Life*) and MGM (*State of the Union*) still distributed these independently produced films.

The major studios valued the independents for providing products the studios could distribute without laying out all the production costs and assuming all the risks. However, due to rising costs, revisions in the tax laws, increased difficulties in securing financing, and other factors, the spurt of important Hollywood studio players turning out independent productions declined significantly by the late 1940s. These types of independent productions never really offered film exhibitors an alternative to Hollywood studio films, since they were both produced by people associated with the studios and distributed by the studios.

Other independent companies sought to fill in gaps in the Hollywood production schedule. A significant number of independent companies focused on the production of B films, since studios were beginning to decrease production of these low-budget films (as discussed earlier). B films produced by independent companies provided a less expensive way for neighborhood theaters featuring double bills to fill screen time.[53] Other more alternative independent projects were also proposed at this time. Documentary director Irving Lerner and scriptwriter Ben Maddow suggested the production of more "specialized" independent films with "limited audience appeal that would play art houses now using foreign pix, plus a small number of regular theatres."[54] Furthermore, as *Variety* suggested, the decreased production schedules at the studios left top Hollywood talent with time to become involved with these smaller independent projects.[55] Although it is not clear what became of such plans, it is significant that producers and industry talent believed these smaller, more specialized films could find an audience in the existing motion picture environment.

Reissues

Reissues, made available by the major studios and a few independent distributors, also offered a less expensive way for exhibitors to fill their screens. In 1947, *Motion Picture Herald* reported an "unprecedented splurge" on reissues as seven major studios released twenty-nine reissues nationally with full promotional campaigns.[56] *Boxoffice* put the number of reissues for the 1946–47 season at four times that of the previous year.[57] The reason for this increase in reissues was clearly explained in *The New York Times* in 1944: "Theatres can't get enough new product to meet the demand of double feature bills. Thus even the big theatre circuits like RKO and Loew's are coming to [reissue distributor] Film Classics to get a double bill."[58] While the major studios' commitment to reissue films fluctuated throughout the late 1940s, smaller theaters grew to rely on these films as inexpensive rentals that generally attracted audiences, sometimes larger audiences than attended subruns of newer films.[59] At times these films even grossed as much or more than the films earned in their original runs.[60] From the eight major and four "lesser" distributors (Eagle-Lion, Republic, Monogram and Film Classics) alone, the number of reissues increased from twelve in 1946 to forty-three in 1947.[61]

In addition to the larger distributors, smaller companies such as Film Classics, Astor Pictures, and Crown Pictures distributed rereleases from both major and independent producers. Film Classics, perhaps the best-known (and largest) of these second-tier reissue distributors, was founded in 1943 to rerelease films from major studios and foreign producers. To foster renewed interest in the films, Film Classics often provided exhibitors with new promotional and advertising materials and even new prints of the older films. As the market for reissues increased, Film Classics expanded. The distribution company purchased exchanges, and by February of 1947, it covered a full 50 percent of the country with thirteen wholly owned exchanges.[62] With this wide reach, Film Classics obviously provided films to a large number of theaters around the country. As discussed above, Film Classics also began distribution of new, independent films in 1947.[63]

The increased number of smaller distributors certainly helped expand the exhibition potential of independent films, such as *The Quiet One* (a documentary/drama about a troubled black youth written by James Agee and distributed by Mayer-Burstyn) and *Lost Boundaries* (a "social problem" film by Louis de Rochemont and distributed by Film Classics that is discussed in detail in chapter 1), which did not have the money-making potential the larger distributors required. Reissue distributors also turned toward rereleasing foreign products. As early as 1944, Film Classics capitalized on the increased interest in England caused by the war by reissuing several Gaumont-British films and some early Alfred Hitchcock films.[64] And in 1947 Film Classics initiated plans to road show four reissues a year, starting with British producer Alexander Korda's *That Hamilton Woman*.[65]

Foreign Films

The move to reissue foreign films capitalized on the increased popularity of new foreign films, which prompted the *Variety* headline "Foreign Film Product Flowing into N.Y."[66] Bruce Austin noted that between 1946 and 1956 the production of Hollywood films dropped 28 percent and the number of imported foreign films rose 132 percent.[67] Foreign films became viable screen-time fillers for small subrun houses suffering from product shortages. As in the 1920s, the relationship between the major U.S. film companies and European countries helped develop film-importing channels. Major studios such as Universal-International and MGM became particularly involved in the importing of foreign films.

Often this interest in importing films stemmed from the desire to create a feeling of mutual respect and cooperation between the United States and European countries trying to protect their national film industries. To demonstrate the U.S. industry's interest in establishing an open trade policy, the studios imported European films for U.S. distribution. Additionally, funds frozen in European countries could be used to purchase the U.S. distribution rights to foreign films[68] and to produce U.S. films (runaway productions) in Europe.[69] Quotas placed on U.S. companies' removal of dollars from Europe also affected the attitudes of the major studios toward European imports. For example, once Britain tied the amount of dollars U.S. companies could take out of Britain to the amount of money British films earned in the United States, the U.S. studios became very interested in encouraging exhibitors to screen British films. European films, then, gained greater access to the U.S. market as the major studios became involved in importing foreign films and promoting their exhibition.

The record-setting (and, at times, supposedly exaggerated) success of films such as *Open City* and *Henry V* (both of which reportedly earned over $1 million at the box office) also increased distributors' enthusiasm about the financial prospects of foreign films.[70] At this time Warner Bros., MGM, 20th Century-Fox, Universal-International, RKO, United Artists, and Columbia all distributed foreign films. These larger film companies tended to be very selective regarding the types of films they distributed, usually handling only films for which their general distribution strategies would be appropriate. To generate large-scale interest in these films, Hollywood distributors offered foreign film producers relatively large promotional and advertising campaigns for their films in comparison to what smaller distributors could offer. Universal-International, for example, reportedly spent over $300,000 (more than many foreign film distributors earned in an entire year) on the national advertising campaign for J. Arthur Rank's Technicolor film *Stairway to Heaven* (produced, directed, and written by Michael Powell and Emeric Pressburger).[71] In their efforts to distribute films with wide audience appeal, most of the major studios' attention focused on British films, which did not require dubbing or subtitles to be shown in U.S. theaters. From a review of the trade press, MGM appears to be the only one of the Big Five studios that actually distributed foreign-language films.

The reasons for giving so much emphasis to British films went beyond the desire to appeal to a wide audience and requires brief consideration. The British Empire, accounting for as much as 75 percent of the U.S. companies' foreign box office,[72] was an important market for the film industry and one the U.S. industry wanted to protect and foster. After World War II, as the British government became more protective of its economy and its national industry, the U.S. companies understood the need to appear to be an open market welcoming British films. British producer J. Arthur Rank became the most prominent British producer in the U.S. market, undoubtedly due at least in part to his ownership of two of the three major theater circuits in Britain as well as theater interests in Australia, Canada, and France.[73] The studios, therefore, relied on Rank for much of their overseas revenue.[74] Rank's theaters appeared to give preference to U.S. films coming from the companies distributing and exhibiting Rank films in the United States.[75] In 1947, in an attempt to appease Rank, who was growing impatient with the U.S. market, the U.S. film industry promised Rank $2 million in play dates from each of the major studios' affiliated theaters and $2 million from the independent exhibitors.[76]

Although the Little Three and other minor studios without theater holdings reported difficulties in getting films booked into British theaters,[77] two minor film companies, Universal and Eagle-Lion, escaped such problems through their reciprocal distribution deals with Rank, whereby they distributed Rank products in the United States and Rank distributed their films abroad.[78] As part of these arrangements, Eagle-Lion and Universal could not limit their selections of Rank films to those with large audience appeal. Universal distributed both general-release films and more specialized films. Rank and Universal teamed up to create the Prestige Picture Program to take advantage of what Rank executive Robert Benjamin called the "prestige pictures market" made evident by the success of *Henry V*.[79] The Prestige unit at Universal distributed, as *Variety* put it, "Rank pix aimed over the heads of the average audience,"[80] mostly to art houses. Although Prestige personnel encouraged the conversion of small, neighborhood theaters to art houses,[81] Prestige did not limit itself to (or remain loyal to) the art house market. When *Brief Encounter,* Prestige's first film, became a breakout art film hit, Prestige quickly switched gears on the film, selling it to interested major circuits. A Prestige executive reported that, should a deal with a major circuit go through, the "idea of playing the film in other art houses may be dropped entirely."[82] Even Prestige, then, although founded to handle specialized films for art houses, demonstrated that its primary interest was in making money through the general distribution of films with crossover potential even if this prevented art houses from exhibiting these financially successful films.

The implementation of quotas and taxes on U.S. films in Britain and Rank's sale of older films for television distribution in 1949 appear to have strained the relationship between Universal and Rank. Universal became more selective about the British films it distributed in the United States. Films originally slated for general distribution in the United States ended up being funneled through Prestige, restricting their possible exhibition outlets.[83] Other large distributors also turned away from foreign films, particularly foreign-language films, with the realization that marketing these films required more specialized care than was allowed for in the studios' general distribution systems.[84] Even though the major studios' handling of foreign films became more cautious, critically and financially successful foreign films such as the British films *Hamlet, The Red Shoes,* and *Quartet* continued to earn money for Rank,[85] allowing the major studios to illustrate that there was space in the U.S. market for foreign films as long as they were of "good quality."[86]

Although the major studios became more selective and wary of foreign films throughout the late 1940s, the number of small independent foreign film distributors increased. According to *Film Daily Year Book,* the number of foreign film importers and exporters increased from 25 in 1946 to 62 in 1949,[87] and the number of foreign films distributed by independents in the United States rose from 21 in 1946 to 113 in 1949.[88] The ranks of independent foreign film distributors operating at the time included Mayer-Burstyn, Siritzky International Pictures, President Films, Artkino, Lux Film Distributors Corporation, Times Film Corporation, Distinguished Films, Lopert Films, Vog Films, English Films, and Superfilm. The increased number of foreign film distributors made these films more available both to art houses and to neighborhood houses.[89] At the same time, however, the growing interest of distributors increased competition, driving up the costs for distribution rights. *Variety* reported that the price normally requested by Italian producers for U.S. distribution rights increased from $3,000 or $5,000 to approximately $10,000 as a result of the box office reports on *Open City*'s high grosses as well as the growing number of distributors clamoring for Italian films.[90] The increased number of foreign films available in the United States also made it more difficult for distributors to find open theaters and get play dates for their films.[91]

The more financially solvent foreign film distributors, concerned by the limited number of outlets for their films and the difficulty of securing playing times, operated film theaters that exhibited their imports. Within the art cinema industry, Noel Meadow of Vog Films reported plans to open an art house, Jean Goldwurm of the Times Film Corporation operated New York's World Theatre and Little Carnegie, and Siritzky International Pictures ran the Ambassador Theatre in New York.[92] Similarly, some art house operators entered the distribution field to ensure that they would have films to screen. Ilya Lopert owned art houses in Washington, D.C., and operated New York's 55th Street Playhouse and Plaza Theatre (acquired in the 1950s) and distributed films.[93] Abe and Charles Teitel, who owned the World Playhouse in Chicago, distributed art films in the Midwest.[94] Los Angeles theater owner Sidney Pink arranged to distribute films west of Chicago.[95] And after converting its newsreel theaters to art houses, the Trans-Lux Corporation also became involved with foreign film distribution.[96]

Trans-Lux executive Richard Brandt explained, "The important thing was that if you were going to run an art theater you had to have films."[97]

Screening Alternative Films

The connections between art film distribution and exhibition illustrate that the availability of alternative films both required and fostered the growth of theaters in which to screen these films. The existence of the films allowed the theaters to flourish, and the growth of art houses encouraged the continued production and distribution of films for the art cinema market. Exhibitors looking to run art film theaters relied on the availability of films from independent companies distributing the less expensive foreign films, reissues, and independent productions. Moreover, to differentiate these theaters as special sites of film exhibition, art houses preferred to exhibit films seen somewhat exclusively at art houses and not at any neighborhood theater. As mentioned earlier, some art house owners requested that the major studios reissue some films on a limited basis only to art houses so that the art houses would not have to compete with general-release theaters for audiences.[98] However, it was not only art houses that showed these films. As Richard deCordova explained in his study of the rise of art houses in Chicago after World War II, "Foreign films appeared most regularly in first-run art houses, but ... they also appeared in major affiliated houses, in legitimate theaters on a road show basis, in second-run art houses, in major circuit houses across the city (in second run, often on a double bill) and in independent and smaller circuit theaters that were struggling for product."[99]

The high box office grosses earned by particular films encouraged mainstream exhibitors to book some foreign films. Following the success of *Open City*, Roberto Rossellini's *Paisan* received play dates in many conventional theaters, probably because the film's dialogue was 80 percent English. *Paisan* was booked into Loew's theaters in metropolitan New York, both the Balaban and Katz and Warner circuits in Chicago, and 260 of Fox-West Coast's houses on the West Coast.[100] *Carmen*, another Italian film (distributed by Superfilm, Inc.), was booked into New York's Skouras, Randforce, Century, and Brandt circuits.[101] As with mainstream films, foreign films booked by major circuits had better chances of being exhibited in independent neighborhood houses than films that remained in the art house circuit because these crossover films already received some promotion (either in print or by word of mouth) to encourage audience attendance.

Despite their willingness to screen potentially successful art films, main-stream exhibitors had hopes for high profits for few of these films. The average potential box office gross for foreign films, particularly foreign-language films, was quite low.[102] However, conditions within the film industry led many exhibitors to feel "forced" to screen art films. The major studios certainly encouraged exhibitors to book the foreign films they imported, and sometimes they even ordered their affiliated circuits to exhibit British (usually Rank) films.[103] The major studios particularly promoted British films, especially after the money that U.S. film companies could take out of Britain was tied to the amount of money earned by British films in the United States. In 1947, *Variety* reported that the president of Paramount Pictures had called for more screen time for British films under the headline "Balaban Urges More Playdates for British Pix."[104] Nate Blumberg, the president of Universal, emphasized that "exhibitors must be made to realize that their welfare and the welfare of the American film industry depends a good deal on their giving British films a fair break here."[105]

Some of the smaller independent exhibitors resented the pressure put on them by the major studios and the industrial circumstances forcing them to book foreign films. R. Navari of the New Penn Theatre in Universal, Pennsylvania, wrote a letter to the editor of *Motion Picture Herald* saying that the major studios "cannot get away with ... pushing [the exhibition of foreign films] down the throats of twelve thousand independent small exhibitors."[106] However, other exhibitors felt they had few alternatives to screening British films, since foreign film distributors charged subrun non–art houses low rental fees, which fit into their limited budgets.[107] This method of marketing the films proved successful, and the trade press estimated that "several hundred indie exhibs, outside of the sureseater circuit, are meantime buying foreign pix ... to plug up gaps left by Hollywood's product shortage."[108] *Variety* reported the situation of one exhibitor who "said that English-made pictures usually flop in his town of 20,000 but he's been forced, nonetheless, to buy the six J. Arthur Rank films being released by Universal. Doesn't know yet if they'll do business."[109] So, even though British films were found to be "box office poison" in small towns, independent exhibitors continued to play these films to fill screen time.[110]

In addition to the large theaters and the neighborhood theaters that were showing some alternative films, still other theaters used foreign films to cater to different audiences. Ethnic theaters, discussed in chapter 2, cultivated audiences speaking foreign languages. Spanish-language films never became a staple of art houses in this period, yet *Motion Picture Herald* reported that approximately four hundred houses in the United States booked Mexican and Spanish films.[111] In its reviews of foreign-language films, *Variety* seemed to distinguish between "foreign-language" theaters and "art houses" when suggesting possible exhibition outlets for the films. Exploitation theaters, which offered audiences films that broke away from the Production Code propriety, also screened foreign films and other art films, advertising their sexual or risqué qualities. Clearly, then, a range of theaters showed foreign-language films, as well as other nonmainstream films.

As one type of theater showing alternative film products, art film theaters blossomed during this postwar period. Just how many art houses operated at this time is unclear; reports of the number of art film theaters vary considerably from source to source. In 1947, Joseph Burstyn estimated that twenty houses in the United States were willing to play French and Italian films on a regular basis, whereas Noel Meadow placed the number at thirty-five to forty houses.[112] Adding in the number of houses occasionally playing any type of foreign film, including British films, seems to swell the number of art houses.[113] A year before Burstyn and Meadow's estimations, a Universal survey found 365 art houses in the United States with an average seating capacity of six hundred.[114] In 1947, *Variety* estimated that the United States had four hundred art houses.[115] These efforts to pinpoint the exact number of art houses in the United States prove hopelessly contradictory, illustrating the ambiguity involved in determining which theaters should be, and were, considered art houses. The one thing that seems clear is that art houses became popular in the major urban centers of the country. By 1947, *Variety* reported that Cincinnati was the only city with a population over 300,000 without a foreign film theater.[116] The popularity of art houses did not go unnoticed by more established theater owners. Circuit theaters converted some of their smaller, less successful subrun theaters to art houses. For example, the Fox-West Coast and ABC circuits in Los Angeles each included art houses, as did the H & E Balaban chain in Chicago.[117] And, as discussed earlier, several newsreel chains (pointing to box office decreases caused by television news coverage) began showing foreign features.[118]

With a range of theaters showing films that might be classified as art films, art house operators distinguished their theaters by mobilizing these films in a unique way. Relying on notions of art and prestige to appeal to audiences, art film exhibitors differentiated the experience of going to an art house. These associations with high culture and status proved successful, attracting filmgoers facing a shifting socioeconomic terrain in the postwar United States.

4

"Any Leisure That Looks Easy Is Suspect": Art House Audiences and the Search for Distinction

The quotation opening the introduction to this project refers to art houses' "subtle snob appeal," "tasteful paintings," films that assume "you have average intelligence," and "top admission prices."[1] This portrait of art film theater attendance illustrates that the appeals of art houses were firmly associated with a sense of exclusivity. Art film–going certainly offered people a place to see adult films that were different from mainstream motion pictures. And art houses also provided an environment in which people could think about film seriously as an art form. Exhibitors packaged these opportunities in theaters with an air of exclusivity and prestige in order to attract as large an audience as possible. To understand how art film theaters functioned, it is necessary to consider why appeals of status, taste, and prestige provided art houses with an effective marketing strategy in the postwar period.

Changing Times: The United States after World War II

To more fully understand the importance of distinguishing leisure pursuits in the postwar period and to consider the approach art house operators took in establishing their niche, it is necessary to look beyond the industrial factors influencing the rise of art houses discussed in chapter 3. We must also look to the sociocultural shifts of the time, including the effects of economic changes, the increased numbers of people moving to the suburbs, the corresponding emphasis on family and home, and the growing number of leisure options available within the United States.

Making Money/Spending Money

Between 1941 and 1950 the U.S. population increased by fifteen million people, the average take-home pay doubled, and family affluence increased.[2] Estimates suggest that by 1950, even after considering inflation, the population of the United States had generally twice as much money to spend as before the war.[3] This increased income meant people could spend more money at the movies; however, other changes at this time also gave people more choices of how to spend their money.[4]

People moved in large numbers out of the cities and into the suburbs. A study done by the J. Walter Thompson advertising agency in 1956 estimated that between 1940 and 1955 the suburban population increased by 59 percent, whereas the U.S. population as a whole only increased by 23 percent.[5] This move to the suburbs related to the reconceptualization of the private sector of life in the United States, which kept people focused on their homes and their families.[6] Encouraged by the GI Bill and the booming economy, more and more people also bought their homes rather than renting them.[7] Items then needed to be purchased for these new homes. The expanding consumer culture in the United States during the 1950s encouraged people with higher incomes to make their lives "easier" and "more enjoyable." Installment buying plans became popular, and people gave up sums of money each week to finance their purchases of television sets and other consumer goods.[8] In many cases this desire to own things certainly cut into the money American people previously set aside for movie-going and other leisure activities.[9] Furthermore, it is probable that once people spent money on their homes, they wanted to spend time in them.

Also in this postwar period, new forms of recreation became popular with the general public. Bowling, night sports, and driving all became viable options for people who normally had gone to the movies at night.[10] Former filmgoers spent more time at home with their suburban baby boom families and took part in more "participatory" family-centered forms of recreation (such as traveling and camping).

You Are What You Enjoy: Hierarchies of Taste

According to John Belton, the appeal of participatory forms of leisure related to changing structures of class and taste cultures.[11] The introduction of new cultural forms (such as television) and the transformation of others (such as the increased distribution of foreign films in the United States) led to changes in the accepted hierarchy of U.S. taste cultures. The rise of the cold war and the ideal of the middle class in the United States in the late 1940s and early 1950s affected many people's conceptions and uses of culture, raising new questions about "legitimate taste." Issues of taste became increasingly important as the postwar United States appeared to eliminate economic inequalities. As Jackson Lears wrote, "For the first time in American history, it was thought, the vast majority of the population had been economically enfranchised."[12]

This ideal of the U.S. middle class, with which more and more people identified themselves, overshadowed realities of the time, creating an image of a classless society.[13] Although many people considered themselves part of the middle-class and aligned themselves with middle-class values and interests, they still sought to distinguish themselves from others in noneconomic ways (or at least not overtly economic ways). The ostensibly larger middle class created hierarchies based on foundations other than economic class. As John Belton has observed: "Given the diversity of occupations within this new middle class, class identity emerged as a highly stratified, heterogeneous phenomenon. Each strata demanded a slightly different kind of entertainment, and, as a class, this new emerging group of consumers sought for ways in which to distinguish themselves socially and culturally from previous generations of audiences and from other classes."[14] Culture and leisure activities became important arbiters of status. Taste became a significant source of distinction among the suburban middle class as members of this group tried to distinguish themselves from one another and from other classes. Intellectuals and opinion leaders, according to Lears, promoted taste as a marker of cultural distinction, and taste relations came to replace previous power relations. Therefore, people's taste—including what films they chose to see and where they saw them— became a significant element of how they viewed their place in society.

The connections between class and culture complicated how people dealt with the increased attention given to culture and taste. Both Pierre Bourdieu and Herbert Gans, in their discussions of taste cultures, emphasized the importance of class in the formation and continuation of cultural distinctions. In *Distinction: A Social Critique of the Judgment of Taste,*

Bourdieu argued that a person's taste culture is strongly determined by factors such as economic wealth, social position, and access to education.[15] Gans, in *Popular Culture and High Culture: An Analysis and Evaluation of Taste,* also privileged economic class as the main element that delimits factors such as education, and therefore a person's taste culture. Gans wrote that "the major source of differentiation between taste cultures and publics is socioeconomic level or *class.*"[16] The emphasis on socioeconomic class is interesting to consider in light of the idea of the "classless" society in the United States after World War II. This approach forces a reconsideration of the extent to which the middle class in the United States really saw society as "classless" and how people marked differences between social groups.[17] Leisure activities and taste replaced economic markers as the means of distinguishing class positions, and art cinema, as a representation of high culture (and high class), could then offer people distinction.

Furthermore, both Gans and Bourdieu paid particular attention to the important role education plays in forming and circumscribing taste cultures. Increased education gives people from outside the traditional realms of "high" culture access to and knowledge of this culture, thus destabilizing the existing hierarchy of cultural capital. The teaching of art, Bourdieu wrote, "provides substitutes for direct experience, it offers short cuts on the long path of familiarization ... thereby offering a solution to those who hope to make up for lost time."[18] The importance of education in forming a person's tastes was particularly relevant in this postwar period, when more and more people in the United States began to receive higher educations. The GI Bill, for example, made college schooling possible for many returning soldiers. Longer schooling (along with television and other media exposing the working class to middle-class ideas, values, and lifestyles), according to Gans, contributed to the shifting of the predominant taste culture following World War II from low culture to lower-middle culture.[19] Bourdieu also explained how an increase in schooling might affect the existing hierarchies of cultural distinctions, writing: "When class fractions who previously made little use of the school system enter the race for academic qualifications, the effect is to force the groups whose reproduction was mainly or exclusively achieved through education to step up their investments so as to maintain the relative scarcity of their qualifications and, consequently, their position in the class structure."[20] This statement suggests that the people who invested in "high" culture would need to shift cultural boundaries to maintain their dominance in the cultural hierarchy, resulting in a reconsideration of the value of certain cultural products and activities. As taste cultures slid closer to the high-culture end of the scale for all people in the United States, a noticeable hostility developed toward middle-class culture (including middle-class activities like mainstream filmgoing) among intellectuals.

INTELLECTUALS AND "MIDDLEBROW" CULTURE

Cultural critics derided "middlebrow" culture, seen as high culture made accessible for middle-class amusement, as unstimulating, passive, and easy. Hollywood films (and their viewing) were certainly critiqued in this manner. This discussion of middlebrow culture in many ways paralleled the arguments against mass culture put forth by Max Horkheimer and Theodor Adorno. In their 1944 essay on the "culture industry," Horkheimer and Adorno referred to the "stunting of the mass-media consumer's powers of imagination and spontaneity," stating that "no independent thinking must be expected from the audience: the product prescribes every reaction."[21] In similar ways, postwar U.S. middlebrow culture became associated with mass culture, which was seen by cultural critics as hopelessly bad. Many intellectuals and cultural critics, such as Dwight Macdonald, Leo Lowenthal, and Clement Greenberg, criticized middlebrow culture (also termed "popular" culture and "mass" culture) as harmful and called for the resurrection of the cultural elite. Lowenthal, who cited Horkheimer in his essay "Historical Perspectives of Popular Culture," listed the qualities of popular culture: "standardization, stereotypy, conservatism, mendacity, manipulated consumer goods."[22] Clement Greenberg referred to middlebrow culture as "insidious."[23] Attacking the "tepid, flaccid Middlebrow Culture that threatens to engulf everything in its spreading ooze,"[24] cultural critics stimulated people's desires to separate themselves from middlebrow culture and to associate themselves with "higher" cultural pursuits.[25]

The critiques of middlebrow taste by cultural reviewers were supplemented by sociological studies warning against the effects of mass/middlebrow culture. David Riesman, in his influential study of postwar culture, *The Lonely Crowd,* argued that the rise of the "other-directed" personality caused people to obsess about fitting in and conforming to the standards and mores of the people around them. Riesman acknowledged the growing importance of taste and culture (as surface-level replacements for more substantive things such as morality and politics), and he saw people tending "to surrender any claim to independence of judgment and taste."[26]

Although fear of this conformity dominated much intellectual writing, some scholars have noted that the terms of compliance were much more complicated than may have been believed. Riesman's work indicates that conformity and "other-directedness" were accompanied by a great deal of anxiety and tension. However, after World War II, anxiety surrounded the ideals of prewar America.[27] For example, the suburban dream, becoming possible for many people, also brought out fears of violence and juvenile delinquency in the suburbs. Many writers have agreed that the conflicting feelings of the desire to conform and the anxiety stemming from this conformity significantly affected the general public's relationship to leisure and culture, upsetting the hierarchies of taste being used to determine status and position in society. As people turned to taste and culture to distinguish themselves from others, they found the accepted structure of status hierarchies shifting under their feet.

Writing in the 1950s, C. Wright Mills noted that people did not maintain a steady status level; their positions in the cultural hierarchy changed according to their activities and choices. Focusing on white-collar workers, Mills observed that many individuals based their leisure choices, whether in their selection of restaurants or their choice of vacation spots, on how these choices might allow them "to act like persons of higher levels and temporarily get away with it."[28] People spent time determining what would make them look as if they belonged to a higher status group. As Mills wrote, "The leisure of many middle class people is entirely taken up by attempts to gratify their status claims."[29] This focus on the cultural value of leisure activities encouraged the embracing of leisure that appeared more participatory, active, and culturally valuable than previous forms of middle-class culture.

CHARTING THE WAY: TASTE CULTURES IN THE POPULAR PRESS

The effects of cultural anxiety and the "experts'" critiques of taste cultures were compounded by popular periodicals' reports on the new cultural hierarchy. These articles helped disseminate the focus on taste cultures, encouraging all members of society to pay attention to how they spent their free time. An example of the coverage of this phenomenon can be seen in two articles, one in *Harper's*, the other in *Life*.

In February of 1949, Russell Lynes, the editor of *Harper's*, wrote an article titled "Highbrow, Lowbrow, Middlebrow," following up his article "The Tastemakers," which had run in *Harper's* two years earlier. "The Tastemakers" had focused on the new emphasis on art and the "campaign against philistinism" in postwar society.[30] The 1949 article expanded on the ways intellectual hierarchies were displacing social hierarchies, noting, "It isn't wealth or family that makes prestige these days. It's high thinking."[31] Lynes broke down the cultural groups into highbrow, upper middlebrow, lower middlebrow, and lowbrow. The main thrust of the article was to consider how and why middlebrow culture came under attack from both the high-brow and the lowbrow taste cultures as people "[jockeyed] for position in the new cultural class order."[32] Although firmly placing *Harper's* at the upper-middlebrow level, Lynes suggested that people at this taste culture position tend to take pleasure in culture only for the sake of being "part of the cultural scene."[33] The upper-middlebrow level also includes those cultural leaders who promote and package highbrow ideas for lower-middlebrows; as Lynes wrote, "It is the upper middlebrows who are the prin-cipal purveyors of highbrow ideas and the lower middlebrows who are the principal consumers of what the upper middlebrows pass along to them."[34]

This "passing along" of high culture to the lower middlebrows in easily accessible form is demonstrated by the fact that after *Harper's* (an upper-middlebrow periodical) reported on this new cultural order, *Life* (a lower-middlebrow magazine) then published a story based on Lynes's article. Compressing Lynes's argument to half a page, *Life*, with Lynes's assistance, created a chart categorizing different cultural forms and practices as high-brow, upper middlebrow, lower middlebrow, and lowbrow. For example, in the category of "Entertainment," *Life's* chart lists ballet as a highbrow cultural pursuit, theater as an upper-middlebrow activity, musical extrava-ganza films as a lower-middlebrow entertainment and western movies as an activity for lowbrows. The "causes" supported by each of the taste cul-tures are categorized as follows: art for the highbrow, Planned Parenthood for the upper middlebrow, P.T.A. for the lower middlebrow, and the lodge for the lowbrow.[35] With the help of this chart, the readers of *Life* could see where they fit into the cultural hierarchy. The accompanying story also acknowledged the stigma of being part of middlebrow culture, thus encouraging people to search to separate and distinguish themselves from the middlebrow culture of the swelling middle class.[36]

Basically, *Life* offered a chart instructing readers how to behave to increase their cultural prestige. By participating in active leisure pursuits rather than passively experiencing mass culture, the middlebrows (mostly the middle classes) might hope to separate themselves from the larger middle class and find the distinction that supposedly could no longer be found in economic divisions. Riesman attributed the search for partici-patory leisure to the desire of people to set themselves apart from the "pulpy recreations of popular culture."[37] In the existing situation, Riesman claimed, "any leisure that looks easy is suspect."[38]

The Film Industry: Reacting to the Changing Times

Status and high culture became ways for factions of the film industry to differentiate themselves from middlebrow culture. Certainly, these were not the only means used to differentiate leisure. Drive-ins catered to family and teen audiences, and exploitation houses appealed to men interested in more sensational films. The promotion of art and culture offered one strategy by which film exhibitors on the financial outskirts of the film industry could create a space for themselves. In his study of the Brattle Theatre, an art house serving the Harvard community in the 1950s, Jim Lane argued that the theater survived off of the "profit of distinction."[39] As discussed in chapter 1, Bourdieu explained that participants in a field who are dominated by a stronger element of the market must find "subversive strategies" by which to differentiate their products.[40] Art house owners who were not able to compete within the field of high-budget Hollywood films instead focused on long-term economic benefits by establishing the importance of art and culture. Bourdieu also noted that the emphasis on art highlights the opposition between commercial and genuine art. This distinction maximizes the longer-term financial benefits associated with art (by making the cultural object valuable over long periods of time). The presentation of art films as a high-culture art form marked these films with longer-term value, made them financially viable for longer periods of time, and provided art cinema participants a niche within the U.S. film industry.

Attracting the "Lost Audience"

Art film exhibitors' methods of differentiation attracted audiences dissatisfied with mainstream filmgoing. The film industry clearly had problems stemming from increased competition for the leisure dollar, the growing emphasis on the family and home, and the backlash against mass culture. Industrial difficulties resulting from declining attendance, changes in film rental policies, and increased production costs (as discussed in chapter 3) also plagued the film industry at this time. In 1948 U.S. audiences reportedly spent a smaller share of their total income for the year on motion pictures than in the previous twenty years.[41] By 1950 the percentage of money spent on recreation that went to the motion picture industry showed a 50 percent decrease.[42] The suburban family acted as a magnet, drawing potential viewers, particularly adults, away from urban theaters. People not only moved away from the location of many of the most popular theaters, located in the cities,[43] but, as discussed earlier, they also spent a great deal of money on their homes and often spent more time within these homes or participating in active recreation with their families.

One of the most important audiences that seemed disenchanted with the mainstream film industry was termed the "lost audience"—people over the age of thirty or thirty-five who did not attend motion pictures. In a study of the motion picture audience, Paul Lazarsfeld found that 80 percent of the domestic film revenue came from people under the age of thirty.[44] Following the war and the resulting increased interest in European culture, it was believed that adults were looking for more mature films than Hollywood provided. Director Henry Koster (*The Time of Your Life*) observed, "The public is no longer interested in seeing the underprivileged maiden marry the millionaire, because everybody knows now it doesn't happen. War experiences made adults out of adolescents."[45] Therefore, the declining audience numbers also related to the changing interests of the postwar audiences.

As John Belton noted in *Widescreen Cinema,* the film industry reacted to decreasing attendance in the 1950s in part by marketing filmic techniques such as wide-screen and 3-D as making filmgoing more participatory, appealing to the middle-class desire for more active recreation. Of course, it is not clear that viewing wide-screen or 3-D films is actually more active than watching academy-ratio flat films. Viewers watching any film work to make sense of the still images passing across the screen at twenty-four frames per second, connect elements within the story world, and interpret the film according to their own understandings of the world. Classical Hollywood films, however, were often critiqued as passive entertainment because they were so clearly laid out as narratives following cause and effect logic that consistently showed viewers what they needed to see to understand the story. There are certainly real differences in the mode of spectatorship involved when watching a wide-screen film as compared to a "narrow-screen" film.[46] However, the idea that audiences participated more while viewing wide-screen films stemmed mainly from industry publicity about how these films brought viewers into the action or brought the action to the viewer, making the audience members part of (and participants in) the film world. Promoters of wide-screen films undoubtedly exaggerated the passivity and ease of "traditional" film viewing. At a time when "easy" entertainment was berated as middlebrow culture, wide-screen film promoters benefited by characterizing flat films as passive entertainment and wide-screen films as active entertainment.

Similarly, art cinema gained prestige by promoting the intellectually active and participatory nature of art films and art film–going. The discussion of art films in chapter 1 considers how many of these films required more audience attention, as the films, especially in the 1950s and 1960s, became increasingly personal and ambiguous. We also saw that the Italian neorealist films and British comedies playing in art houses of the late 1940s also required more work on the part of spectators. Films like *Open City* and *Tight Little Island*, for example, used various techniques (including a documentary style of shooting, moving cameras, and long shots) to avoid giving spectators the optimal viewpoint from which to follow the story. The filmgoing experience at art houses bolstered the intellectually participatory image of art films. Furthering the association of art films with active high culture, art houses offered spaces that encouraged audience members to think and talk about the films in an intellectual manner. Again, it is not certain that this atmosphere constructed for audience interaction actually required more "activity" on the part of the spectator than did the experience of viewers discussing elements of classical Hollywood films (such as the costumes, the acting, or the plot) in a more informal and unstructured manner; however, people invested in art cinema (from the producers to the critics) mobilized the categories of active and passive leisure to set art cinema apart from mainstream filmgoing.

The unique nature of art film–going gave audiences a reason to return to the urban centers to attend art houses. As a marketing strategy, the conversion of a theater to an art house offered a theater owner a way to expand the audience, since people came from outside the neighborhood to see art films.[47] As art house operator Richard Stern recalled, "We did draw from a wide area in addition to the near north [where the theater was located]. We drew from other parts of the city [and] suburban areas because there were very few theaters running that type of policy."[48]

It can be seen, then, that in addition to the changes within the film industry that fostered the growth of art houses (as discussed in chapter 3), art houses also grew out of the interrelated factors of the increased emphasis on taste and culture in U.S. society, the growing interest in European culture, and the supposed desire on the part of the audience for more mature and intellectually stimulating screen entertainment.

The Prestige of Art Cinema

Although, as discussed in chapter 3, the exact number of art houses existing at this time is open to debate, they clearly grew in number during this postwar period and came to be viewed as viable businesses. Writing in

Theatre Arts, Herman Weinberg, who wrote the English subtitles for many foreign-language films, observed, "At no time in the history of the distribution of foreign films in America have there been so many theatres showing them."[49] *Variety's* accounts support Weinberg's assessment, reporting that a "sweep of conversions by nabes [neighborhood theaters] and hand-to-mouth first-runs to sureseater policy has blanketed the 30 top towns in population since the end of the war."[50] Throughout the late 1940s *Variety* headlined upbeat stories about art houses, reporting "7 Out of 10 Sure-seaters Click," "Sureseaters Now Surefire B.O.," and "Click of Certain 'Arty' (Foreign) Pix in America's Sureseaters has H'wood Eyeing that 'Special' B.O."[51] The potential profitability of art house ownership was further supported by the eagerness of participants in the art house industry to hold onto and expand their territory. The art house field became contested terrain when, in 1947, two groups fought over the lease to the Little Carnegie Theatre in New York City.[52] In 1948, distributors Joseph Burstyn and Ilya Lopert each disclosed plans to set up foreign film exhibition outlets on the West Coast,[53] prompting *The Hollywood Reporter's* front-page headline, "Foreign Film War Looms Here," characterizing the foreign film market as an important and serious area of business.[54]

The Mainstream Film Industry and Art Cinema

The reported success of art cinema at a time when the mainstream industry appeared to be taking a downturn resulted in two distinct reactions from the mainstream U.S. industry. On the one hand, Hollywood praised art cinema, tried to learn from these films, and wanted to benefit from the prestige they brought to the film industry. On the other hand, the mainstream industry reacted with suspicion and fear, trying to keep "outsiders" from usurping too much of the mainstream industry's business. I discuss the former reaction here; the latter is considered at the end of this chapter.

Most often the issues of prestige and status associated with art houses and art films were foregrounded by the film industry's support of the art film industry. Well aware of changes in the recreational patterns of people in the United States, film industry participants understood the need to adapt to changing times.[55] Eric Johnston, president of the Motion Picture Association of America (MPAA), reported the need to create more adult films, since audiences were more educated and would not tolerate being talked down to.[56] The major industry long had recognized that one way to expand the filmgoing audience was to increase the prestige value of films. In the early 1900s, filmmakers and film exhibitors interested in attracting the middle classes had turned to legitimate plays (like those of Shakespeare) and longer, more complex narratives to attach status to filmgoing. The construction of picture palaces in the 1920s had also brought more middle-class viewers to theaters by making filmgoing an elegant and sophisticated experience. When attendance declined in the 1940s, the major studios once again sought ways to bolster the connection between filmgoing and high culture to attract adult audiences to theaters. Art films and art houses offered Hollywood examples of how this strategy worked. MGM, after a brief entry into the distribution of foreign-language films in the United States, shifted toward producing and distributing English-language films made abroad, such as *The Search*. Distribution of *The Search*, according to *Variety*, offered MGM "impressive prestige value."[57] This prestige value was expected to serve MGM by bringing in new adult viewers not just for *The Search*, but for all MGM films.

Charles Skouras, who owned a circuit of sixty-two neighborhood the-aters in New York, announced in September of 1947 that, based on surveys of the interests of his customers, all his theaters would play foreign films as part of double bills with Hollywood films. *Variety* reported, "Acceptance of these films by his customers, [Skouras] declared, indicates a rise in the general American taste, because the hallmark of these pictures is quality, naturalism and realism and not glamour, elemental sensation or the pho-tographic spectacular."[58] Clearly, Skouras associated interest in foreign films, which in those years ranked high on critics' lists of the best films, with improved taste and rising standards.

Universal's art film unit, the aptly named Prestige, sought tie-ins with national charity organizations and "the more artistically pretentious stra-tum on main street" to develop subscriptions series for Prestige's British and foreign-language films.[59] A final example of the exploitation of the prestige value of art films by the major studios is the treatment received by *The Quiet One*, an independent film written by James Agee, which tells the story of a "10-year-old Harlem Negro boy, cruelly rejected by his loved ones but rescued by the people of Wiltwyck School."[60] *The New York Herald Tribune* devoted an entire editorial to praising this art film's intelligent handling of the issue of juvenile delinquency, and the MPAA (dominated by the major studios) reportedly used the film to demonstrate the educa-tional value of motion pictures to civic groups such as women's clubs.[61] Although the major Hollywood studios used the artistic and educational values of art films to make the entire film industry seem high culture and important, the mainstream industry also reinforced the prestige value of art cinema.

Film Critics

Critics and film reviewers also bolstered the qualities and benefits of art cinema and impacted the success of certain art films. *Variety* reported that critics had "the actual life-or-death say on British and foreign imports," particularly in larger cities (such as New York, Chicago, and Los Angeles), where people demonstrated a "slavish devotion" to newspaper reviewers. The same article stated that film stars did not strongly influence a film's art house box office take.[62] Herman Weinberg also noted, "Bad reviews will ruin a foreign film, since their audiences are generally more discerning. Bad reviews of an American film featuring a popular star hardly make an appreciable dent in the box office receipts."[63]

Film critics who went beyond plot summary and opinion but also attempted to analyze the meanings and values of films played a particularly important role for art cinema. Critics like *The New York Times'* Bosley Crowther; James Agee and Manny Farber, both writing for *The Nation;* Robert Hatch at *The New Republic;* and John Mason Brown of *The Saturday Review* were significant, as writers for upper-middlebrow periodicals, for their willingness to discuss art films and their abilities to reach the audiences sought by the art film industry. These reviewers drew attention to certain films (not all art films were reviewed) and may have offered some filmgoers their only means of hearing about art films. In larger cities, where film reviewers were most important to art film–goers, critics helped audience members faced with more choices to determine which films to see.

Reviewers also helped audience members start to think seriously about films and provided the terms of analysis for some of the films. Critics of the time, as discussed in chapter 1, focused on issues of realism when discussing films, noting if a film handled a serious issue in an adult and mature manner and if the style of the film broke away from the mainstream Hollywood form. The nationality of a film and its method of production were also frequently mentioned in reviews, with the effect of tying films to European culture or separating films from the Hollywood studio system. Reviewers mentioned film directors, although the auteur theory had yet to be developed wholeheartedly. Rather than consistently privileging a film's director, critics also referred to film producers and writers. Offering these terms of film analysis, film critics not only gave viewers a means by which to approach and discuss these films; they also provided the films with the element of respectability required to keep them from being considered exploitation films.[64] *Open City,* a film that could have been attacked for its depiction of lesbianism, drug use, and torture, was instead praised by critics for its "realism." The approach taken by these film critics certainly helped to ensure that this film was taken seriously and categorized as art rather than exploitation.

The importance of the critic in drawing attention to art films and in offering intelligent and thoughtful ways to understand these films (an importance that did not necessarily exist for critics reviewing Hollywood films) helped raise the status of critics nationwide. By the 1950s, Crowther was noted for his role in making or breaking art films,[65] and in the 1960s and 1970s, serious film critics like Pauline Kael, Andrew Sarris, and John Simon were seen as "stars." Film critics within the art cinema movement were the cultural elite who guided people through the complex world of art films.

The Art House Audience

Despite the power granted film critics by the art film movement, as early as the 1940s, some critics suggested that art house audiences and supporters were so blinded by ideas of high culture and prestige that they accepted both good and bad films playing in art houses as "art." Writing in *The New York Herald Tribune*, Otis Guernsey Jr. described the "true Art theatre patron" as a "die hard."[66] According to Guernsey, despite the decreasing quality of art films being imported into the United States, uncritical filmgoers refused to diminish their enthusiasm for art films. Many critics rejected the position that art films were inherently better than Hollywood films and questioned the motivations of the art house audiences.

Although many filmgoers were interested in the artistic and adult films offered in these theaters, this critique of art house audiences illustrates that there were various ways to think about these audiences and multiple reasons for art film attendance. Certainly, art houses offered a product different from the films available at mainstream theaters. Art films often dealt with more serious issues in a more mature manner and allowed people to experience art from different cultures. Some art film patrons also appreciated the atmosphere at art film theaters, which, as is discussed in chapter 5, provided a quieter, more intimate atmosphere in which to see films. Art house operators Charles Teitel and Richard Stern emphasized the unconventional interests of the art house audiences. Teitel explained that art houses had to attract "people who wanted to see something unusual, something different."[67] Stern described art house audiences as people who were "more discriminating, more sophisticated ... people ... who went to opera and ballet and ... [who were] more sophisticated and in some cases, I suppose maybe you might say, a better-educated audience."[68] Real pleasures and cultural values drew people to art houses. However, these were not the only reasons people went to art houses. Social and economic forces also made art houses attractive sites of leisure. These factors allowed art houses to appeal not only to upscale highbrow audiences, but also to middle-class and middlebrow audiences.

Audience Demographics

Studies of the art house audience (conducted since the 1950s) generally support the idea that art houses appealed to more discriminating and sophisticated audiences. Art houses attracted upscale, educated, "adult" audiences (who tended to be single men). Art film audiences of the post-war period were also avid filmgoers, people who tended to go to many films, but also planned their filmgoing and did not go out of habit. Art film–goers also made more active use of other cultural products, going to the opera, ballet, and symphony more often than did people who went to mainstream theaters. And, as discussed earlier, art film–goers were more likely to be influenced by reviews and word of mouth rather than advertising.[69] The age of the art house audience, over thirty years, was of particular interest to film industry observers, since art films seemed to appeal to the "lost audience" discussed earlier.[70] We can see, then, that the people who attended art film theaters tended to be adult audiences interested in high culture and more likely to think of film as an art form rather than as light entertainment.

Location

The geographic location of the majority of art houses also influenced the makeup of the art house audience. As many studies and reports have shown, most art houses were located in either urban areas or university towns. The New York Times reported in 1948 that foreign-language films earned approximately 60 percent of their revenue in New York City.[71] According to a report in Variety, revenue from New York, Washington, D.C., Los Angeles, San Francisco, Boston, Philadelphia, Baltimore, and Chicago accounted for half of Universal's Prestige unit's take on its films.[72] Prestige encouraged the exhibition of British films in small-town neigh-borhood theaters, recommending that these theaters set aside at least one day a month to show British films for the "carriage trade." According to Lewis Blumberg, the assistant general sales manager of Prestige, "By fixing a specific date for each month, the so-called 'upper crust' and others who generally stay away from films can book the event on their social calendars."[73]

However, despite efforts, small towns still seemed resistant to foreign films. For example, following are two reactions to the film *Caesar and Cleopatra* (a British film distributed by United Artists) from two small-town theater operators: "This isn't a small town picture, although the trade papers tell us it was a box office champion. We cannot say we did business. The story was poor. It looked like a lot of wasted film to us."[74] And, "Very good feature. Not received well by small town and rural patronage. Schools did not recommend the picture to students."[75] Therefore, the art film industry focused on "sophisticated" urban viewers, and art houses continued to blossom primarily in urban centers.

Taste Cultures and Audiences

The intellectual highbrow and upper-class audiences dominated much of the discourse surrounding art houses (Elmer Balaban described the audience for his Chicago art houses, the Esquire and the Surf, as being the "Gold Coast" audience).[76] Theaters' services and promotional strategies, however, also attracted middlebrow and middle-class audiences. Art houses offered a cultural activity that did not require an extensive knowledge base or a large cash outlay. Advanced schooling was not necessary for the understanding of most films; film knowledge could be self-taught by watching the films, reading reviews, and learning the names of prominent directors, writers, and producers. Perhaps most important, the relatively low cost of film attendance (when compared with that of other "high-culture" pursuits such as theater, opera, or symphony attendance) allowed intellectuals (often not financially well off) and those seeking distinction the opportunity for cultural stimulation, "the pursuit of maximum 'cultural profit' for minimum economic cost."[77]

The "foreignness" of foreign art films and their status as European culture also helped to make them culturally valuable. Interest in European culture, long considered more legitimate than U.S. culture, increased after the war. Foreign-language recordings, for example, had a "banner year" of sales in 1946.[78] *Motion Picture Herald* noted that the people interested in seeing (subtitled) foreign-language films not only included the "intelligentsia, but also many thousands of GIs whom the war had brought into contact with European languages and customs."[79] Furthermore, art houses were considered part of upper-middlebrow culture, and as part of this culture their appeal would undoubtedly spread to the lower-middlebrow audiences who frequently looked to culture from the upper middlebrow to elevate their status. Therefore, it is probable that art houses attracted many people from within the middle class who used art cinema as a means of attaining distinction. Or, as Douglas Gomery put it, "The motto seemed to be: sell the art films to the rich and well educated and a sizable group of the middle class might follow."[80]

Organizing the Audience: The Foreign Films Movie Club, Inc.

The growth of film clubs and societies raises interesting questions about the types of audiences attracted to art houses and the motivations behind art film attendance. The success of several film groups and societies at the time suggests the abilities of the art film industry to appeal to both upper-middlebrow audiences and the more numerous lower-middlebrow audiences, as well as the upper class and the middle class. As noted in chapter 2, *Variety* estimated in 1949 that "about 5,000 private and semi-private film clubs are currently operating in the U.S., mostly within cities of 50,000-or-over populations."[81] Although some of these private clubs, such as New York's Cinema 16 and San Francisco's Art in Cinema, were mostly associated with highbrow audiences, many of them also seemed interested in appealing to the middlebrow audiences.

As Mike Budd discussed in relation to art cinema in the 1920s,[82] some film societies generated mixed messages, demonstrating a tension between the desire for exclusivity and democratic leanings toward inclusion and uplift. The Foreign Films Movie Club, Inc., for example, incorporated different promotional and operational strategies to engage the conflicting interests and priorities of different members. The club combined appeals of culture and prestige with middle-class interests in monetary savings to form what seems to have been a call for a more middlebrow audience interested in increasing its cultural capital with the least outlay of economic capital. Connections can be drawn between the Foreign Films Movie Club and other organizations such as the Book-of-the-Month Club, which began in 1926. Joan Shelley Rubin has considered how the Book-of-the-Month Club appealed both to people trying to "get ahead" in an information-driven society and to "readers who clung to genteel perceptions." Rubin noted that this ability to adapt to the different values and needs of potential consumers "was the 'middleness' of middlebrow culture, as the Book-of-the-Month Club exemplified it: the embodiment in a single institution of competing assumptions about reading and criticism, rooted in changing historical circumstances, that accommodated a variety of needs."[83] Similarly, the Foreign Films Movie Club sought to meet several needs within the postwar art film movement.

Arthur Davis started the New York City-based Foreign Films Movie Club in 1948. Davis served as president of the club and editor-in-chief of the club's newsletter, *The Foreign Films News* (coincidentally, or not, the Book-of-the-Month Club also published a newsletter called *Book-of-the-Month Club News*). As *The Foreign Films News* declared in its first issue in May 1948, "After two years of careful planning, the Foreign Films Movie Club has finally become a reality. Thousands of moviegoers from coast to coast are joining this new type of film society because they enjoy a different kind of screen entertainment and are interested in seeing foreign films gain in popularity throughout the nation."[84] Through language such as this, the Foreign Films Movie Club created an image for itself as an organization for highbrows in order to attract people who aimed to establish their distinction or to increase their cultural status. This approach allowed the club to attract the widest possible audience—the diverse and large middle class.

The Foreign Films Movie Club's appeal to audience interests in prestige becomes clear in reviewing its promotional literature for new members (who had to submit "applications" for membership to the club). One brochure read, "The Directors and Artistic Collaborators of the Foreign Films Movie Club, Inc. cordially invite you to become a member" of "a group of discriminating moviegoers who enjoy the better pictures."[85] Potential members were also offered "private showings," "previews," and "special exclusive showings."[86] All these phrases implied the prestigious standing of members of the club. Because of its private club status, the Foreign Films Movie Club was also able to offer members the opportunity to see films ineligible for public screenings due to censorship regulations. Members of the club were "permitted to see these fine pictures of adult entertainment in their original versions—complete—nothing cut!"[87] These screenings added to the exclusive and special nature of membership in the film club. Additionally, the list of honorary members of the club, including Bosley Crowther, Jean Cocteau, James Mason, Basil Rathbone, and Charles Boyer, allowed members to imagine themselves among high-status company.[88]

The club's newsletter actively sought to assist in the advancement of the cultural knowledge desired by many middlebrows by acting almost as a textbook for people hoping to access high culture through self-teaching. *The Foreign Films News* stated:

Until today it was not possible for the foreign film fan to gain much information about forthcoming film releases, the real stories behind the various
productions, news and items of interest concerning the people who create
these fine films, and stories and biographies of the stars. Members of the
club will now be afforded all that knowledge through reading the pages of
the club publication, The Foreign Films News. This authoritative monthly
publication will be devoted to news, reviews, and items of interest to foreign film fans and will deal exclusively with the international cinema and
the better type of documentary film, regardless of country of origin.[89]

The Foreign Films News, then, offered viewers knowledge about art film
culture, reviews on which to base discussions of these films, and a sense of
being "in the know."

The Foreign Films Movie Club also indicated an interest in attracting
middlebrow audiences through its seeming support of the star system
within the art film movement, asking potential members, "Would you like
to personally meet such international film favorites as Jean Cocteau,
Michele Morgan, Jean-Louis Barrault, Viviane Romance, Jean Gabin, Louis
Jouvet, and others? All of them have thrilled you on the screen, and all of
them have promised to appear in person at our special private showings
whenever they are visiting our shores."[90] This promotional piece combined
interests in the star system with feelings of prestige and status: "As a member
of THE FOREIGN FILMS MOVIE CLUB you will join a roster of prominent
names in the fields of literature, art, education, and the professions, who
like yourself, take pride in calling themselves 'discriminating moviegoers.'"[91]

In addition to fostering ideas of status and high culture, the Foreign
Films Movie Club and The Foreign Films News also promoted the club's
economic benefits. Figure 6 shows the front and back pages of a promotional brochure sent out by the Foreign Films Movie Club in 1949, which
highlights the potentially conflicting appeals of prestige and monetary savings.[92] The Foreign Films Movie Club publicized the membership cost of
"only $2" and stated that membership in the club entitled members to
reduced admission rates at some New York art houses. The brochure pro-
claimed, "As a member you can attend your favorite Foreign Film theatre at
sensational reduced rates ranging up to 50%!"[93] Issues of The Foreign Films
News also informed members which theaters offered "cut-rate tickets" and
the prices available at these theaters. These promotional techniques indicate that this club did not aim to enlist the upper classes, who were probably unconcerned with the inflated admission prices at art houses, but
rather sought more middle-class viewers, including intellectuals with little
money and people trying to self-educate themselves.

Finally, the promotion of the risqué nature of foreign films by the Foreign Films Movie Club must be considered. As noted earlier, the club offered members the opportunity to see censored films "not shown elsewhere in their original, uncut form."[94] This indication that some of the club's films were deemed unfit for public screening automatically instilled these films with some amount of sensationalism. Furthermore, the photos and advertisements featured in the newsletter sometimes tended toward the lurid. Although the copy always promoted the cultural values of the films, the photos often featured women wearing little clothing or a man and a woman holding each other. As *Variety* noted, "While these groups [such as the Foreign Films Movie Club] are pitching for support mainly from among 'intellectuals,' their promotional literature is frequently angled like an exploitation house's marquee."[95]

The question becomes, then, Did clubs like the Foreign Films Movie Club intend to create an exclusive organization for people who wanted to separate themselves from the mass audience, or did the clubs want to expand the audience for art films to include the maximum number of people? The balance of these two conflicting interests—retaining the prestigious appeal of films and making them more popular and accessible—influenced how such societies, and art cinema in general, operated. In the search for this balance, the Foreign Films Movie Club worked to make art films palatable both culturally (by reinscribing the star system) and economically (by offering discounts) as tools by which middlebrows (and the middle classes) could increase their cultural capital and achieve distinction.

Seeing the Audience Differently: Sex and the Art Film Audience

Variety's charges that groups like that the Foreign Films Movie Club used sex and lurid promotions to attract audiences illustrate an alternative model of the postwar art house audience. Some critics suggested that art films attracted not only high-culture intellectuals, but also people simply interested in seeing the more "realistic" presentations of sex generally associated with art films (particularly foreign films). These groups attempted to weaken the connection between art films/art houses and high culture by highlighting their exploitation of sex to make money. In other words, as discussed in the consideration of the art film in chapter 1, these groups brought to the foreground the economic side of the art film industry generally hidden by the concepts of art and culture. Although the most fervent attacks on the art film industry as perverse did not come until the 1950s, their beginnings can certainly be seen in the late 1940s. By attacking art

Announcement

SEASON 1949

The Directors and Artistic Collaborators of

The Foreign Films Movie Club, Inc.

cordially invite you

to become a member

FULL INFORMATION INSIDE

YOU CAN NOW SEE ALL FOREIGN FILMS AT REDUCED RATES

Figure 6. Front and back pages of a Foreign Films Movie Club brochure.

films and the promotion of these films for their emphasis on sex, certain groups, such as the mainstream Hollywood movie industry and procensorship groups, suggested that art film audiences were not highbrow, but were oversexed and tasteless.

The mainstream U.S. film industry perhaps felt the most pressure from the success of these alternative theaters and their films. Although, as noted above, the U.S. industry looked to art films as a model for recapturing the adult audience and as a tool to promote the benefits of the motion picture industry, Hollywood was nonetheless threatened by the financial success of art films and art houses. While learning ways to attract adult audiences and reconceptualize the treatment of sex in motion pictures from art films, the mainstream industry also tried to limit the success of art films. The refusal of the foreign film industry and art houses to conform to the standards of the Production Code Administration (PCA) led the Hollywood film industry to label these films "immoral." Art films frequently offered more graphic depictions of love and sex than those seen in mainstream U.S. films (see chapter 1), and these qualities were clearly noted in trade reviews of art films, particularly foreign films. For example, *The Hollywood Reporter* headlined two film reviews: "French Import Has Some Racy Passages" (a review of *The Room Upstairs*) and "'Incorrigible' Apt Name for Import."[96] The refusal of the PCA certificate of approval for *The Bicycle Thief,* discussed in chapter 1, illustrates how Hollywood both praised and fought against the "adult artistry" of art cinema.

Those involved in the procensorship movement took the lead in accusing art house culture and foreign films of perversity. For those guardians of U.S. morality, foreign films provided proof that films needed to be censored. In 1948, a group of Catholics picketed two New York neighborhood theaters, getting the double feature of *Passionelle* and *Torment* pulled from two Randforce circuit theaters.[97] The 1949 annual conference of Catholic bishops charged that the moral quality of films was deteriorating. This statement was supported by the increased number of films deemed objectionable by the Legion of Decency. In reporting this story, *Variety* noted that the majority of the films receiving the "Condemned" label issued by the Legion were foreign films: between November of 1948 and November of 1949 the Legion objected to only 19 percent of domestic films as opposed to 47 percent of imported films.[98] The growing popularity of art films made them ripe for attack. *Variety* noted that "before the war, when foreign pix were confined to a narrow circuit of arty houses, censorship groups didn't care one way or another how much 'realism' they depicted on the screen."[99] However, that foreign films could now be seen in neighborhood theaters "perked up the guardians of public morality," making them interested in art films no matter where they played.[100]

Ironically, although the move of art films away from art houses and into more mainstream theaters encouraged increased criticism of the films, this same move also triggered the increased exploitation of the sex in art films. As will be discussed in chapter 5, the promotion of art films playing *outside* of art houses seemed to rely most on exploiting the risqué qualities (whether real or fabricated) of art films. It was while *Passionelle* and *Torment* played in mainstream New York circuit theaters, not art houses, that the promotion of the films was found objectionable.[101] *Variety* reported that for art films to be successful outside of art houses they needed "a strong sex hook on which to hang some razzle-dazzle exploitation."[102] This article estimated that although the average foreign film earned 60 percent of its revenue from the urban New York theaters, films with sex or other exploitation angles earned only 25 percent of their revenue from New York, making these films more successful throughout the rest of the country.[103]

The audiences seeing art films outside of art house environments were those people most drawn by the sensational nature of the films. Art houses, at least in the mid- to late 1940s, retained an emphasis on art and sophistication to distinguish art film theaters and art film audiences. As we have seen, industrial and economic pressures of the film industry, as well as social and cultural factors (including the increasing number of people getting a higher level of education, the rising incomes and number of leisure hours of many workers, and the growing diversity of leisure options), shaped this marketing strategy. The combination of these industrial and social factors led art film exhibitors to develop a strategy of film exhibition focusing on high culture, prestige, and status to appeal to highbrow and middlebrow people. To attract these potentially diverse filmgoers, art house operators relied on various promotional strategies and theater services designed to strike a balance between exclusiveness and inclusiveness and maximize the art house audience.

"Demitasse Intermissions and Lobbies Hung with Paintings": The Techniques of Running an Art House

Joseph Springer, the general manager of the Century Theatres circuit in the New York City area, discussed the planned conversion of a theater to an art house policy in order to improve business:

> Right now we're instituting a radical policy change as well as a physical change in a theatre whose grosses leave something to be desired. The house is big, barn-like, and has a late run. We're planning to make it an "arty" theatre, hoping to attract students of the motion picture and intellectuals from all over, rather than from the area surrounding the theatre. We'll run class revivals, foreign films, and occasional documentaries. We'll "warm" up the house by changing its name, the manager will be a man of culture, with some knowledge of letters, music and art; he will wear slacks and sport jackets and will smoke a pipe. We plan to change the name of the theatre, add a music and game room; one large foyer will become an art gallery in which we'll show and sell the finest in contemporary art. We're also going to try some special new services. And, who knows, maybe it will work. We believe it will.[1]

As Springer's comments suggest, switching to an "arty" theater involved a range of changes that went beyond simply screening art films, such as alterations in theater decor and the manager's wardrobe. While attempting to reach beyond neighborhood audiences by offering nonmainstream films, these theaters also relied on the appeals of prestige and status associated with high art to attract people who considered themselves "in the know" and who wanted to be among their own kind. The attractions of culture and status also drew people who aspired to a higher level of sophistication and wished to use cinema to elevate and display their cultural taste. To reach all these potential filmgoers, art film exhibitors created a theater environment projecting an image of art and high culture. This alternative filmgoing experience allowed viewers to separate themselves from the supposedly passive middle-class audiences of mainstream films and helped art film–goers find their place in the shifting cultural hierarchy.

Art house operators deliberately planned their theaters to foster an image that would distinguish art houses from other theaters, such as neighborhood theaters and ethnic theaters, which occasionally showed art films. Although neighborhood subrun theaters attracted an audience through their low-priced mass audience appeal and ethnic theaters targeted specific nationalities, art houses focused on notions of prestige and status to create an atmosphere of "high culture" for more "discriminating" filmgoers. The high-culture image of art films, therefore, did not emerge solely from any inherent aesthetic qualities of these films, but was also a construction of art house operators attempting to find a niche within the film exhibition market. Art theaters needed to find a balance between exclusiveness and inclusiveness, to create sites of filmgoing that were accessible yet alternative. To attract audiences, a later article in *Variety* suggested, art houses "tend to create a 'loyal' clientele of their own which knows the house, appreciates it and doesn't mind paying the extra charge for extra comforts, the service, the feeling of being with one's own."[2] This chapter examines the specific techniques used by art theater operators to attract this audience and create for art cinema an image of prestige associated with highbrow culture.

Although the strategies employed by art houses certainly varied by location and theater ownership, this discussion provides an overview of the art house industry in the United States. Though most of the examples here are drawn from New York City or Chicago, this is not meant to suggest that the situations in these two urban areas were the same as everywhere else in the United States. Rather, these two cities are singled out because of the important information each can provide about the art house movement at the time.

As mentioned in the introduction, New York was an incredibly important spot for art houses. Douglas Gomery noted that in the 1940s, 60 percent of the revenue from a typical art film came from New York and 40 percent of the two hundred art houses in the United States before 1950 were in the New York City area.[3] As late as 1957, *Variety* reported, "it's difficult to get a good import off the ground without launching it in New York."[4] The importance of New York City as a showcase for art films seems to have made the running of an art house in New York more complex and elaborate. Distributors recognized that a film's ability to get booked for screenings outside of New York City was heavily dependent on how well it did at the box office in New York. Chicago, on the other hand, although an important urban location for art houses, also provides balance to the enthusiasm of New York City for art houses by virtue of its Midwest location, where audiences seemed to be more resistant to art films.[5] The art house movement began in Chicago in the early 1930s with the opening of the Cinema Theatre, which specialized in British films, and the World Playhouse, which exhibited foreign-language films. Following World War II a number of additional art houses opened in downtown Chicago and in the surrounding neighborhoods. By 1950, art houses in Chicago included the Cinema, the World Playhouse, the Astor, the Surf, the Essex, and the Esquire.

Art houses actively created a filmgoing experience that could be differentiated from conventional filmgoing through theater operations, theater environment/services, and theater promotions. This "alternative" filmic atmosphere supported the association of art cinema and highbrow intellectual culture and appealed to those people who wished to separate themselves from the mass audience and from supposedly passive viewers. Techniques examined later, such as using mailing lists and programs, refusing admission to children, charging high admission prices, and selling coffee instead of popcorn, fostered a sense of sophistication and exclusivity at these small theaters.

Theater Operations

Although theater environment and promotions are certainly elements of theater operations, this section examines the more specific business decisions and day-to-day activities involved with running art theaters (such as determining theater location and size, the films shown, admission prices, and the length of film runs). Art house operators utilized these different aspects of theater operation to help foster an image and cater to their target market of viewers searching to maintain or achieve cultural distinction.

Theater Location

As *Variety* observed, art houses had to "build an arty patronage of steady consumers who come because of the theatre rather than the billing."[6] Undoubtedly, the film programs attracted viewers; however, as theater owner Elmer Balaban indicated, when people had several art houses to choose from, they often became loyal to a particular theater.[7] Theater location was instrumental in helping an art house find such a dedicated audience. To attract audiences, art houses needed to be accessible to educated, highbrow, upper-class audiences as well as middlebrow and middle-class audiences. A well-situated art house could reach beyond the immediate surrounding neighborhood to a broader pool of potential viewers interested in seeing something different. As the quotation opening this chapter illustrates, the Century Theatres circuit switched some neighborhood theaters to art houses to attract an "all-borough" patronage, not just the neighborhood crowds.[8] Theater owners, however, needed to attract select audiences, and therefore situated their theaters in neighborhoods that offerred them contact with these audiences. Art houses, as previously noted, often thrived in rich cultural centers: university towns and urban areas like New York, Los Angeles, Boston, and San Francisco.[9] Small cultural centers developed around art houses in some neighborhoods. For example, the Eighth Street Bookshop opened in 1947 next to the Eighth Street Playhouse (formerly the Film Guild) in New York City's Greenwich Village. These cultural centers included attractions such as art houses, bookshops, and cafés. These businesses thrived in neighborhoods comprised of their target audiences, and it is also likely that the opening of bookstores, art houses, and cafés in close proximity attracted people to these neighborhoods.

Art theaters found outside of urban centers were frequently located in affluent neighborhoods. According to Richard Brandt, Trans-Lux selected theaters to become art houses "based on population. In other words, you needed people who were reasonably well educated. So that depended on where you were ... so it depended on location.... But where you were—it was the more or less upper-class areas."[10] When selecting locations for art houses that would give them access to their target audiences, art house operators considered issues of class and culture alongside concerns about attracting the largest possible audience.

Theater Size

The small size of the art houses (averaging between 300 and 750 seats)[11] allowed these theaters to keep their operating costs down, since electricity bills and other maintenance costs were lower for smaller theaters.[12] The small seating capacity of art houses also allowed these theaters to play films longer while still keeping seats filled. *Variety* reported that Samuel Cummings, the general manager of Pix Theatres Company, believed that a smaller theater was in a "better strategic position to reap exploitational benefits and word-of-mouth business from foreign films, since quite often that type of product ... needs 'two or three weeks to establish itself.'"[13] Larger houses, on the other hand, as *Variety* explained, "can't afford to wait while the picture gains momentum."[14] The small size of art houses also added a sense of exclusivity to these theaters. Audience members saw themselves as part of a select few, not a mass audience.

Admission Price

Since art houses had lower rates of attendance than many conventional theaters, both because of the smaller seating capacity and because of the limited appeal of the films, art houses often charged higher admission prices than more mainstream theaters. Although the higher prices allowed art house operators to meet their costs, they also added to the impression that art houses offered more sophisticated entertainment and that the audience consisted of a more select group that was willing to pay a higher admission cost for a more mature cinematic experience. *Time* observed that art house audiences were "increasingly willing to pay premium prices (up to $2.40) while admission prices elsewhere are slipping."[15] In 1947, *Motion Picture Herald* listed the top ticket price for a first-run downtown theater in Chicago as 95 cents,[16] and in 1948, *Variety* reported that the average adult admission price for theaters in cities with populations over 500,000 was 59.1 cents.[17] Meanwhile, Pathé's Paris theatre charged $1.10 for its evening screenings and 85 cents for matinees.[18] An advertisement for *The Red Shoes* at the Los Angeles Fine Arts Theatre promoted the reserved seating policy for the film, which was shown twice daily, with extra matinees on Sundays and holidays. The three-tiered price breakdown for the matinees was $1.20, $1.50, and $1.80 and for the evening performances $1.20, $1.80, and $2.40.[19]

Some art films were also road shown (opened in select cities where viewers reserved seats for the film shows) or four-walled (played in theaters rented out by the films' distributors for a set fee that often included part of the box office grosses). The usual admission price for both road shown and four-walled films in the late 1940s was $2.40.[20] The price for art film viewing, therefore, could potentially be more expensive than that for viewing conventional films. However, in comparison to the cost of going to the legitimate theater, the symphony, or the opera, art houses offered a relatively inexpensive way to participate in more highbrow culture and increase one's cultural capital.[21]

Film Schedules

As discussed previously, selecting films for art house exhibition necessitated a consideration of issues of prestige and culture (as evidenced by the tendency to screen subtitled films rather than dubbed films) as well as economics (such as the inability of most art house operators to afford the rental fees for mainstream films). Art house operators sought a balance between their policy of exhibiting more specialized, esoteric films and their interest in maximizing theater attendance. The importance of art theaters maintaining their policies of screening "specialty" films is highlighted by the fact that the Bijou Theatre in New York City canceled a booking of *The Best Years of Our Lives* when the French film *Revenge* became available for rental. The theater may have attracted a larger audience for *The Best Years of Our Lives,* but the theater operator felt it more important to uphold the theater's identity as a foreign-language house.[22]

Elmer Balaban agreed that the selection of films was crucial. Despite playing some Hollywood films, Balaban's Esquire Theatre was known as an art house in the late 1940s. Because of this, Balaban noted, he had to carefully select the theater's more mainstream films. He explained that his high-class clientele and the reputation of his theater often resulted in the Esquire's making more money at the box office with a British Rex Harrison film than with certain Hollywood films.[23] Some art houses also screened more specialized programs. Richard Stern explained that there were films his father used to call the "arty of the art." These types of films, Stern said, included "opera films, ballet films, films about art. So those were even specialized in the art field."[24] Programs such as these added even greater cultural appeal to art house programs, marking them as sites of education and highbrow culture.

To round out the presentation of select art films, art houses offered other filmic novelties. Further mobilizing the association between European and highbrow culture, some art houses in the late 1940s arranged to exhibit Italian newsreels with English commentary.[25] Pathé planned to screen its French newsreel, the *Pathé Journal,* at its Paris Theatre in New York City.[26] The Surf Theatre in Chicago presented the "Surf Digest," and

Chicago's Esquire Theatre featured the "Esquire Hour," sixty minutes of newsreels, shorts, and clips from classic films (such as the hitchhiking sequence from *It Happened One Night*).[27] The Surf also hosted the Chicago Film Council's 16 mm "Films of the World Festival," ran a Museum of Modern Art series of films, and presented a program of short subjects on New Year's Eve 1947.[28] Leon Siritzky, who owned several art houses on the East Coast, found another way to differentiate his film programs. At his Ambassador Theatre in New York City, Siritzky planned to present stage shows in which the nationality of the performer corresponded with the nationality of the film being screened. For example, Siritzky signed Maurice Chevalier to perform the stage show for the theater's premiere of the French film *The Well Digger's Daughter* (directed by Marcel Pagnol).[29]

Although Siritzky used stage shows to internationalize his film programs, other art houses moved away from stage shows and other devices that stretched out the film-viewing experience. Many art houses tended toward single bills rather than double bills. Double bills, as Gomery explained, were associated with children and lower-class audiences as early as 1937.[30] Some theater operators believed that more intellectual art house audiences did not want to spend too much of the day staring at a screen. Art film exhibitors also found it difficult (in the late 1940s) to find motion pictures considered appropriate for art houses. These adult, highbrow audiences were supposedly more particular about their screen entertainment. Balaban explained that double bills could not work at his Esquire or Surf Theatres because art house audiences were "more selective. Because it was difficult to find two suitable pictures for them. It was hard enough to find one."[31]

Length of Film Runs

Films at art houses tended to have longer runs than most films at conventional theaters. Richard Brandt of the Trans-Lux Corporation explained that art film distributors were willing to give art houses long runs: "That was one of the advantages of having a picture that was specialized. It could play a long time, and [distributors] didn't feel they had to release it [to other theaters] fast."[32] Art films were described as having more staying power, since they built up an audience over time. *Variety* noted that these films did not have the immediate box office rush at the beginning of a run as did most U.S. films. However, they also did not have the same "drop-off" in attendance in the second and third weeks, but continued to gross a consistent amount at the box office. "Consequently," *Variety* observed, "extended runs of 10 to 12 weeks is almost the norm."[33] In 1950 *The New York Herald Tribune* reported that after seventeen months in operation New York's Paris Theatre (operated by Pathé) had run only two films (*Symphonie Pastorale* and *Devil in the Flesh*).[34] According to Brandt, the Trans-Lux Theatre in Philadelphia ran *The Red Shoes* for one year in 1948. Brandt also recalled that in 1949 the first Trans-Lux newsreel theater in New York switched to an art house policy, opening with the British film *Tight Little Island*, which played for twenty-six weeks.[35] Even more remarkable was the run of *Open City*, which, according to *Variety*, reopened at a New York City first-run theater after running for a hundred straight weeks at various theaters in the Times Square area.[36] These long runs allowed art houses to gain momentum from word-of-mouth promotion and to publicize, and profit from, the phenomenal lengths of film runs.

Theater Environment/Services

The one hundred weeks *Open City* spent playing in the Times Square area most probably included play dates at theaters that were not art houses. As I have stressed, screening art films such as *Open City* did not automatically make a theater an art house. The atmosphere in the theater and the services provided created a specific filmgoing environment that became associated with art houses. As Richard Stern remembered, the art house atmosphere aimed to make the theaters "appealing to a more sophisticated, discriminating audience."[37] Art house operators created intimate, club-like environments in which viewers could see films with others who, like themselves, were presumably intellectually engaged with films.

Theater Decor

Defining themselves against the larger downtown theaters which had more ornate and garish architecture, art houses, like little cinemas, adopted more modern stylistics. As discussed in chapter 2, precedents for the modern art house style can be found in little cinemas such as the Film Guild in New York City (see Figure 4), newsreel theaters, particularly the art deco Trans-Lux theaters (see Figure 5), and the upscale subrun theaters, such as Chicago's Esquire Theatre. The interior designs of art houses also displayed the simplicity and elegance of the modern styles. The decor, like the architecture, turned away from the more grandiose stylistics of the larger downtown theaters and instead stressed simplicity and refinement. Art houses offered viewers unique (and supposedly more sophisticated) decorations, featuring, for example, art galleries (often displaying the work of local artists) through which audience members could browse before or after the film.

Much of the publicity surrounding Pathé's Paris Theatre, which Douglas Gomery refers to as a "posh house,"[38] stressed the decor of the theater. According to the *Theatre Catalog of 1948–49,* "There's been a conscious and highly successful attempt to give the theatre an intimate, personal warmth of a home environment rather than a commercial public atmosphere."[39] *The Foreign Films News* described how the Paris went about creating this warmth: "Modern simplicity in design is the keynote of the interior decorations at the 'Paris.' ... Downstairs there is a lovely lounge, and to add to the home atmosphere, the powder room includes small, individual dressing tables with fully equipped cosmetic shelves. There are bridge tables in the lounge and facilities for chess, checkers and backgammon. The lounge is decorated daily with flowers and the lobby and exterior also have seasonal flowers and plants to enhance the visual appeal."[40] *The New York Times* noted the Paris Theatre's "limestone and marble facade, an unusual marquee, herculite glass doors and terrazzo flooring in the lobby."[41] *Time* admired the 571 "natural birch seats," and *Variety* explained that "exhibits of various Gallic products will be made in the lounge, giving the theatre a 'continental aspect.'"[42] Again, this association of the interior design with elegant European culture differentiated art houses from the more ostentatious style of the larger film theaters and imbued them with the markings of highbrow culture.

Theater Atmosphere

In addition to "upgrading" the surrounding visual environment, attempts were also made to create a more social and intimate atmosphere in art houses. To promote art film–going as a more participatory leisure activity, art houses often attempted to give viewers the impression of being part of a society or a club rather than a passive audience. Universal's Prestige distribution unit, when encouraging smaller neighborhood theaters to switch to art film policies, stressed "the need for intimate surroundings as an added lure for the customers."[43] Lounges in art theaters offered a space for people to sit together and discuss cultural issues. Frequently theater owners provided newspapers and magazines in these lounges for audience members to read before and after the films. Some art houses also featured writing rooms and television viewing or radio listening rooms, again giving the theater the feel of a clubhouse rather than a commercial theater.

Furthermore, roomy seats in both the lounge areas and the theaters made filmgoers more comfortable and more relaxed in their "clubhouse."

To create a specific environment, the Cinema Theatre in Chicago, which specialized in showing British films, piped in FM (classical) music, provided British magazines in the lobby, and served coffee and free candy ("kind of a little better class candy").[44] Additionally, many art houses featured cafés rather than concession stands. Instead of offering popcorn and lower-priced candy, snacks associated with "lower-class" amusements,[45] many art houses offered coffee and pastries.[46] The Trans-Lux theaters used the cafés to add an even greater air of cosmopolitan sophistication to their theaters. Richard Brandt described the "Parisian Sidewalk Motif" adapted by several Trans-Lux theaters (see Figure 7):

> You have some place that someone can actually sit at a table like a Paris café, and while [in] no theaters in the major cities could you put a table outside on the sidewalk —you couldn't do that—in one of our theaters, the Eighty-fifth Street Theatre, we made the interior lobby as you walked in, we designed it with trees (they were fake trees) and everything to make them look like an exterior ... We did this in Washington, we did it in Philadelphia. Not everyone the same. Each theater was different. But that's the kind of thing. You wanted to make it upscale and look good and look different than the average theater.[47]

Figure 7. The "Parisian Sidewalk Motif" at Trans-Lux's Eighty-fifth Street Theatre, New York City. Reprinted courtesy of the Trans-Lux Corporation.

Some art houses even offered demitasse, tea, "better-class" candies (mints at the Cinema Theatre), cigarettes, and perfume (in the women's lounges) free of charge. Art house operators spent time and money distinguishing their theaters for those audience members who were searching for motion picture entertainment that was more upscale and highbrow than the conventional filmgoing experience. As Christine Grenz wrote in her history of Trans-Lux, "Demitasse intermissions and lobbies hung with paintings were vying successfully with the giant popcorn palaces."[48]

In addition to providing an intimate and high-culture atmosphere, art houses also created an "adult" environment for filmgoers. Many art houses had a policy that excluded children, keeping the filmgoing experience quieter and more sedate than in many mainstream houses. Those art theaters that permitted admission of children rarely featured films to attract their attendance. Furthermore, censorship apparently became less of an issue for theaters known to exclude children. Louis Sher, the owner of the largest chain of art houses in the United States in terms of number of theaters, in 1958 explained that "when [censors] find out that we cater only to adults—and even exclude children—the pressure usually disappears."[49]

Art house operators who started film societies centered around their theaters further promoted an adult and intellectual appreciation of films. The five hundred–seat Kimo Theatre in Kansas City began the Kimo Theatre Guild. In 1947, the *Motion Picture Herald* focused on this theater guild as an example for other theaters to follow, reporting that this film society had approximately two thousand members and attracted people from as far as a hundred miles away "to see unusual pictures at the Kimo, mostly imports."[50] As the discussion of the Foreign Films Movie Club in chapter 4 demonstrated, film societies could combine appeals of structured cultural education with the attractions of exclusive club membership to help art houses foster a sense of prestige and culture while maximizing their audience.

Theater Programs

Since, as Stern explained, art film–goers liked to read information about the films, some art house operators distributed programs to their customers. This procedure connected art film attendance to the attendance of highbrow events such as the legitimate theater, the symphony, and the opera, which also handed out programs. Sometimes theater operators mailed the programs to a select list of regular patrons.[51] Programs frequently featured production details about the films and sometimes reprints of film stills and cast lists. Announcements of upcoming films and events were also included to inform audience members of expected future programs and to encourage their return to the theater. It is interesting to observe that more programs seemed to be produced for New York City art houses than for Chicago art houses. Balaban never used programs in his Esquire and Surf Theatres.[52] The Cinema in Chicago did not produce programs regularly, but Stern occasionally distributed flyers about the films being screened.[53] The larger number of programs produced in New York City art houses makes sense when considered in terms of the relatively large number of art houses in New York at the time. Art theaters had to differentiate themselves not only from conventional theaters, but also from other art houses. Furthermore, theater owners, who sometimes also distributed films, understood the importance of an art film's New York run in determining its national run. These art film exhibitors attempted to attract as many people as possible in New York to illustrate a film's box office potential.

The programs distributed by New York art houses offer insights into how art theaters presented themselves to their audience members. Programs were produced on paper ranging from heavy-stock glossy paper to plain copy paper; some flyers were simple two-sided documents, but others were more elaborate and "traditional" programs. Theaters frequently used mottoes (of sorts) on their programs to describe the theater. The Apollo Theatre's mailings/programs referred to the theater as the "Home of the world's finest foreign films."[54] The Ambassador's program declared that this theater was the "Broadway Showcase for Great International Films,"[55] while Siritzky's Elysée Theatre's mailing designated the theater "New York's Newest and Most Exquisite International Showplace" and stated, "The finest International Motion Pictures are presented by Siritzky International."[56] The Fifth Avenue Playhouse announced that it was "the only cinema on the eastern seaboard whose board of directors attempts to procure films with an intellectual and artistic appeal."[57]

These promotional tools fostered the idea that the theaters presented high-quality films for a more highbrow audience in a more discriminating setting. The Fifth Avenue Playhouse's two-sided half-sheet handout for its special program of three French films (Carl Dreyer's *Day of Wrath,* Jean Cocteau's *Blood of a Poet,* and Jean Vigo's *Zero for Conduct*) declared that the showing of these films "for the first time together" offered its patrons "a trio of camera poetica to dispel 'ennui mortel de l'immortalite [sic].'"[58] The reverse side of this handout from the Fifth Avenue Playhouse provided information about the three films being screened. The handout extolled the "exquisite photography" in *Day of Wrath,* the "witty score" of *Blood of a Poet,* and the "irony, humor and quick silver beauty" of *Zero for Conduct's* script. This practice of providing information about the films also offered viewers a preset way of understanding and talking about the films with others.

The different ways art house programs established relationships between viewers and theaters can be seen by comparing programs from the Paris Theatre and the Park Avenue Theatre. The Paris Theatre's program for its gala opening on September 13, 1948, provided a schedule of the films to be seen (*A Visit with Henry Matisse* and *Symphonie Pastorale*),[59] a cast and credit list, information on the theater's staff (such as who painted the artworks on the walls, who arranged the exhibition in the lounge, and the names of the house managers) and detailed information headed "About the Picture." The back of the program welcomed audience members to the Paris Theatre, telling them that "In this sumptuous Gotham locale Pathé Cinema, the original French company, has built a new motion picture theatre to present films from its own studios and from other Gallic producers. The Paris will bring to its screen the most noteworthy films made abroad, combining artistry and talent of leading Continental writers, directors and artists."[60] Also on the back of the program was a listing of the "Honorary Committee" of the "Gala Benefit Premiere," including the French ambassador to the United States, the mayor of New York City, and Eleanor Roosevelt. All of these elements—the production information, the listing of the prominent honorary committee members, and the information about the theater—encouraged audience members to think about the theater as a facet of highbrow culture, laden with prestige and sophistication.

Unlike the program for the Paris Theatre, which stressed status and upper-class leisure, Universal Pictures' program for the "Premiere American Engagement" of *Stairway to Heaven*[61] at the Park Avenue Theatre illustrated the tension between the inclusive and exclusive culture of art cinema. *Stairway to Heaven* opened at the Park Avenue in 1946, when Universal leased the theater, and ended the policy of theater subscriptions implemented by theater owner Walter Reade.[62] This program, like the Paris Theatre program, offered a schedule of "events": musical interlude, newsreels, a cartoon (*Chopin's Musical Moments*), and finally the feature presentation (*Stairway to Heaven*). The program also provided a list of "The Players." The back page of the program, however, presented the Park Avenue differently than the Paris program presented that theater. Instead of simply listing the staff members, the Park Avenue introduced its staff: the snack bar attendant, the checkroom attendant, the chief of service staff, and the ladies' room attendant. Next to each person's name and position title was a quote related to that person's job. For example, the quote next to the snack bar attendant's name reads, "May I invite you to visit the Snack Bar in the downstairs lounge, before or after the performance, and enjoy our freshly brewed coffee or tea."[63] Underneath the list of names, two lines in italics read, "Yes! It's our pleasure to serve you and therefore we ask that you refrain from offering us any gratuities." Introducing the staff to the theater patrons made the theater seem more friendly and at the same time focused on the importance of service.

Although the programs for both the Park Avenue and the Paris provided the viewer with a schedule of the evening's entertainment and information about the program, the Park Avenue's program fostered feelings of relaxed intimacy, whereas the Paris focused on culture and status. This difference may relate to the fact that Universal used the Park Avenue to exhibit its British films, which, as discussed in chapter 1, had a more popular acceptance than the foreign-language films exhibited by the Paris Theatre. Universal's creation of a more casual atmosphere may have been an attempt to make middlebrow (and middle-class) audiences feel welcome and to appeal to a wider, more socially diverse group of people. On the other hand, the Paris, showing foreign-language films, may have decided to strictly target those people (whether highbrow or middlebrow) who wanted to use their filmic entertainment to gain the prestige and status associated with sophisticated culture.

Theater programs, then, like theater decor and other services (such as cafés and film societies), clearly contributed to the way audience members, and potential audience members, saw art houses and the values of art film–going.

Theater Promotions

Theater promotion was essential for furthering the association between art houses and highbrow culture. For the most part, art houses relied on many of the same promotional tools as did mainstream theaters: film reviews, lobby/marquee displays, and advertising. However, the ways these techniques were used differed for art film exhibitors, who were attempting to imbue their theaters with an air of sophistication. Art houses rarely mobilized the glamor that conventional theater operators often tried to associate with their films. Rather, as discussed in chapters 1 and 4, art films were presented as adult, realistic, and intellectual leisure.[64] Art houses generally attempted to use relatively small promotional campaigns to start people talking about the films and encourage word-of-mouth publicity.

To keep promotional costs low, media outlets were carefully selected to reach the targeted audiences. Richard Brandt explained that although *The Daily News* may have had the largest circulation of all the newspapers in New York City, art houses tended to advertise in *The New York Times*, because it had "the upscale readership that you were looking for."[65] Newspapers were essential outlets for art film promotion, since most of this promotion centered on print advertising.[66] As discussed, film reviews encouraged potential audience members to attend art films. Placing photos and small stories about art films in select newspapers could also help ticket sales. Charles Teitel of Chicago's World Playhouse remembered spending a great deal of time cultivating his relationship with the newspaper film staff.[67] Furthermore, instead of just giving the newspapers photos and cast lists for upcoming films, Teitel made it easier for the papers to run items on his films by writing "about two or three paragraphs on each [film] so that I had a little better chance [of getting these films mentioned]."[68]

Marquees and Mailings

Art houses also tended to be selective about the art that they used inside and outside of their theaters. Mainstream theaters often used these displays to lure people into or back to the theater. Obtrusive displays of posters and signs attracted attention. Most art houses, however, took a more reserved approach toward these displays, assuming their preferred clientele would want to see films based on the artistic and intellectual qualities of the films not poster and photo displays.[69] Douglas Gomery noted that the Esquire Theatre in Chicago did not use posters, publicity photos, or on-screen previews, but used only a simple card outside the theater.[70] Art theaters were more likely to simply announce the name of a film and perhaps the name of the director on their marquees.

Rather than using posters and displays, art houses notified people about upcoming features by sending out flyers to regular patrons. Mailings, sometimes simply a postcard with an announcement of a film, at times also included information about the film. Similar to the programs (some of which exhibitors mailed to patrons), mailings could be printed on anything ranging from heavy-stock glossy paper to cardboard and created particular images for the theaters and the films. As a mailing from the Midtown Theatre illustrates, even the simplest mailings relied on critics' quotes to attract previous audience members back to the theater.[71] Maintaining mailing lists not only helped theaters keep their customers informed, but also reinforced for filmgoers, the sense of being part of an exclusive group. The Esquire Theatre sent out seven thousand announcements each week in the late 1940s (as well as sending two free tickets to each person for Christmas).[72] Some art house operators found problems with mailings, however. Stern pointed out that he never sent out mailings for his Cinema and Wilmette Theatres because he was never completely certain of his upcoming schedule. Sending out mailings could potentially hold a theater to an economically unfavorable schedule, requiring that the theater keep running a film that was not doing business or that it change over the current film when it could still do business for a few more weeks.[73] Therefore, mailings could be sent out only if exhibitors knew, without a doubt, that a film would begin playing on a certain date and run a certain amount of time.

Advertising

Advertising received a great deal of attention and money from art house operators. The images created through advertising impacted the entire conceptualization of film theaters and the film industry. The ability of advertising to create and control a film theater's image made this a powerful tool by which theaters could support their distinct qualities and emphasize the differences between the mainstream and the alternative. Art house operators could create and shape potential audience members' understanding of the distinctive qualities not only of art houses, but also of art films. As Mary Beth Haralovich wrote, "Film advertising is an arena which interlocks the promotion of a single film, individual studios, the film industry, and the pleasure of filmgoing."[74] Although referring mainly to studio advertising for Hollywood films, Haralovich's idea that the advertising of each film reflects on the entire film industry and the desires of the filmgoers is certainly pertinent for an understanding of art cinema advertising.

As discussed previously, studies showed that art film-goers were less affected by advertising and more likely to be influenced by reviews and word-of-mouth.[75] Some reports suggested that art houses did not need to use much advertising because "a sureseater hit automatically woos the kind of audience that is eager to seek out a good film."[76] However, interviews with people who ran art houses in Chicago and an examination of theater advertisements in *The Chicago Tribune* illustrate that advertising was essential for attracting audiences to art film theaters. Richard Stern said that advertising was actually even more important for art houses than for mainstream theaters and that his family often spent more on advertising for the Cinema art house than for the mainstream theaters they ran. Stern explained that for an art house, "your advertising was much, much higher, more involved than when you just ran a Hollywood type theater. ... If you ran a small ad you couldn't put a picture over. You had to spend more money on ads to get the people into an art type of operation."[77] Furthermore, art house operators did not just have to advertise; they had to tailor their advertising to attract their particular intended audiences. Charles Teitel explained that, next to the actual changes in films, modifications in advertising techniques were the most important changes made in a theater's conversion to an art policy. Teitel said, "They had to change their whole concept of advertising. That was the main thing. You see that was the key to the whole thing—the presentation of the product."[78]

Athough they recognized the importance of advertising, art film exhibitors did not have access to the same measure of financial resources as did the studios and their affiliated theaters or the larger theater chains. Additionally, unlike the studio-controlled theaters, art houses did not have organized, centralized, and systematized publicity departments to provide promotional support. The smaller exhibitors, therefore, worked with limited advertising budgets to come up with innovative advertising ideas for each film as it came along. Even though film distributors supplied many of the advertising materials (such as graphics and quotes) to exhibitors, these packages often did not include ad mats small enough to fit into the modest ad spaces taken by independent houses.[79] Furthermore, according to Balaban, all distributors (both of art films and of mainstream films) paid part of the advertising costs, but distributors offered less money to art house operators because there was less grossing potential at these sites.[80] Economic concerns, therefore, influenced the amount of advertising and the stylistic options available to art film exhibitors.

Art house operators used their limited advertising space to strengthen the association between their theaters and the appeals of status and prestige of high culture. According to Richard Brandt, the advertisements for art films, "promoted the values of the films that we were playing, which were different values than [those of] the American pictures that were playing around."[81] *Motion Picture Herald* reported that a theater in Rhode Island had a successful run with *Open City* by stressing that this was the first local showing of the film and by using critics' quotes in its advertisements.[82] In addition to laudatory quotes from critics, art houses also promoted film directors. This strategy, Stern explained, differed from the techniques of most mainstream theaters: "In the neighborhood theater they'll advertise the star but they'll never advertise the director."[83] Promoting the importance of the director in advertisements supported the idea of the director as an artist/auteur (a theory that would soon become popular in film criticism), further connecting the art film industry with traditional art and dissociating art films from the factorylike studio system.

Art film exhibitors sometimes included in their ads brief copy telling readers something about the film.[84] According to Balaban, the ads for the Esquire and Surf Theatres took him hours to write.[85] In a small box, Balaban included the theater name, brief text on the film, and perhaps a quote from a critic. Balaban tried to tell audience members something about the film, "whether it was ... well-made, interesting. Those were the things that were important."[86] Charles Teitel used white space to help his ads stand out. Teitel recalled that, to compete with the large ads placed by the major theaters, "I used maybe a fiftieth amount of the space they did, but I would leave a lot of white space in all my ads. . . . I would just have the name of the film and the name of the theater and maybe one line, and I tried not to clutter them up too much."[87] So they would stand out even more, Teitel also requested that his ads be placed near the larger, more cluttered ads.[88]

Like the Esquire and the World Playhouse, other art theaters generally used simple advertisements to connote sophistication and elegance. These ads were frequently quite small (often, as noted, for economic reasons), and they rarely used graphics, except perhaps when opening a film. Many of the art houses also adopted logolike designs for their theater names, so their ads jumped out from the rest of the smaller theater advertisements. Figure 8, for example, illustrates how the Esquire ad for *Never Say Goodbye* and the Cinema ad for *On Approval* stand out from the other small ads

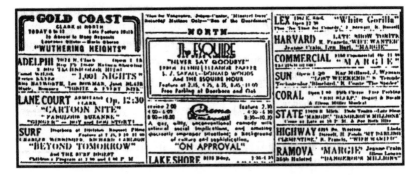

Figure 8. Theater advertisements, illustrating the distinctiveness of ads for the Esquire and Cinema Theatres. *Chicago Tribune,* 15 March 1947.

because of their more stylized typeface, which they used in all their advertisements.[89] This use of standard type for the theater names helped make the ads easily recognizable.[90]

Advertising and Sex

Although in interviews art house operators clearly foregrounded their attempts to promote the qualities of high culture and prestige surrounding art houses, art films continued to be identified by their sexual (and other risqué) qualities. If, as I argue, art house operators found their niche in selling highbrow culture to filmgoers, we must also consider whether advertising for art films ever capitalized on their more lurid elements. Forces outside of the traditionally defined art film industry certainly helped shape the public's view of art films. Yet the art film producers, distributors, and particularly the exhibitors were the people charged with exploiting sex to sell films.

Advertising for mainstream motion pictures after World War II must be considered as the yardstick against which advertising for art films was judged. Haralovich noted that in the 1940s, after a brief relatively conservative period in the 1930s, the film industry returned to the use of sexually provocative advertising to sell films. She quoted a 1950 article in *Advertising Agency* that observed, "Within recent months, newspapers seem to be carrying an increasing amount of copy decorated with busomy gals, overstandard cheesecake and clinch close-ups, all amply larded with text suggestive of lurid sex episodes in movies."[91] In a profile featured in the *Saturday Evening Post*, the theater manager for Loew's Richmond (Virginia) listed "sex" as the number-one appeal used in advertising and promotions to attract audiences to his theater.[92] Conventional theaters certainly used sex appeal to attract audiences. Some exhibitors complained about ads sent out for the film *Enchantment*, which featured "a mammoth-bosomed Teresa Wright ... in a clinch with Farley Granger" and used a "spotlight effect ... to play up the points that count."[93] However, other exhibitors used these ads despite being sent more modest replacements by the film's distributor, RKO.

The advertising for *The Outlaw* offers an example of the ways the Hollywood industry both used and reacted to the use of sensational sex in advertisements. The Howard Hughes film lost its Production Code Administration (PCA) certificate of approval because of its over-the-top advertising after this film was rereleased in 1946 with an advertising campaign focusing on Jane Russell's figure. Following the controversy over *The Outlaw*, the film industry expressed concern over the quality of cinema advertising and the Motion Picture Association of America (MPAA) strengthened its Advertising Code,[94] yet this seemed to have little effect on advertisements, which stayed just a bit more conservative than those for *The Outlaw*. For example, we can compare the advertisements for the film *Smash Up* of the RKO Grand and the Esquire Theatres. The large RKO Grand advertisement featured a busomy graphic of Susan Hayward and the copy "The men who loved her called her 'Angel' . . . but no angel could ever do what 'Angel' did!"[95] The Esquire ad, a fraction of the size of the RKO Grand advertisement, simply advertised the film's stars (Susan Hayward and Lee Bowman), the name of the film, the "Esquire Hour," the show times, and the free parking.[96] This small ad did not include any of the sexual allusions of the larger ad and attempted to instill a sense of dignity in the film in order to attract the usual Esquire audience to see this subrun Hollywood film.

Some art film exhibitors claimed that *avoiding* sexualized film promotion helped them maintain their adult audiences. According to an article in *Business Week*, art house operator Louis Sher "makes no effort to exploit by life-size nudes or flamboyant billboards any sensational films. Pictures are advertised in a subdued and straight forward way."[97] At least publicly, then, art house managers claimed to aim their advertising at sophisticated adults who could develop into loyal audience members. Richard Brandt adamantly stressed the fact that the lurid qualities of art films were particularly *not* exploited. He said that a risqué film "was very carefully handled. No, it wasn't promoted as a sex film. No, not at all. That was not where this whole art film was coming from. It was not that at all."[98]

Despite this apparent focus on sophisticated promotion, it would be incorrect to suggest that art theaters never used sensationalized advertising to attract audiences. Richard Stern explained that when a film was considered risqué, the line "for mature adults" or "an adult drama" would sometimes be used to advertise the film, though he claimed that this would have been the extent of using sex to sell the film.[99] Advertisements for Chicago's most prominent foreign-language film theater, the World Playhouse, show that sex was occasionally used more blatantly to promote films. For example, the World Playhouse's advertisement for *Open City*, prominently displayed (in bold capital letters) the "adults only" tag line.[100] In the advertisement for *Portrait of a Woman*, a French film directed by Jacques Feyder, the World Playhouse included a quote from *The New York Post* declaring the film "AS DARING as is permitted in the Gallic manner!" and a quote from *The New York Sun*: "Lusty humor . . . a triumph!"[101] The selection of critics' quotes for this ad clearly emphasized the more sensational qualities of the film. The World Playhouse was not the only art house to promote the more lascivious side of its films. For example, the Surf Theatre featured an ad for the French film *Jenny Lamour* with a graphic of a scantily clad woman, a tag line referencing the Kinsey report, and the suggestive line "French—English Titles, but the language of this film is international."[102]

Some art cinema participants acknowledged the importance of sex and scandal to art film box office revenue. As mentioned in chapter 1, in his 1953 autobiography art film distributor and exhibitor Arthur Mayer acknowledged that "frank sex content" helped art films attract audiences.[103] Mayer charged exhibitors (not distributors or filmmakers) with promoting the sexual nature of films: "*The Bicycle Thief* was completely devoid of any erotic embellishments, but the exhibitors sought to atone for this deficiency with a highly imaginative sketch of a young lady riding a bicycle."[104] However, that this same sketch, which Mayer found objectionable, was included in many different theaters' advertisements for the film (see Figure 9) has two possible implications. First, exhibitors may have copied the ad from each other, with mainstream theaters particularly relying on the sexual imagery. Second, it is also possible that this was actually a pre-prepared advertisement supplied by the film's distributors (Joseph Burstyn and Mayer himself).[105]

Art film exhibitors, then, did not produce all of the advertisements for art films. Art film distributors and businesses altogether outside of the art film industry also created art film advertising. The promotion of sex actually seemed to affect business outside of art houses more than it affected art house attendance. *Variety* observed, "The biological lure is the strongest pulling force outside of the coterie of regular patrons." As discussed in the previous chapter, *Variety* also noted that films that could be exploited for their sexual content were less dependent on New York for their gross. This was most certainly related to the willingness of smaller theaters and independent chains outside of New York to play films that could be promoted in such a manner.[106] Because of the connection between foreign films and risqué entertainment, "grind houses" specializing in exploitation films, such as Chicago's LaSalle and Studio Theatres, also showed foreign films. Grind houses, predominantly run by independent operators, searched, like art houses, for inexpensive films to fill their screen time. Foreign films offered these theaters, like art houses, a practical alternative. Not surprisingly, these theaters tended to promote the sensational attractions of art films. The Studio Theatre's advertisement for *Waltz Time* referred to the film as "a spicy tale of old Vienna when the waltz was considered Naughty!

Immoral! Illegal!"[107] In contrast, another theater previously had advertised *Waltz Time* simply as "a rare treat for those who love good music."[108] Similarly, the LaSalle Theatre advertised *Open City* as a "drama of love and lust" and used a silhouette of a profile of a well-endowed woman to advertise *Germany Year Zero,* in which the ad copy read, "Rossellini does it again!"

Independent exploitation houses were not alone in their lurid promotion of art films. Mainstream theater chains also exhibited successful art films, and they frequently resorted to sensational means to promote them. The Balaban and Katz theater chain (at the time owned by Paramount)

Figure 9. Two advertisements featuring the same graphic for *The Bicycle Thief*
for the World Playhouse (*Chicago Tribune,* 11 March 1950, 15) and the
Alex Theatre (*Chicago Tribune,* 28 April 1950, part 2, 14).

advertised *Open City* with the tag line "SAVAGE LOVE UNLEASHED!"[109] whereas the Imperial Theatre, part of a chain of neighborhood theaters, described the film as a "SAVAGE ORGY OF LUST!" (see Figure 10).

Although following the signing of the consent decree (discusssed in chapter 2) some theater chains were no longer owned by the film studios, most large theater chains (such as the Balaban and Katz chain) still claimed to abide by the PCA's policies, including the Advertising Code. This policy did not prevent theaters from advertising art films in a sensational manner. The double feature of the French film *Passionelle* and the Swedish film *Torment* (discussed in chapter 4), became controversial when playing at mainstream neighborhood theaters in New York City, where, according

Figure 10. Advertisement for *Open City*. *Chicago Tribune*, 13 October 1946, part 6, 19.

to *Variety*, "in all situations, emphasis in advertising and lobbies has been on the lurid side."[110] A comparison of the advertisements created by Balaban and Katz and the Cinema Theatre for *Blithe Spirit* illustrates the different ways a mainstream theater and an art house advertised the same British comedy. Whereas the Balaban and Katz ad featured a sketch of a woman in a suggestive pose, the Cinema ad simply featured a quote from a critic declaring the film "an exquisite piece of light and fanciful entertainment."[111]

Clearly, sex served as an important tool for promoting art films. However, as this discussion demonstrates, we must consider the sources of the sensational promotion. Discussing neorealist films, Richard deCordova noted, "One of the points that emerges very clearly in surveying the record of this period is that the success of foreign language films, and particularly the success of these Italian films, followed from their sexual content more than their serious themes."[112] DeCordova's statement, however, raises questions about whether he was considering the audience for these "successful" Italian films the art house audience or the audience outside of art houses. This examination of art film advertising suggests that the use of sex to promote the films was not a technique used by most art houses. Art film exhibitors, or even art film distributors, clearly cannot be held solely accountable for the type of advertisements used to promote art films. Beside the fact that major studios and theaters outside of the art film industry also took part in exploiting art films, we must also remember that art houses were commercial businesses competing with more conventional theaters for audiences. The increasing sexual emphasis of mainstream film advertising certainly influenced the boundaries set by art film advertisers. And, although it cannot be denied that art film exhibitors used sex to sell films, it also cannot be argued that they did so any more than owners of conventional theaters.

Art house operators, like all film exhibitors, attempted to find a place for their theaters within the changing film culture. At times this meant advertising the sexual nature of their art films to attract audiences. However, as interviews, newspaper articles, and examinations of the theaters and their promotional materials indicate, most often art house operators targeted potential viewers by associating their theaters with the values of highbrow culture, prestige, and sophistication. Although these qualities appeared to emerge from the films themselves (as natural values emanating from art films), clearly art house operators worked carefully to create this highbrow image to appeal to audiences searching for identity and distinction within the shifting cultural hierarchy.

CONCLUSION

Ranges of Difference: Alternative Cultures in a Commercial Industry

As the 1940s drew to a close, the techniques of art film theaters were fairly well established. By the time the *Film Daily Year Book* began listing the art film theaters in the United States, most people attending art film theaters knew what to expect at these exclusive, sophisticated, adult-oriented sites. And many art house operators understood how to appeal to these audiences not only by creating a distinctive filmgoing environment, but also by promoting their theaters and their films in particular ways. By foregrounding the image of prestigious, highbrow culture, art house operators sold their audiences the image of being involved with a unique alternative culture. Examining this image and the factors that shaped it, we begin to understand the operation of the U.S. film industry (such as the role of independent exhibitors); the layers of historical, socioeconomic, and industrial factors that shaped postwar U.S. culture (including the significance of the rise of middle-class culture); and the functions of leisure in the United States, particularly in relation to socioeconomic hierarchies (for example, the relationship between alternative cultures and taste cultures).

Most significantly, viewing the highbrow image of art houses as a construction with its basis in socioeconomic and industrial conditions highlights the role of monetary interests behind the creation of art cinema.

Despite art house operators' attempts to focus attention on art cinema's refined artistry, the rise of art cinema following World War II was an industrial reaction to changes in the film industry and in U.S. society. Factors such as the low rental costs of foreign films and the importing of foreign films by the major studios made art films available to independent theater owners for a relatively low price at a time when competition made mainstream Hollywood products increasingly expensive and scarce. Therefore, while many art house operators advanced the role of foreign and independent films in U.S. culture and supported the artistic potential of film, they also searched for the best way to succeed financially in the field of film exhibition. The screening of art films in theaters that featured cafés rather than concession stands, displayed art exhibits instead of movie posters, and distributed printed programs offered exhibitors an opportunity to draw audiences dissatisfied with Hollywood films and mainstream filmgoing.

That film exhibitors turned to appeals based on status, prestige, and art as ways to promote audience attendance illustrates the significant role of taste and culture in the postwar United States. Many people in the United States sought ways to distinguish themselves from the growing middle class; taste and culture became significant means of distinction. Involvement in art house culture offered potential audience members a way to achieve this distinction and shape their identities by being part of something different or alternative.

The introduction to this project draws on Raymond Williams's work to define an alternative culture as a culture that is different and is left alone to remain different.[1] Regardless of the films shown in art houses (in some cases quite different than mainstream films in terms of structure and content, but in some cases not so different), the atmosphere of art houses was constructed to provide a different type of filmgoing experience. As an emergent culture in the 1940s, art cinema developed in response to the social and industrial changes taking place after World War II. Art films and art houses offered audience members and filmmakers opportunities for difference and also influenced mainstream cinema. In fact, the history of art cinema may be seen as a process of negotiation with the mainstream Hollywood film industry to maintain unique properties for art cinema while still attracting a substantial audience. It was not, however, completely the influence of mainstream cinema that initiated this mediation. The interests of participants in the art film culture contributed to the ways art cinema functioned as an alternative culture. Importantly, art houses were still commercial theaters that did not subvert the commercial capitalist system, but rather worked within it. Additionally, the audiences and business personnel behind art cinema often expressed values of class and culture embedded within the dominant society.

Both art house audiences and business participants helped determine whether art film culture would remain alternative or lean toward the dominant. Although audiences at art houses may have wanted to retain their exclusive status and prevent art house attendance from becoming too mainstream, it is also important to note the push/pull role of conformity in postwar culture that made people want to both stand out from the crowd and be part of the crowd. The extent to which art house audiences truly wanted to be seen as significantly different from others is, then, an ambiguous social question. The financial interests of this commercial mass culture encouraged attempts to attract the largest audiences possible to maximize art cinema profits. Many art film industry participants appeared interested in finding a niche that they could exploit to further incorporate their businesses into the mainstream (while still encouraging increasing numbers of people to think of film as an art form). Therefore, it was not solely the power of the dominant culture that determined the fate of the emergent culture; rather the participants in the alternative/oppositional culture clearly played a substantial role in determining its position in relation to the dominant culture. The commercial and cultural interests of the people operating within these cultures must also be addressed in a realistic (rather than in a nostalgic) manner.

Art house operators solely interested in advancing the notion of film as an art form would have had a difficult time staying afloat within the field of commercial film exhibition. As Jonas Mekas said about an art film theater opening at the Brooklyn Academy of Music in 1998, "If your survival depends on the box office you cannot really serve the film community, because then you are looking for films that make money and then your mission disappears. You need a sponsor."[2] In the late 1940s some film exhibitors who wanted to focus more on art found "sponsors" in their audience members. Nonprofit film societies, such as Cinema 16 in New York and Art in Cinema in San Francisco, offer more concrete examples of how film exhibition might operate as a true alternative culture.[3] Film societies certainly faced the same shifting social, cultural, and industrial terrain as did all other film exhibitors. Like art houses, film societies tended to appeal to upper-class, highbrow audiences (or those trying to become highbrow) who were looking for a different type of film culture. All Cinema 16 members, for example, had to be able to afford the dues.[4] Additionally, Cinema 16 gave these people of means an opportunity to join with the

New York elite, and therefore offered them an element of prestige and status.[5] Cinema 16 also attracted patrons dissatisfied with conventional filmgoing and interested in expanding their cultural horizons (whether for aesthetic, social, or educational reasons). However, Cinema 16 utilized its nonmainstream position differently than did art houses.

Although the commercial art theaters had qualities of alternative culture, their operators, for the most part, strove toward integration into the mainstream. Cinema 16, on the other hand, was an alternative culture with inclinations toward the oppositional. Art film industry participants readily used art cinema's alternative qualities to create an image that would help them carve out a niche and maximize their audience. Additionally, while seeking to exploit their distinctions, art houses had to be careful not to be *too* different so as to avoid alienating any potential viewers. Amos Vogel's nonprofit organization, with its seasonal subscription policy, featured films more markedly different than those screened at art houses and circumvented the systems of governmental censorship, which limited the differences between art films and mainstream films. Furthermore, Vogel focused on film's potential to educate and effect social change.[6] In trying to attract audiences, Cinema 16 promoted its alternative film culture, whereas art houses promoted the status of being associated with such a culture.[7]

Cinema 16's appearance of embracing its alternative/oppositional cultural position raises questions about the role of the relatively more conventional art cinema in relation to the dominant motion picture industry. It is possible, however, that art cinema's closeness to dominant cinema, its existence on the edge of the mainstream industry rather than as a separate culture, allowed it to more forcefully impact Hollywood films. New textual techniques—from improvised dialogue to hand-held camera movement to the jump cut—first made their way into cinema through art films; and, when eventually incorporated into mainstream filmmaking, these techniques brought exciting possibilities to Hollywood films.

The popularity of art cinema also illustrated audiences' interest in more adult themes (including a more "realistic" handling of issues and a more overt portrayal of sex). Additionally, art cinema illustrated the benefits (and potential profit in) attracting highbrow, upper-class, adult audiences through specialized marketing. As discussed previously, the mainstream film industry certainly took note of art cinema's abilities to attract the adult "lost audience." Art and independent cinema helped Hollywood identify a particular niche within the U.S. market. Recognizing that art houses appealed to audiences that tended to avoid mainstream films, the Hollywood industry began to make more serious adult films. Over time, the mainstream film industry moved further away from the conventional family marketing of the studio era (when films were made that were expected to appeal to all viewers) and began to rely more on niche audiences such as teenagers and adults.[8] Additionally, art cinema promoted film as an art form, creating an association that spread into mainstream consciousness and strongly influenced how people thought about film.

Art film culture, as well as the number of art houses, grew in the 1950s. According to Eric Schaefer, "The number of first run art cinemas almost doubled between 1954 and 1960, jumping from 226 to 399."[9] However, there were already signs that the techniques of art films and art houses were moving into the mainstream industry. The serious themes of many art films were picked up by Hollywood filmmakers, resulting in what Bosley Crowther referred to as a trend of "downbeat" films (such as the 1951 releases *A Place in the Sun, Death of a Salesman,* and *A Streetcar Named Desire*).[10] Additionally, there were references in the press to mainstream theaters' reaching for the "more sophisticated" audience members by providing them with "smaller, more intimate, more 'modern' and more 'livable' theatres."[11] In the late 1950s, a few theaters in New York City were adopting some of the techniques of art houses (such as eliminating popcorn sales and removing busy, "hard-sell" theater fronts) to attract upscale audiences to road shows and special wide-screen performances.[12] The Hollywood studios also began to recognize that art houses were potential exhibition sites for their own films. In 1953, Arthur Knight noted that art houses had been "weakened since Hollywood's recent discovery of them as a profitable outlet for their less colossal pictures."[13]

Despite this "weakening" of art houses, the number of theaters specializing in art films grew in the 1960s. A *Newsweek* article titled "Art House Boom" stated that there were five art houses in Los Angeles in 1957, and by 1962 this number had increased to twenty-six.[14] Art house operators expressed concerns about whether there were enough films to fill the growing number of screens showing art films.[15] Film societies also continued to grow in number, developing around a film culture that moved away from the "realist" films of the late 1940s and toward the personal cinema of filmmakers such as Jean-Luc Godard, Ingmar Bergman, Michelangelo Antonioni, and Akira Kurosawa. However, in the middle to late 1960s, art films found themselves in competition with U.S. films for audience attention. Hollywood officially abandoned the Production Code (moving to the ratings system) and began to produce more serious films that included the adult themes and sexual elements of art films. With the demarcation between art film and Hollywood film blurred, theaters also began to cross over and show different types of films. For example, mainstream theaters and drive-ins in the Chicago suburbs screened art films at this time.[16] With mainstream theaters showing films similar to those shown in art theaters, art houses became less important for film distribution.

Increased competition from Hollywood, the development of suburban film theaters, and a decrease in the importation of foreign films (in part as a reaction to the growing number of independent U.S. films) made it more difficult for art houses to fill their screen time.[17] Art houses began to close or change their programming policies. Christine Ogan wrote, "By 1969, the [*Film Daily*] *Year Book* had dropped the art theater category from its listings of U.S. theaters."[18] Many art houses, Eric Schaefer explained, once again looked for alternative product to differentiate their theaters: "Just as lack of product caused exhibitors to turn to the art film in the 1950s, a decline in foreign releases in the 1960s caused art theatre operators to turn to sexploitation."[19]

In their last years, then, some art houses, in search of film product, exhibited pornographic and sexploitation films.[20] This was the case at Charles Teitel's World Playhouse in Chicago, which closed in 1972 after a few years of showing "sex films."[21] Only a couple of years earlier, in 1970, Richard Stern had closed his Cinema Theatre. Across the United States (no longer comprised of a growing middle class, but a country facing war, social change, and eventually recession), the number of art film theaters continued to dwindle. Many of the theaters that continued to screen art films focused on New Hollywood films by young American auteurs such as Robert Altman, John Cassavetes, and Martin Scorsese (films often distributed by the major studios).[22] These films replaced foreign language films as the art house staples. According to one estimate, in 1960 almost forty foreign-language films played in first-run theaters in New York City. By 1973, that number was down to eighteen foreign-language films.[23] Saul Tureli of Janus Films, which distributed foreign films, said in 1973, "American film-goers can see brilliant, sophisticated movies of their own. . . . So the entire market has been shaken up. It's a costly game of Russian roulette. Everyone here is extremely cautious."[24]

By the end of the 1970s, however, the major studios (and their new corporate owners) turned away from the independent New American film-makers and focused on high-concept films—films like *Jaws, Star Wars,* and *Saturday Night Fever*—that attracted large audiences to suburban the-aters.[25] With corporate takeovers of Hollywood studios increasing, potential profits became the central concern of the dominant film industry in a manner even stronger than in previous years. The line between mainstream U.S. films and art or independent films once again became clear. Although Hollywood still produced smaller films, its focus turned to the high-concept films that appealed to the largest number of people during these lean economic years.[26] By the end of the 1970s, the rise of the blockbuster and high-concept films increased the interest in art films—or, as they were now called, "specialty" films—on the part of audiences once again alienated by Hollywood practices.

The bottom-line interests of the industry also affected film theaters. Instead of presenting people with unique experiences, film theaters of the 1970s turned toward offering options, not experiences. Run-down theaters often remained that way, while new theaters were built with an eye toward economizing whenever possible. The major changes in film exhibition (other than the improvements in sound quality) involved the increased numbers of twin and multiplex theaters.[27] However, the environments of these theaters were not considered priorities, and theaters perhaps resembled nickelodeons more than they did the ornate picture palaces of the 1920s or the modern art houses of the 1940s. Gomery wrote, "It was as if, having realized they had 'lost' the battle with television and the living room, these movie theatres gave up all pretense of struggle at the level of architectural fantasy and the viewing experience and actually produced interiors with less to offer than at home."[28]

In the 1980s more multiplex theaters (especially in or near shopping malls) sprang up, the major studios focused increasingly on blockbusters and high-concept films, and the box office earnings of foreign-language films continued to decline (although there was hope for their success in videocassette form).[29] Within this market a group of U.S. independent films once again proved the potential for movies that separated themselves from the mainstream.[30] Sparked by this seemingly new interest on the part of audiences, several of the major studios developed "specialized" divisions (such as 20th Century-Fox's Fox International Classics, later renamed TLC, Columbia's Triumph Pictures, and Universal's Universal Classics) to distribute smaller independent films as well as rereleases of the companies' older films.[31] The majors' involvement drove up the costs for distribution rights as well as the prices of film rentals for imports and U.S. independent films and forced many independent distributors out of the business. Soon, after rediscovering what they had supposedly learned in the 1940s, the difficulties of marketing these films, most of the major studios closed their specialty divisions.[32] Despite the shake-up caused by the involvement of the major studios, the specialized film market expanded. The aging of film viewers prompted the continued production of "prestige" films for audience members past their teen years who, for the most part, were not being served by the dominant film industry.

Several new independent distributors used the success of specialty films to move into more "commercial" markets.[33] New Line Cinema, for example, began in 1967 as the distributor of alternative films (such as *Reefer Madness* and Godard's *Sympathy for the Devil*). As the company became more successful in the 1980s, New Line founder Bob Shaye moved the company toward more mainstream films (including *Nightmare on Elm Street* and *Teenage Mutant Ninja Turtles*).[34] By 1990 New Line had moved so far into the mainstream film market that Shaye created Fine Line Features as its specialty film distribution arm.[35] Again we see that alternative film distributors—even those focusing on art films—did not desire to remain within the alternative market, but hoped to achieve mainstream success.

As in the 1940s, the sites of exhibition for specialty films continued to be an important concern. Douglas Gomery perhaps overgeneralized when he wrote, "With the coming of the conservative 1980s, coupled with the rise of home video, the art house phenomenon came to an end. Home video made it too easy to see foreign films at home."[36] While many revival theaters closed (due in large part to the availability of older films on videocassette and through cable), the number of screens for specialty films has grown since the 1970s. In Chicago, the Fine Arts Theatre opened on the site of the World Playhouse in the early 1980s (and is now a full-time commercial art theater owned by Sony Theaters).[37] In 1986, USA Cinemas announced plans for a chain of art houses.[38] Even multiplexes began to set aside screens for specialized films.[39]

The Carnegie Screening Room, a seventy-five–seat auditorium, opened in 1987 to screen films "more specialized than traditional major art films."[40] The opening of a theater designed to screen films more alternative than specialty films highlights the differences that exist even within the category of art (or specialty) theaters. Some theaters focused on the more mainstream (yet still alternative) art films, while others specialized in more alternative (yet still commercial) films. Interestingly, the more mainstream art houses (such as Chicago's Fine Arts Theatre) offered settings that looked remarkably like mainstream theaters being built at the time. Some of the newer art houses had more than one screen, and some were part of the growing art house chains. However, many of the more alternative spaces, instead of being more sophisticated and higher class than the new theaters, were often old and worn. The Carnegie Screening Room stood out when compared to art houses, which could afford to show these more alternative films only by screening them in older spaces. Still other art houses took another approach and operated out of old picture palaces, returning to the elaborate and ornamental theaters that art houses had originally rejected. The Music Box Theatre in Chicago and The Stanford Theatre in California are two examples of theaters that offer patrons large theaters (at least theaters larger than those in the 1980s multiplexes) in which to see revival, independent, foreign, and other alternative films. The art house as it was known in the 1940s—as a site of cultural distinction and atmosphere, elegance and modernity—had changed, replaced by small, boxy theaters; older, run-down theaters; or renovated picture palaces.

The changes in art houses could be seen as a reflection of the changes in the cultural position of art cinema. The idea of film as art, which was reflected in art film culture, moved from a position as emergent culture in the 1940s and 1950s to an idea accepted by mainstream culture in the 1960s and early 1970s. However, in the later 1970s and 1980s, the dominant film culture retreated from the position that film is an art form, returning to the use of cinema mainly as a form of entertainment.[41] The focus on film as an art form remained a residual culture left over from earlier times. Therefore, in the 1980s, the function of art film theaters (as well as their looks) changed as they moved from embodying groundbreaking modern ideas to a remnant of the culture of previous generations.

Recently, however, we have seen a renewed focus on art cinema. Perhaps the economic boom that created a larger upper middle class has again created an interest in taste as a tool of distinction. The older art houses (both those that were not renovated and those established in old picture palaces) still exist, and more mainstream art houses have joined them. Modeled after the newer multiplexes that focus on theater atmosphere and environment (many of which include stadium seating, game rooms, and gourmet snacks), these art houses, like their mainstream counterparts, once again focus on atmosphere and distinction. As the motion picture audience ages and the studios continue to move into the production, distribution, and exhibition of specialty films (as well as the exhibition of mainstream films), the market for these films grows. Richard Stern now operates the Wilmette Theatre in the northern suburbs of Chicago. Stern has estimated that 80 percent of the films he screens are art films and that he may run the only suburban theater in Chicago featuring practically all art films.[42] Despite others' gloomy visions of art cinema, Stern has indicated that the opportunities for the exhibition of art films may not have declined considerably since the immediate postwar period. Noting that many theaters now have more than one screen, Stern said, "While there's maybe fewer theaters, there's, just maybe, as many screens."[43]

However, the gap between types of art films as well as between their exhibition sites also continues to widen. Some art films (such as *Elizabeth,* *The Red Violin,* and *Life Is Beautiful*) are clearly more dominant than others, being produced and distributed by major studios and displaying the possibility of crossing over into mainstream theaters. Other films (like *Pi,* *Run Lola Run,* and *Buena Vista Social Club*), often distributed by smaller independent firms, seem clearly reconciled to screenings in the more specialized art houses. Similarly, specialty theaters have become big business in the United States. Landmark Theatre Corporation is the largest chain of art film theaters, operating approximately fifty-two art houses across the United States.[44] The Sundance Institute, Robert Redford's organization dedicated to independent cinema, has expressed plans to enter art film exhibition.[45] And City Cinemas acquired New York City's six-screen art house Angelika Theatre for $12 million in 1996.[46] The Angelika offers its downtown New York customers the opportunity to be on a theater mailing list; to attend lectures, seminars, and classes; and to eat in the theater's café (which does not require a theater ticket for admittance).[47] City Cinemas has started to open up a chain of multiscreen "artplexes" using the Angelika brand name. An eight-screen Angelika Theatre opened in Houston in 1998.[48]

Our examination of art cinema and the role of art houses in the 1940s illuminates the issues we might explore to understand art film culture today. Certainly we must inquire after the industrial and economic operations behind this latest art house "boom." We can also think about how the sociocultural context (such as the supposedly strong economy of the 1990s and the increased wealth of many American families) may be increasing art house attendance. Most interesting, though, is the continued operation of the smaller, older, more specialized art houses. The turn away from modern and sophisticated environments for art houses must be considered not only in terms of its industrial and economic causes (such as the increasing costs of rent and film acquisitions), but also in terms of what it tells us about the role of art cinema in leisure culture today. Questions that remain to be asked concern how art houses currently market their films, what these theaters offer audience members, and who attends these films in theaters. Today's art houses must be tied to the role of leisure in the contemporary social hierarchy and the possible position of the current art film culture as a residual culture of the postwar art film movement.

These questions about art film theaters today highlight the ambivalence of cultural values and the importance of understanding the development of image and industry when considering how culture functions in society. As the dominant Hollywood industry moves further into the art film industry, we see the emergence of another art film culture that is attempting to define its position, as did art cinema of the 1940s. The terms on which we can examine art cinema today and the role of art houses in shaping our understanding of art cinema rely on our knowledge of the rise of art cinema in the United States and its negotiation for space within the U.S. film industry.

Art cinema is still clearly influenced by the activities of art film exhibitors of the immediate postwar period. In the late 1940s, before art cinema had firmly established its position within the U.S. film industry, art houses helped to support and shape the emerging art film culture. Art cinema of the 1940s also developed into a social phenomenon that stressed the importance of separating oneself from the mass audience and fostered the ongoing changes in the cultural hierarchy. The art house movement, through its promotion of status and prestige to create a niche in the film exhibition market, illustrated to the mainstream industry the benefits of market segmentation and consequently influenced the development of the conventional industry. The growing popularity of art houses in the United States following World War II also suggested the potential of a different type of film. These sophisticated and adult art films attracted viewers, showing film producers not only new ways to make films, but also that audiences' interests in motion picture content were changing. Furthermore, the ways in which art film exhibitors positioned their theaters within the new cultural environment attached new values to film and helped to associate cinema with legitimate art and highbrow culture. The prestige of art cinema, supported and molded by the postwar art house, affected how people thought about film and influenced the significance and functions of film in cultural life. In the end, the attempts by art house operators and art cinema participants to carve out a niche helped to shape the economic, social, and industrial structure as well as the cultural significance and values associated with the film industry from which they were originally excluded.

Notes

Introduction

1. Stanley Frank, "Sure-seaters Discover an Audience," *Nation's Business*, January 1952, 69.

2. *Film Daily Year Book* (New York: J. W. Alicoate, 1950), 1036; *Film Daily Year Book*, (New York: J. W. Alicoate, 1964), 1033–36. It should be noted that this number does not include the theaters that specialized in exhibition of subrun art films—which probably greatly outnumbered the first-run theaters. Furthermore, it is interesting to note that the number of art houses increased at a time when the total number of theaters in the United States declined. Although there were almost 17,000 four-walled theaters (this figure excluded drive-ins) in the United States in 1950, by 1963 that number had decreased to 12,500. *Film Daily Year Book* (1964), 117.

3. For example, see Pierre Bourdieu, *Distinction: A Theoretical Critique of the Judgment of Taste*, trans. Richard Nice (Cambridge: Harvard University Press, 1984); Pierre Bourdieu "The Production of Belief: Contribution to an Economy of Symbolic Goods," *Media, Culture and Society* 2 (1980): 261–93; Herbert Gans, *Popular Culture and High Culture: An Analysis and Evaluation of Taste* (New York: Basic Books, 1974).

4. John F. Kasson, *Amusing the Million: Coney Island at the Turn of the Century* (New York: Hill and Wang, 1978); Lawrence W. Levine, *Highbrow/Lowbrow: The Emergence of Cultural Hierarchy in America* (Cambridge: Harvard University Press, 1988); Kathy Peiss, *Cheap Amusements: Working Women and Leisure in Turn-of-the-Century New York* (Philadelphia: Temple University Press, 1986).

5. Andrew Ross, *No Respect: Intellectuals and Popular Culture* (New York: Routledge, 1989); Joan Shelley Rubin, *The Making of Middlebrow Culture* (Chapel Hill: University of North Carolina Press, 1992).

6. Jackson Lears, "A Matter of Taste: Corporate Cultural Hegemony in a Mass-Consumption Society," in *Recasting America: Culture and Politics in the Age of Cold War*, ed. Lary May (Chicago: University of Chicago Press, 1989), 38–57; C. Wright Mills, *White Collar*

(New York: Oxford University Press, 1956); David Riesman with Nathan Glazer and Reuel Denney, *The Lonely Crowd* (New Haven: Yale University Press, 1961).

7. For example, Dwight Macdonald, "A Theory of Mass Culture," in *Mass Culture: The Popular Arts in America*, ed. Bernard Rosenberg and David Manning White (New York: Free Press, 1957), 59–73.

8. In contrast, an oppositional culture is a culture that questions the dominant order. Dominant culture tends to either automatically incorporate or destroy oppositional cultures, whereas alternative cultures are given more room in which to exist. Raymond Williams, "Base and Superstructure in Marxist Cultural Theory," *New Left Review* 82 (November/December 1973): 3–16.

9. Chuck Kleinhans examines some of these issues in relation to independent film production of the 1990s in "Independent Features: Hopes and Dreams," in *New American Cinema*, ed. Jon Lewis (Durham: Duke University Press, 1998), 307–27.

10. "Art House Boom," *Newsweek*, 28 May 1962, 102.

11. For more information about the role of the "major independents," see Justin Wyatt, "The Formation of the 'Major Independent': Miramax, New Line and the New Hollywood," in *Contemporary Hollywood Cinema*, ed. Steve Neale and Murray Smith (London: Routledge, 1998), 74–90.

12. See, for example, John Brodie and Monica Roman, "H'wood May Be Too Big for Its Niches," *Variety*, 10 June 1996, 1; Josh Young, "Sundown," *The New Republic*, 10 April 1995, 22.

13. The case of *Burstyn* v. *Wilson*, quoted in Richard S. Randall, *Censorship of the Movies: The Social and Political Control of a Mass Medium* (Madison: University of Wisconsin Press, 1968), 29. *The Miracle*, a short film directed by Roberto Rossellini, was distributed by Joseph Burstyn (who also distributed *Open City* and *The Bicycle Thief* with Arthur Mayer) as part of the *Ways of Love* trilogy (the other films in the trilogy were the French films *A Day in the Country* and *Jofroi*). *Ways of Love*, which played at New York's Paris Theatre throughout the court case, attracted standing-room-only audiences to the theater. Robert Wohlforth, "People and Pickets," *The New Republic*, 5 February 1951, 13.

14. The case of *Mutual Film Corporation* v. *Ohio*, quoted in Randall, 19.

15. *Newsweek*, 8 August 1955, 50–51.

16. Thomas Elsaesser, "Putting on a Show: The European Art Movie," *Sight and Sound*, April 1994, 25.

17. Quoted in Walter Spencer, "Modern Movies: No Kids, No Popcorn," *World Journal Tribune* (New York, N.Y.), 17 October 1966, 13. Art cinema additionally influenced the public's acceptance of sex as part of motion pictures by associating sexual content with adult and sophisticated films. In this instance, art cinema became part of a growing adult culture in the postwar period that related to the emergence of *Playboy* in the 1950s and the "bachelor" culture that was depicted in films of the 1950s, such as those featuring Doris Day and Rock Hudson.

18. See Jim Lane, "Critical and Cultural Reception of the European Art Film in 1950's America: A Case Study of the Brattle Theatre (Cambridge, Massachusetts)," *Film History* 24 (1994): 49–64.

19. See, for example, David Bordwell, "The Art Cinema as a Mode of Film Practice," *Film Criticism* 4 (Fall 1979): 56–64; Robert Self, "Systems of Ambiguity in the Art Cinema," *Film Criticism* 4 (Fall 1979): 74–80.

20. Richard Schickel, "Days and Nights in the Arthouse," *Film Comment* 28 (May–June 1992): 32.

21. Each of the following authors, to differing degrees, considers the economic context of art cinema: Mike Budd, "Authorship as a Commodity: The Art Cinema of *The Cabinet of Dr. Caligari*," *Wide Angle* 6 (1984): 12–19; Peter Lev, *The Euro-American Cinema* (Austin: University of Texas Press, 1993); Michael Mayer, *Foreign Films on American Screens* (New York:

Arco, 1965); Steven Neale, "Art Cinema as Institution," *Screen* 22 (1981): 11–39; John Twomey, "Some Considerations on the Rise of the Art Film Theater," *Quarterly of Film, Radio and Television* 10 (Spring 1956): 239–47.

1. Reading for Maximum Ambiguity

1. Otis L. Guernsey, Jr., "'Art Movies' Low in Quality but 'Art Theaters' Thrive," *The New York Herald Tribune,* 30 October 1949, "Cinema—Foreign-U.S." clippings file, Billy Rose Theater Collection, Performing Arts Research Library, New York Public Library at Lincoln Center, New York.

2. Herbert Mitgang, "Transatlantic 'Miracle' Man," *Park East,* August 1952, 36.

3. Mike Budd, "Authorship as a Commodity: The Art Cinema and *The Cabinet of Dr. Caligari,*" *Wide Angle* 6 (1984): 13.

4. Peter Lev, *The Euro-American Cinema* (Austin: University of Texas Press, 1993), 5.

5. David Bordwell, "The Art Cinema as a Mode of Film Practice," *Film Criticism* 4 (Fall 1979): 61. This is not to suggest that Bordwell did not recognize that art films exist within a unique, and perhaps alternative, industrial framework. However, his method of defining the art film in this essay focused on textual rather than industrial factors.

6. Steven Neale, "Art Cinema as Institution," *Screen* 22 (1981): 13.

7. Budd, "Authorship as a Commodity," 13.

8. John E. Twomey, "Some Considerations on the Rise of the Art Film Theater," *Quarterly of Film, Radio and Television* 10 (Spring 1956): 240.

9. Lev, *The Euro-American Cinema,* 4.

10. Ibid., 38.

11. "U Showcase in NY as Test Run for Rank," *Variety,* 4 February 1948, 4.

12. Bordwell, "The Art Cinema as a Mode of Film Practice," 57.

13. See David Bordwell, Janet Staiger, and Kristin Thompson, *The Classical Hollywood Cinema: Film Style and Mode of Production to 1960* (New York: Columbia University Press, 1985) and David Bordwell, *Narration in the Fiction Film* (Madison: University of Wisconsin Press, 1985).

14. Lev, *The Euro-American Cinema,* 5.

15. Thomas M. Pryor, "Foreign Films Become Big Business," *The New York Times,* 8 February 1948.

16. Sergio Amidei, "'Open City' Revisited," *The New York Times,* 16 February 1947.

17. "Italo 'Open City' Freak B.O. in U.S.," *Variety,* 19 June 1946.

18. Ibid.

19. Review of *Lost Boundaries, The Exhibitor,* 6 July 1949, 2645.

20. Thomas M. Pryor, "Hoeing His Own Row," *The New York Times,* 26 June 1949.

21. Richard Brandt, telephone interview by author, 5 September 1996, tape recording.

22. Other qualities of classical Hollywood films include the use of a double plot line, one of which is generally a love story, that tie together at the end of the film; the attempt to make the techniques of filmmaking "invisible" (through conventions such as continuity editing) in order to foreground the narrative and create an illusion of reality; and the tendency toward a strong sense of story closure at the end of the film. See Bordwell, Staiger, and Thompson, *The Classical Hollywood Cinema,* 1–84.

23. Bordwell, "The Art Cinema as a Mode of Film Practice," 57.

24. Ibid., 60.

25. Robert Self, "Systems of Ambiguity in the Art Cinema," *Film Criticism* 4 (Fall 1979): 77.

26. Pamela Falkenberg, "'Hollywood' and the 'Art Cinema' as a Bipolar Modeling System: *A Bout de Souffle* and *Breathless,*" *Wide Angle* 7 (1985): 44–53.

27. Charles Barr, *Ealing Studios* (London: Cameron and Tayleur Books, 1977), 115.

28. On realism, see Erich Auerbach, *Mimesis: The Representation of Reality in Western*

Literature, trans. Willard R. Trask (Princeton: Princeton University Press, 1953), 538; on naturalism, see Mordecai Gorelik, *New Theatres for Old* (1940; repr. New York: Octagon Books, 1975), 10.

29. Linda Nochlin, *Realism* (London: Penguin Books, 1971), 13.

30. Ibid., 34.

31. André Bazin, "De Sica: Metteur en Scene," *What Is Cinema?* Vol. 2 (Berkeley: University of California Press, 1971), 62.

32. Bosley Crowther, review of *Open City, The New York Times,* 26 February 1946, 21.

33. Manny Farber, review of *Open City, New Republic,* 15 July 1946, 46.

34. Review of *Open City, Life,* 4 March 1946, 111.

35. Nora E. Taylor, "British Film Goal: Realism," *Christian Science Monitor,* 14 December 1946, 9.

36. Manny Farber, review of *Lost Boundaries, The Nation,* 30 July 1949, 114.

37. Bosley Crowther, review of *Lost Boundaries, The New York Times,* 1 July 1949, 14.

38. The review in *The Exhibitor* lists the film's genre as "Documentary Drama." Review of *Lost Boundaries, The Exhibitor,* 6 July 1949, 2645.

39. Review of *Lost Boundaries, Variety,* 29 June 1949, 20.

40. Review of *Lost Boundaries, Theatre Arts,* October 1949, 96.

41. Though it is important to remember that the film was written, directed, and produced by white people.

42. John Mason Brown, review of *Lost Boundaries, The Saturday Review,* 10 September 1949, 33.

43. Neale, "Art Cinema as Institution," 32.

44. Review of *Open City, Life,* 111.

45. Joseph Burstyn, "Talent Surplus in France," *The New York Times,* 27 August 1939, "Joseph Burstyn" clippings file, Billy Rose Theater Collection, Performing Arts Research Library, New York Public Library at Lincoln Center, New York.

46. "Lots of New Foreign Films," *PM New York,* 10 November 1947, "Foreign Films" clippings file, Billy Rose Theater Collection, Performing Arts Research Library, New York Public Library at Lincoln Center, New York.

47. Bosley Crowther, quoted in "Foreign Films Dominate Crix Lists of '10 Best,'" *Variety,* 1 January 1947, 10.

48. "Rank-Young Interviewers Evidence that U.S. Press Seems Plenty Sold on British Pix," *Variety,* 14 May 1947, 6.

49. At the time the trade organization was known as the Motion Picture Producers and Distributors Association.

50. *The Motion Picture Almanac* for 1944–45, quoted in Ruth A. Inglis, "Self Regulation in Operation," in *The American Film Industry,* rev. ed., ed. Tino Balio (Madison: University of Wisconsin Press, 1985), 385.

51. Richard Brandt, telephone interview by author, 5 September 1996, tape recording.

52. The other Legion of Decency ratings were A-I (a film approved for all viewers), A-II (a film approved for adults only), and B (a film morally objectionable in part). The Legion also instituted a pledge that churchgoers could (but were not required to) take once a year vowing not to attend any films condemned by the Legion. "How Do You See the Movies? As Entertainment and Offensive at Times or as Candid Art?" *Newsweek,* 8 August 1955, 51. It is important to note that the Legion did not represent all factions of the Catholic Church. For example, the Catholic magazine *Commonweal,* which was not an official magazine of the church and focused on cultural and social rather than theological issues, frequently disagreed with the Legion regarding film censorship.

53. The Legion, however, could always send people to see a film in the theater and rate it during the film's run. By condemning a film at this time, the Legion did not stop a theater

from initially renting a film, but could prevent people from attending the film and provoke the exhibitor to pull the film out of the theater.

54. Mitgang, "Transatlantic 'Miracle' Man," 36.

55. "Treasury Passes Buck to Atty Genl on French 'Diable' Pix, Too Sexy?" *Variety*, 9 July 1947, 4; "'Diable' Finally OK'd but U Won't Distrib in U.S.," *Variety*, 1 September 1948, 18.

56. "Moral Breach," *Time*, 30 October 1949, 76. One way around state and local censorship was the formation of private film societies, such as New York's Cinema 16, which were not subject to prior censorship rules for public showings since the screenings were private. Private film societies will be discussed in greater detail in chapter 2 and Cinema 16 is discussed in the conclusion.

57. Herman G. Weinberg, "I Title Foreign Films," *Theatre Arts*, April/May 1948, 51.

58. Charles Teitel, telephone interview by author, 4 August 1996, tape recording.

59. Ibid.

60. Irwin Course, acting director of Motion Picture Division, letter to Arthur Mayer and Joseph Burstyn, Inc., dated 6 February 1946, file 47909, box 1209, Motion Picture Records of the New York State Department of Education's Motion Picture Division, New York State Archives, Albany, New York. According to Course, the specific torture scenes to be eliminated were "where hypodermic needle is being jabbed into prisoner's arm," "where flame of flow [sic] torch is thrown against man's breast and view of flesh burning," and "where implement of torture is bound to man's finger, and other man with pliers starts to take off nail." Dr. Ward Bowen, the acting director of the New York State Department of Education's Motion Pictures Division (the state's censor board) attempted to explain why the New York censor board was more lenient toward foreign films such as *Open City*. Bowen said, according to *Variety*, that "such films are approved mainly because they depict such things in the light of a foreign atmosphere and not in that of the U.S." See "NY Censor Chief Explains Breen OK Not Always OK; Stance on Foreign Pix," *Variety*, 26 March 1947, 4. This justification foregrounds how easy it would have been for foreign films to get contradictory reactions from different censor boards.

61. Quoted in "Moral Breach," *Time*, 31 October 1949, 76.

62. Gunnar D. Kumlien, "The Artless Art of Italian Films," *Commonweal*, 22 December 1953, 177.

63. "Miracle on 58th Street," *Harper's*, April 1951, 107.

64. That the New York state archives have no record of requiring changes for *Tight Little Island* shows that the film's name had already been changed before being submitted for permission for public exhibition in New York. This suggests either that a national organization (such as the Production Code Administration or the Legion of Decency) requested the change or that the film's producers or distributors made the change on their own to avoid any potential problems.

65. Richard deCordova, "The Rise of the Art Film in Post-War Chicago," paper presented at the College Art Association Convention, Boston, 1987.

66. Thomas F. Brady, "The Hollywood Wire," *The New York Times*, 14 November 1948; Pryor, "Hoeing His Own Row."

67. Cyril Ray, "These British Movies," *Harper's*, June 1948, 5.

68. Ibid.

69. Quoted in Pierre Leprohon, *The Italian Cinema* (New York: Praeger, 1972), 92.

70. "Independent Producer Ranks Swelled Considerably During 1947," *Variety*, 7 January 1947, 43.

71. "Small Seaters Pitch to Majors on Reissues," *Variety*, 3 August 1949, 5.

72. "Par Clicks with Dualer Reissues at Art Houses as Linguals Fade," *Variety*, 31 August 1949, 3.

73. Ibid.

74. "Film Chain Finds Cure for Box Office Blues," *Business Week,* 22 March 1958, 75.

75. Richard Stern, interview by author, 8 October 1996, Wilmette, Ill., tape recording.

76. "Brit Pix Bloody but Unbowed," *Variety,* 28 April 1948, 24.

77. However, even some mainstream theaters played foreign-language films, particularly neighborhood theaters that needed to fill screen time. The reasons for this will be discussed in greater detail in chapter 3. "Big New York Play for Foreign Pix," *Variety,* 30 April 1947, 11.

78. "Universal to Continue Big Rank Release," *The Hollywood Reporter,* 25 January 1949, 2.

79. "Rank," *Motion Picture Herald,* 7 June 1947, 8.

80. "U Showcase in NY as Test Run for Rank," *Variety,* 4 February 1948, 4.

81. "Rank," 8.

82. DeCordova, "The Rise of the Art Film in Post-War Chicago." Some major distributors participated in foreign-language film distribution, particularly MGM, which experimented with foreign-language film distribution beginning in 1946, but quickly abandoned the project after discovering the difficulties of tailoring a distribution plan for foreign-language films. "MGM Gets Foreign Films," *Motion Picture Herald,* 2 June 1946, 60.

83. "Stix Nix British Pix," *Variety,* 18 June 1947, 18.

84. To name just a few, 20th Century-Fox, RKO, Samuel Goldwyn, and MGM all produced films overseas. See "Rossellini-Bergman (Goldwyn) Pic Due for Release Via RKO," *Variety,* 9 February 1949, 4, and "20th Using Its Foreign Pix Coin for Production Abroad Says Skouras," *Variety,* 16 February 1949, 5.

85. See "Loew's Conflict on Foreign Pic for Top Dates," *Variety,* 18 February 1948, 6; "Metro's Yankee-Doodle Bally on 'Search' to Offset 'Foreign' Pic Hex," *Variety,* 14 April 1948, 19; and "Pix Like 'The Search' OK for Distrib—Rodgers," *Variety,* 22 December 1948, 18.

86. "Azteca Seeks Dates in U.S. Art Theatres," *The Hollywood Reporter,* 23 June 1949, 3.

87. Ibid.

88. "Average French or Italian Film Nets Only 20–40G in U.S. Market," *Variety,* 17 November 1948, 15.

89. "Sureseaters in '46 Do Triple of '41 Because of Better Foreign Pix," *Variety,* 4 December 1946, 6.

90. Neale, "Art Cinema as Institution," 36.

91. Elmer Balaban, interview by author, 19 April 1996, Chicago, tape recording.

92. "Still Another Rank Unit (Prestige Pix) Aims at Sureseaters," *Variety,* 10 July 1946, 9.

93. Pierre Bourdieu, "The Production of Belief: Contribution to an Economy of Symbolic Goods," *Media, Culture and Society* 2 (1980): 268.

94. Ibid., 269.

95. Film societies such as San Francisco's Art in Film and New York's Cinema 16 came closer to questioning the commercial basis of the industry by organizing as nonprofit private organizations. These societies offered a different type of organization for film exhibition based on memberships rather than single admissions. Some film societies also exhibited motion pictures outside of the conventional theatrical venues, in school or museum auditoriums. It is important that, for the most part, these film societies operated on a not-for-profit basis, eliminating the possibility of making money by showing these films.

96. Ways in which theater owners supported this distinction, through means such as theater environment and marketing, will be considered in chapter 5.

97. *Variety,* 19 June 1946, 4; 17 November 1948, 15; 8 December 1948, 7.

98. Falkenberg, "'Hollywood' and the 'Art Cinema,'" 44.

99. "Foresees More Imports Here," *Motion Picture Herald,* 4 January 1947, 32.

100. DeCordova, "The Rise of the Art Film in Post-War Chicago."

101. Thomas M. Pryor, "Front Runner in Foreign Film Sweepstakes," *The New York Times,* "Joseph Burstyn" clippings file, Billy Rose Theater Collection, Performing Arts Research Library, New York Public Library at Lincoln Center, New York.

102. "French too Get That American Idea ($)," *Variety,* 22 October 1948, 2.

103. "Foreign Film Bubble Bursts," *Variety,* 31 August 1949, 22.

104. Thomas J. Brandon, "Foreign Film Distribution in the U.S.," interview by Edouard L. de Laurot and Jonas Mekas, *Film Culture* 2 (1956): 16.

105. "Rene Clair Cautions Against Overdoing Bi-Lingual Technique," *Variety,* 29 October 1947, 6.

106. Lev, *The Euro-American Cinema,* 5.

107. "Joe Breen to Cue Brit. Pix on U.S. Production Code, Save Costly Cuts," *Variety,* 10 July 1946, 1.

108. "Breen Compromise or OK on Certain Rank Pix; New Tag for 'Narcissus,'" *Variety,* 17 September 1947, 3.

109. "Global Interest in Aid for Foreign Films," *Christian Science Monitor,* 2 September 1950, 15.

110. Jane Cianfarra, "Italian Film Industry Is Wary of Americans," *The New York Times,* 2 May 1950.

111. "Global Interest in Aid for Foreign Films," 15.

112. Arthur Mayer, *Merely Colossal* (New York: Simon and Schuster, 1953), 233.

113. "Sexacious Selling Best B.O. Slant for Foreign Language Films in U.S.," *Variety,* 9 June 1948, 2.

114. Though it was clearly not necessarily true that sex was responsible for the success of art films. As Richard Griffith points out, not all films with sex became mainstream box office successes. Richard Griffith, "European Films and American Audiences," *Saturday Review of Literature,* 13 January 1951, 85.

115. Eric Schaefer, "Art and Exploitation: Reconfiguring Foreign Films for American Tastes, 1930-1960," paper presented at the New England American Studies Association Conference, Brown University, Providence, Rhode Island, 7 May 1994.

116. Bosley Crowther, "Unkindest Cut," *The New York Times,* 2 May 1950.

117. "Banned Bicycle," *Newsweek,* 13 March 1950, 78.

118. Crowther, review of *Lost Boundaries,* 1950.

119. Falkenberg, "'Hollywood' and the 'Art Cinema,'" 44.

120. Ibid., 46.

121. Neale, "Art Cinema as Institution," 37.

122. Budd, "Authorship as a Commodity," 16.

123. Bourdieu, "The Production of Belief," 278.

124. Lev, *The Euro-American Cinema,* 5.

2. Around the Corner from the Big Top

1. The Little Three, however, did have distribution deals with the Big Five theater chains. The studio-affiliated theater chains needed films from all of the eight major studios to fill their screen time. Therefore, despite their competition, the major studios cooperated with each other to maximize their profits.

2. Mae D. Huettig, "Economic Control of the Motion Picture Industry," in *The American Film Industry,* rev. ed., ed. Tino Balio (Madison: University of Wisconsin Press, 1985), 297.

3. Tino Balio, "A Mature Oligopoly, 1930–1948," in *The American Film Industry,* rev. ed., ed. Tino Balio (Madison: University of Wisconsin Press, 1985), 254–55.

4. Huettig, "Economic Control of the Motion Picture Industry," 298.

5. Ibid., 299.

6. Ibid., 303.

7. In a 1940 consent decree, the studios agreed to limit blocks of films to no more than five. David Bordwell, Janet Staiger, and Kristin Thompson, *The Classical Hollywood Cinema: Film Style and Mode of Production to 1960* (New York: Columbia University Press, 1985), 331.

8. Balio, "A Mature Oligopoly," 258.

9. "'47: Year of New Sales Policies," *Variety,* 31 December 1947, 5.

10. Ruth A. Inglis, "Self Regulation in Operation," in *The American Film Industry,* rev. ed., ed. Tino Balio (Madison: University of Wisconsin Press, 1985), 385.

11. Kristin Thompson, "Dr. Caligari at the Folies-Bergère, or, The Successes of an Early Avant-Garde Film," in *The Cabinet of Dr. Caligari: Texts, Contexts, Histories,* ed. Mike Budd (New Brunswick: Rutgers University Press, 1990), 157.

12. Eric Clarke, quoted in "Special Theaters Urged for Artistic Pictures," *The New York Times,* 10 October 1926.

13. Anthony Henry Guzman, "The Exhibition and Reception of European Films in the United States during the 1920s," Ph.D. diss., University of California at Los Angeles, 1993, 263.

14. Ibid.

15. Mike Budd, "The National Board of Review and the Early Art Cinema in New York: *The Cabinet of Dr. Caligari* and Affirmative Culture," *Cinema Journal* 26 (Fall 1986): 7.

16. Guzman, "The Exhibition and Reception of European Films in the United States," 3.

17. Robert E. Sherwood, "Motion Picture Album," *The New York Evening Post,* 4 December 1946.

18. Guzman, "The Exhibition and Reception of European Films in the United States," 78.

19. For example, Parufamet was developed in 1926 (ibid., 206), and a subsequent distribution deal was made between United Artists and the German film company Phoebus Films (ibid., 232).

20. Jan-Christopher Horak, "The First American Film Avant-Garde, 1919–1945," in *Lovers of Cinema: The First American Film Avant-Garde, 1919–1945,* ed. Jan-Christopher Horak (Madison: University of Wisconsin Press, 1995), 27.

21. Guzman, "The Exhibition and Reception of European Films in the United States," 32.

22. Charles Teitel, telephone interview by author, 4 August 1996, tape recording.

23. Michael Mindlin, "The Little Cinema Movement," *Theatre Arts,* July 1928, Michael Mindlin Collection, Film Study Center, Museum of Modern Art, New York.

24. Horak "The First American Film Avant-Garde," 24.

25. Harold Lefkovits, "The Little Cinema Marches On," *The New York Times,* 6 February 1938.

26. "The National Board of Review," *Film Year Book,* 1927, 477.

27. Ibid.

28. Horak, "The First American Film Avant-Garde," 18–19.

29. Budd, "The National Board of Review," 4.

30. Lefkovits, "The Little Cinema."

31. Peter DeCherney, "Cult of Attention: An Introduction to Seymour Stern and Harry Alan Potamkin (Contra Kracauer) on the Ideal Movie Theater," *Spectator* 18 (Spring/Summer 1998): 19.

32. Guzman, "The Exhibition and Reception of European Films in the United States," 833.

33. The small size, though promoted as an appeal for little cinema audiences, prompted critic Roscoe McGowan to refer to one little cinema as a "glorified projection room." Roscoe McGowan, "Easy Now, Critic'll Keep His Shirt On—Regular One," *The New York Daily News,* 29 October 1926, Michael Mindlin Collection, Film Study Center, Museum of Modern Art, New York.

34. "The Year with One Little Film Group," *The New York Sunday World,* Michael Mindlin Collection, Film Study Center, Museum of Modern Art, New York.

35. For example, see the description of Michael Mindlin's plans for a theater in Hartford, Connecticut. "Ultra-Smart Movie House for Hartford," *The Hartford Courant,* December 1926, Michael Mindlin Collection, Film Study Center, Museum of Modern Art, New York.

36. *The New York Times,* 22 September 1926, Michael Mindlin Collection, Film Study Center, Museum of Modern Art, New York.

37. Julia Older, "I Hate the Movies," *Mayfair,* December 1926, Michael Mindlin Collection, Film Study Center, Museum of Modern Art, New York.

38. Lisa Phillips, "Architect of Endless Innovation," in *Frederick Kiesler,* ed. Lisa Phillips (New York: Whitney Museum of Art, 1989), 16.

39. DeCherney, "Cult of Attention," 24.

40. Seymour Stern, "An Aesthetic of the Cinema House: A Statement of the Principles Which Constitute the Philosophy and the Format of the Ideal Film Theatre," *The National Board of Review Magazine* 2.5 (May 1927); rpt. in *Spectator* 18 (Spring/Summer 1998): 30–1.

41. S. J. O'Brien, editorial, *Electrical News Letter* 4 (15 February 1927), Michael Mindlin Collection, Film Study Center, Museum of Modern Art, New York.

42. Leonard Hall, *Washington Daily,* 1 April 1927, quoted in Bettina Gunczy, "The Bloodless Revolt," *National Board of Review Magazine* 2 (May 1927): 1.

43. Douglas Gomery, *Shared Pleasures: A History of Movie Presentation in the United States* (London: British Film Institute, 1992), 173.

44. Guzman, "The Exhibition and Reception of European Films in the United States," 209.

45. *Variety,* June 1927, Michael Mindlin Collection, Film Study Center, Museum of Modern Art, New York. The failure of the Greenwich Village Theatre (which, in 1928, charged $2.00 to $3.50) suggests that there was a cap on what people were willing to spend at little cinemas. Guzman suggested that the admission price was too high to be afforded by the bohemians and intellectuals living in Greenwich Village, and the theater closed within a month of its opening. Guzman, "The Exhibition and Reception of European Films in the United States," 304.

46. Guzman, "The Exhibition and Reception of European Films in the United States," 690.

47. Though Arbuckle was acquitted of the murder of actress Virginia Rappe, his career was destroyed by the accusations against him. Robert Sklar, *Movie-Made America: A Cultural History of American Movies* (New York: Random House, 1975), 78.

48. Forming private clubs allowed little cinemas and film societies to get around the public screening rules applied by state and local authorities.

49. Guzman, "The Exhibition and Reception of European Films in the United States," 221.

50. The more suggestive nature of the art films probably also led little cinemas to attract an audience simply interested in the lurid aspect of foreign films. According to Guzman, however, the sexual nature of these films tended to be glossed over by critics and the popular press and was only really discussed by intellectuals. Ibid., 704. This surely reflects not whether people actually attended these films for erotic pleasure, but that moral watchdog groups did not consider them enough of a "problem" to warrant public consideration.

51. Budd, "The National Board of Review and the Early Art Cinema," 8.

52. Clarke, quoted in "Special Theatres Urged."

53. Ibid.

54. Budd, "The National Board of Review and the Early Art Cinema," 6.

55. Guzman, "The Exhibition and Reception of European Films in the United States," 377.

56. John Hutchens, "L'Enfant Terrible," *Theatre Arts Monthly,* September 1929, Michael Mindlin Collection, Film Study Center, Museum of Modern Art, New York.

57. Horak, "The First American Film Avant-Garde," 24.

58. A 1938 article in *The New York Times* stated that the little cinema movement had been dead for the past ten years. Lefkovits, "The Little Cinema."

59. Gomery, *Shared Pleasures,* 174.

60. Guzman, "The Exhibition and Reception of European Films in the United States," 312.

61. Ibid., 692.

62. "Newark to Have Unusual Theater," *The Newark News,* 30 October 1929, Michael Mindlin Collection, Film Study Center, Museum of Modern Art, New York.

63. Though the Michael Mindlin scrapbooks at the Museum of Modern Art show that little cinemas clearly received coverage in and advertised in the foreign-language press.

64. Gomery, *Shared Pleasures*, 175.

65. Ibid., 174. As sound films grew in popularity, language barriers became important for foreign-language films. Although this decreased interest for mainstream audiences, ethnic audiences, on the other hand, probably appreciated the opportunity to hear their native tongues.

66. Ibid., 180.

67. Nick John Matsoukas, "The Unconventional Punch and Judy," *Exhibitors Herald-World*, 25 October 1930, 35.

68. "Chi's Class Nabe, Esquire, a Mecca for Showmen on Deluxe Operation," *Variety*, 25 May 1938, "Esquire" clippings file, Billy Rose Theater Collection, Performing Arts Research Library, New York Public Library at Lincoln Center, New York.

69. Ibid.

70. Lynn Abbie, "Esquire Theatre," *Chicago Art Deco Society*, Spring 1986, "Esquire" clippings file, Theatre Historical Society, Elmhurst, Ill.

71. Papers of Joseph Ducibella, Society Designs, "Esquire" clippings file, Theatre Historical Society, Elmhurst, Ill.

72. "Talk of the Town," *New Yorker*, 16 November 1946, 24.

73. Christine Grenz, *Trans-Lux: Biography of a Corporation* (Norwalk: Trans-Lux Corporation, 1982), 9.

74. "New Type of Theatre for Newsreels Opens," *The New York Times*, 16 March 1931.

75. Ibid.

76. Ibid.

77. Gomery, *Shared Pleasures*, 147.

78. Richard Brandt, telephone interview by author, 5 September 1996, tape recording.

79. Horak, "The First American Film Avant-garde," 25.

80. Charles Wolfe, "The Poetics and Politics of Nonfiction: Documentary Film," in *Grand Design: Hollywood as a Modern Business Enterprise, 1930–1939*, ed. Tino Balio (Berkeley: University of California Press, 1993), 351.

81. Films in the series included the German films *Student of Prague* and *Metropolis* and the Soviet *Ten Days* and *Old and New*. Ibid., 359.

82. "5,000 'Private Clubs' Become Big Outlet for Out-of-the-Way Films," *Variety*, 16 February 1949, 8.

83. Lauren Rabinovitz, *Points of Resistance: Women, Power and Politics in the New Avant-Garde Cinema, 1943-71* (Urbana: University of Illinois Press, 1991), 44.

84. Scott MacDonald, "Amos Vogel and Cinema 16," *Wide Angle* 9 (1987): 44.

85. Ibid., 45–46.

86. "Private," *New Yorker*, 5 May 1962, 35; Amos Vogel, "Cinema 16: An Interview with Amos Vogel," interview by Scott MacDonald, *Film Quarterly* 37 (1984): 21.

87. A blizzard in December 1947 prevented people from attending one of the early Cinema 16 programs. The blizzard effectively wiped out the Vogels, who had put all their money into mounting and promoting the program and planned to use the money from admissions to continue exhibition. Vogel, "Cinema 16," 21.

88. MacDonald, "Amos Vogel and Cinema 16," 43.

89. Cecile Starr, "Occasion for Cheers," *The Saturday Review*, 9 December 1953, 36. Cinema 16 screened films in art houses at times when the theaters did not have their own commercial screenings scheduled. It is not clear how much Cinema 16 paid for the use of these exhibition sites and what resources of the theaters (e.g., the cafés or the reading rooms) were available to Cinema 16 members at these off-hours.

90. Starr, "Occasion for Cheers," 36.

91. Ibid.

92. Ibid., 37; "Private," 36.

93. Vogel, "Cinema 16," 23.

94. Starr, "Occasion for Cheers," 37.

95. Vogel, "Cinema 16," 29. In addition to its regular monthly screenings, Cinema 16 provided other services and programs. Vogel organized diverse ventures that ran the gamut from trips to the Eastman House in Rochester, New York, to college film courses associated first with New York University and later with the New School. MacDonald, "Amos Vogel and Cinema 16," 33. Cinema 16 presented the Robert J. Flaherty Award, recognizing achievement in documentary film, and cosponsored Maya Deren's Creative Film Foundation's acknowledgment of avant-garde films. MacDonald, "Amos Vogel and Cinema 16," 33–34. Rabinovitz, *Points of Resistance*, 82. Vogel offered planning services to other people trying to establish film societies throughout the United States, and Cinema 16 became a leading distributor of avant-garde films in North America. MacDonald, "Amos Vogel and Cinema 16," 46. Cinema 16 began advertising film distribution in 1948, and in 1951 it produced a catalogue of films available for rental. By 1963, Cinema 16 offered 240 films by 140 filmmakers. MacDonald, "Amos Vogel and Cinema 16," 46.

3. Limited Audience Appeal

1. *Motion Picture Herald*, 15 February 1947, 14; *Variety*, 19 February 1947, 19; *Variety*, 30 April 1947, 11; *Motion Picture Herald*, 7 June 1947, 22; *The Hollywood Reporter*, 1 April 1949, 6; *The Hollywood Reporter*, 1 June 1949, 2.

2. "Trans-Lux Going to Features," *The Hollywood Reporter*, 20 December 1948, 1.

3. "New Feathers for Pathé," *Time*, 20 September 1948, 92. See also "Foreign Showcase," *Newsweek*, 20 September 1948, 98.

4. Douglas Gomery, *Shared Pleasures: A History of Movie Presentation in the United States* (London: British Film Institute, 1992), 84.

5. Paris Theater program for *Symphonie Pastorale*, 13 September 1948, "Paris" clippings files, Billy Rose Theater Collection, Performing Arts Research Library, New York Public Library at Lincoln Center, New York. This program is considered in greater detail in chapter 5.

6. "New Feathers for Pathé," 92.

7. Ibid.

8. Paris Theatre program for *Symphonie Pastorale*.

9. "New Feathers for Pathé," 91.

10. Tino Balio, "Retrenchment, Reappraisal, and Reorganization," in *The American Film Industry*, rev. ed., ed. Tino Balio (Madison: University of Wisconsin Press, 1985), 405.

11. "Exhibs Welcome Dropping 'B' Product by Majors," *The Hollywood Reporter*, 20 January 1949, 14.

12. "Movies Worry," *Business Week*, 16 March 1946, 8.

13. Stanley Frank, "Sureseaters Discover an Audience," *Nation's Business*, January 1952, 34.

14. Gomery, *Shared Pleasures*, 188.

15. Albert Warner, "Production Costs the No. 1 Concern for Entire Industry," *Variety*, 8 January 1947, 6.

16. "Yates Sees Pix Aided by Decree," *Variety*, 4 September 1946, 11.

17. "'B' Pix B.O. Chasers—Schenck," *Variety*, 18 May 1949, 3.

18. "Independents' Day," *Time*, 17 May 1948, 91.

19. "Nelson in Movies," *Business Week*, 30 June 1945, 26.

20. "Federal Court in Final Decree Is Industry's Boss," *Motion Picture Herald*, 4 January 1947, 10a.

21. "Distribs' Selling Practices Face Heavy Attack from TOA and Allied," *Variety*, 28 September 1949, 4.

22. For example, see "Plan Still Longer Runs," *Variety*, 15 May 1946, 5, and "More Pix on Shorter Runs," *Variety*, 22 May 1946, 3.

23. Although the 1940 consent decree in which the major studios agreed to limit blocks to no more than five films expired by the late 1940s. "Nelson in Movies," 26.

24. Robert Sklar, *Movie-Made America: A Cultural History of American Movies* (New York: Random House, 1975), 282.

25. This certainly contributed to the reduced production of B films, since studios could no longer guarantee rentals of the low-budget films by tying them to A films.

26. "Majors Now Can't Sell Pix to Own Theaters Unless Bids Asked First," *Variety,* 1 December 1948, 3.

27. Sklar, *Movie-Made America,* 274.

28. "Small-Town Independent Exhibitors Appear Hardest Hit by Decision," *Variety,* 19 June 1946, 6.

29. "MPTOA-NY Meet Attacks Auction Phase of Decree," *Variety,* 3 July 1946, 6.

30. "Exhibs Overwhelmingly Vote to KO Auctioning," *Variety,* 9 October 1946, 7. That the studios did, in fact, benefit from competitive bidding over the independent exhibitors is suggested by the fact that some studios continued with this system of selling even after the Supreme Court ruled against making it mandatory. "Exhibs Point to Bidding As Jacking Up Prices As Much As 100 percent Over Prewar," *Variety,* 16 June 1948, 9.

31. "Bids Set Sales Policies on Ear," *Variety,* 4 June 1947, 5.

32. "Decree Appeal Boxscore," *Motion Picture Herald,* 8 March 1947, 20.

33. The level of mistrust that existed between the independent exhibitors and the studios can be seen in the independent exhibitors' holdup of a Motion Picture Association of America survey on the industry by refusing to answer questions that the exhibitors feared would provide the major studios with too much information about their operations. "Indie Exhibitors Balk MPA Survey by Their Suspicion," *Variety,* 6 August 1947, 3.

34. "'Not Hoarding Pix': Balaban," *Variety,* 25 September 1946, 3.

35. "Major Companies Deny 'Shortage' of Prints Nips Indie Exhibitors," *Variety,* 6 August 1947, 17.

36. "'Quality of U.S. Film Is Getting Bad,' Plaint of N.Y. Indie Circuit Chiefs," *Variety,* 4 June 1947, 7.

37. "Irate Exhibs Sing 'Don't Blame Me,' Claim Majors Stifle Exploitation Plans," *Variety,* 17 July 1946, 20.

38. "N.W. Distribs Charge Ganging Up by Indies in Adopting Exhib Tactics," *Variety,* 11 April 1946, 29.

39. "Checkers Figure Exhibitors Get Away with As Much as $25,000,000," *Variety,* 2 October 1946, 9.

40. "'Lazy' Exhibs Rapped for B.O. Lag," *Variety,* 21 January 1948, 1.

41. "Distribs Hit Exhib Ad 'Chiseling,'" *Variety,* 10 March 1948, 11.

42. This discussion does not focus on the countries that were occupied by the United States following World War II. These nations, such as Germany and Austria, clearly did not have the same relationship with U.S. industries and also (and perhaps because of this) did not make significant contributions to the U.S. art film industry at this time. For a consideration of the relationship between the United States and occupied countries in the late 1940s, see Ralph Willett, *The Americanization of Germany, 1945–1949* (London: Routledge, 1989) and Reinhold Wagnleitner, *Coca-Colonization and the Cold War: The Cultural Mission of the United States in Austria after the Second World War,* trans. Diana M. Wolf (Chapel Hill: University of North Carolina Press, 1994).

43. Thomas H. Guback, "Hollywood's International Market," in *The American Film Industry,* rev. ed., ed. Tino Balio (Madison: University of Wisconsin Press, 1985), 474.

44. Gomery, *Shared Pleasures,* 182.

45. Sklar, *Movie-Made America,* 275.

46. "U.S. Exports: End of Boom," *Business Week,* 16 August 1947, 103.

47. "Provisions of Anglo-U.S. Film Pact," *Variety,* 17 March 1948, 9.

48. Eric Johnston, "The Motion Picture on the Threshold of a Decisive Decade," in *Motion Picture Association of America 24th Annual Report*, 25 March 1946, 46.

49. "Box Office Pinch," *Business Week*, 4 October 1947, 62.

50. Walter Waldman, "Foreign Film Showings Are on the Upswing," *Boxoffice*, 29 November 1947, 18.

51. Balio, "Retrenchment, Reappraisal, and Reorganization," 416.

52. Independent producers paid the lower capital gains tax rather than income tax. "Independent Income," *Time*, 5 November 1945, 84.

53. "Exhibs Welcome Dropping of 'B' Product by Majors," *The Hollywood Reporter*, 20 January 1949, 14.

54. "Low Budgeters for Specialized U.S. Audiences, a la Foreign Film Ideas," *Variety*, 4 August 1948, 4. Any of Maddow's plans for the film industry were halted when he was blacklisted for his refusal to answer questions about his (and others') political beliefs before the House Committee on Un-American Activities in the early 1950s. It is believed that Maddow eventually (and privately) testified before the committee in order to return to work. Victor S. Navasky, *Naming Names* (New York: Viking Press, 1980), 374.

55. "Low Budgeters for Specialized U.S. Audiences, a la Foreign Film Ideas," 4.

56. "Seven Majors Releasing 29 Reissues This Season," *Motion Picture Herald*, 26 April 1947, 12.

57. "Reissues in Current Year Four Times Over 1945–46," *Boxoffice*, 31 May 1947, 9.

58. Thomas M. Pryor, "Boom Market for Yesteryear's Movies," *The New York Times*, 30 January 1944.

59. "So. Calif. Exhib Finds Reissues Pay Off Better than Milked New Films," *Variety*, 1 October 1947, 11.

60. "Reissues Still Keep to Wartime Peak in Boff Sales, Repeat Bookings Spurt," *Variety*, 13 February 1946, 7.

61. "8 Majors, 4 Lesser Distribs Released 428 in '47 vs. 405 in '46," *Variety*, 31 December 1947, 6.

62. "Film Classics Now Owns 100 percent of 13 Branches," *Variety*, 26 February 1947, 20.

63. "Harris-Broder Reissues Sought by Classics," *Variety*, 20 August 1947, 5.

64. Pryor, 30 January 1944.

65. "FC Plans Roadshow of 4 Reissues Yearly," *Variety*, 4 June 1947, 7.

66. "Foreign Film Product Flowing into N.Y.," *Variety*, 23 November 1949, 13.

67. Bruce A. Austin, *Immediate Seating: A Look at Movie Audiences* (California: Wadsworth Publishing Co., 1989), 81.

68. Ellen Draper, "'Controversy Has Probably Destroyed Forever the Context': *The Miracle* and Movie Censorship in America in the Fifties," *Velvet Light Trap* 25 (Spring 1990): 76.

69. Gomery, *Shared Pleasures*, 182.

70. "100 Weeks Played on B'way, in Nabes, 'City' Reopens in First Run," *Variety*, 11 February 1948, 4; "Henry's Million," *Motion Picture Herald*, 5 April 1947, 9. There were also reports, though, that the numbers for *Open City* were exaggerated. "Exaggerated U.S. Reports on 'Open City' Inflate Other Italo Pix Prices," *Variety*, 28 May 1947, 6.

71. "Rank to Release 23 Pictures in the U.S. This Year," *Motion Picture Herald*, 26 April 1947, 22.

72. "Encourage Top British Films: Silverstone," *Motion Picture Herald*, 1 March 1947, 38.

73. "World Pictures," *Business Week*, 8 December 1945, 44.

74. "Stix Nix British Pix," *Variety*, 18 June 1947, 6.

75. Abel Green, "Slap Rank's Anglo-U.S. 'Cartel'," *Variety*, 4 June 1947, 3.

76. Abel Green, "Rank's $12,000,000 U.S. Pact," *Variety*, 11 June 1947, 1. Unsurprisingly, Rank did not earn this $12 million; rather, his films were expected to earn approximately $4 million for 1947. "Rank Combine Hit by B.O. Dip in U.S.; '47 Take Only 40% of $10,000,000 Dream," *Variety*, 17 December 1947, 4.

77. Green, "Rank's $12,000,000," 1.

78. Universal had first choice of Rank product and Eagle-Lion second choice. Other Rank films were at times distributed by United Artists as well as smaller distribution companies. "Sears Would Like Rank Pix for UA," *Variety,* 18 May 1949, 5.

79. "Prestige," *Motion Picture Herald,* 29 June 1948, 8.

80. "Prestige Pix Seeking School Aud. Outlets," *Variety,* 24 July 1946, 29.

81. *Variety* reported that, in its first year of operation, Prestige prompted 15 theaters in "medium sized towns" to switch to an art house policy. "N.Y. DC, LA and Frisco Best B.O. for Rank's Prestigers; Stix Still Nix 'Em," *Variety,* 10 September 1947, 4.

82. "British Pix Finally Click in U.S.," *Variety,* 11 September 1946, 3.

83. "U's Sales on Rank Pix in U.S. to be Highly Selective," *Variety,* 18 August 1948, 3.

84. As discussed earlier, MGM had difficulty figuring out how to sell foreign-language films even to its own circuit theaters. And Columbia reported the formation of a special unit to handle foreign films. "House Divided within Metro Typifies General U.S. Resistance to Foreign Pix," *Variety,* 12 March 1947, 29; "Col. Another to Recognize Need for Special Selling of Foreign Pix," *Variety,* 21 December 1949, 15.

85. "Rank's $3,000,000 from U.S. This Yr.," *Variety,* 16 November 1949, 7.

86. "Paramount Pledges More Bookings for Rank but Indie Circuits Still Skeptical," *Variety,* 4 June 1947, 3. Exhibitors (affiliated and independent) repeatedly stated that they would be willing to exhibit foreign films as long as they were of high quality—meaning that they would appeal to audiences and earn money at the box office.

87. "Importers and Exporters," *Film Daily Year Book,* (New York: J. W. Alicoate, 1946), 599; "Importers and Exporters," *Film Daily Year Book,* (New York: J. W. Alicoate, 1949), 648.

88. "General Industry Statistics," *Film Daily Year Book,* (New York: J. W. Alicoate, 1950), 75.

89. "Hinterland Cool to Foreign Pix," *Variety,* 12 March 1947.

90. "Exaggerated U.S. Reports on 'Open City,'" 6.

91. "Italo Pix Production Worsening; Increasing Import Glut Market," *Variety,* 8 September 1948, 15.

92. "Lingo Pix Spreading Into Stix," *Variety,* 1 January 1947, 5; "Jean Goldwurm," press release, "Jean Goldwurm" clippings file, Billy Rose Theater Collection, Performing Arts Research Library, New York Public Library at Lincoln Center, New York; "Siritzky Company to Produce in Hollywood," *Motion Picture Herald,* 29 March 1947, 51.

93. "Ilya Lopert Dies; Film Official, 65," *The New York Times,* 1 March 1971, "Ilya Lopert" clippings file, Billy Rose Theater Collection, Performing Arts Research Library, New York Public Library at Lincoln Center, New York. In 1950 Lopert combined his distribution efforts with those of British film producer Alexander Korda and City Investing (which owned two theaters in Manhattan and one in Syracuse, N.Y.) to form Lopert Films Distributing Company. "Dowling, Lopert, Korda Form Distributing Co.," *Boxoffice,* 16 December 1950, 37.

94. Charles Teitel, telephone interview by author, 4 August 1996, tape recording.

95. "Foreign Language Chain Planned by Sidney Pink," *Boxoffice,* 22 March 1947, 35.

96. Richard Brandt, telephone interview by author, 5 September 1996, tape recording.

97. Ibid.

98. "Small Seaters Pitch to Majors on Reissues," *Variety,* 3 August 1949, 5.

99. Richard deCordova, "The Rise of the Art Film in Post-War Chicago," paper presented at the College Art Association Convention, Boston, 1987.

100. "'Paisan' Booked Into All Loew's N.Y. Houses," *The Hollywood Reporter,* 8 March 1949, 1; "Clips from Film Row," *Variety,* 25 May 1949, 21; Fox-West Coast reported plans to eventually play *Paisan* in 500 to 600 theaters in its chain. "FWC Books 'Paisan' into 260 Calif. Units," *The Hollywood Reporter,* 12 January 1949, 1.

101. "Circuits Book 'Carmen,'" *Motion Picture Herald,* 7 June 1947, 43.

102. "Average French or Italian Film Nets Only 20–40G in U.S. Market," *Variety,* 17 November 1948, 15.

103. "Upbeat Anglo Pix in U.S. Markets Already Seen: From 30G to 42G Weekly," *Variety*, 19 May 1948, 3.

104. *Variety*, 21 May 1947, 5.

105. "British B.O. in U.S. NSG—Blumberg," *Variety*, 21 May 1947, 5.

106. R. Navari, "Exhibitor Comments on Foreign Films," *Motion Picture Herald*, 25 May 1946, 34.

107. "Foreign Pix' Quality Ebb Plus Peak U.S. Distrib Fees K.O.ing Imports," *Variety*, 6 April 1949, 25.

108. Ibid.

109. "Pix Shortage for Rural Exhibs," *Variety*, 10 April 1946, 11.

110. "Small Town Exhibitors Frankly Cold to Brit Pix," *Variety*, 28 May 1947, 8.

111. "Import Boom Bringing 125 Foreign Films This Year," *Motion Picture Herald*, 1 February 1947, 21.

112. "Disputes Importer's View on New Comers," *Variety*, 12 February 1947, 11.

113. These estimates do not seem to include foreign film theaters catering to ethnic audiences.

114. "Click of Certain 'Arty' (Foreign) Pix in America's Sureseaters has H'Wood Eyeing that 'Special' B.O.," *Variety*, 10 November 1946, 36.

115. "Cincy Lone Key Sans Foreign Pix As Denver House Takes on British," *Variety*, 19 November 1947, 22.

116. Ibid. It is interesting to consider Cincinnati's lack of an art house despite its large German population. German films may have been seen in ethnic theaters in Cincinnati, not at art houses (leading to questions about the status position of German films at this time). It is also possible that the war affected Cincinnati's German population's desire to publicly associate themselves with their culture. Or Cincinnati's residents may have lacked interest in art films because few German films were distributed along the art house circuit at this time; perhaps Cincinnati would have had an art house had German films been included more.

117. "15 Art Houses Now Operating in LA," *Variety*, 2 November 1949, 25; Elmer Balaban, interview by author, 19 April 1996, Chicago, tape recording.

118. In 1948, Trans-Lux announced plans to convert its theaters to an emphasis on foreign films. "Trans-Lux Going to Features," *The Hollywood Reporter*, 30 December 1948, 1. In 1949 the Embassy newsreel circuit in New York made plans to switch three of its five New York houses to feature film houses with a heavy reliance on Rank films. "N.Y. Newsreel House Goes First Run," *The Hollywood Reporter*, 13 May 1949, 2. That same year, the Chicago Northside Telenews, after one month as a newsreel theater, switched to an art house policy and changed its name to the Carnegie. "Clips from Film Row," *Variety*, 21 December 1949, 20.

4. "Any Leisure That Looks Easy Is Suspect"

1. Stanley Frank, "Sure-seaters Discover an Audience," *Nation's Business*, January 1952, 69.

2. Gilbert Seldes, *The Great Audience* (New York: Viking Press, 1950), 15.

3. Ibid.

4. Jack C. Ellis, *A History of Film*, 2nd ed. (Englewood Cliffs: Prentice-Hall, 1985), 272.

5. "American Suburbs Gain 15,000,000," *Variety*, 11 January 1956, 1.

6. Phillipe Aries, "The Family and the City in the Old World and New," in *Changing Images of the Family*, ed. Virginia Tufte and Barbara Myerhoff (New Haven: Yale University Press, 1979), 38.

7. Nicholas Schenck, "Pix Still a Big Business—Company President Fully Alerted to Maintain Its Prosperity," *Variety*, 3 January 1951, 6.

8. Frank E. Beaver, *On Film* (New York: McGraw-Hill, 1983), 346.

9. Schenck, "Pix Still a Big Business," 6.

10. Beaver, *On Film*, 346.

11. John Belton, *Widescreen Cinema* (Cambridge: Harvard University Press, 1992), 82.

12. Jackson Lears, "A Matter of Taste: Corporate Cultural Hegemony in a Mass-Consumption Society," in *Recasting America: Culture and Politics in the Age of Cold War,* ed. Lary May (Chicago: University of Chicago Press, 1989), 39.

13. Belton, *Widescreen Cinema,* 81.

14. Ibid.

15. Pierre Bourdieu, *Distinction: A Social Critique of the Judgment of Taste,* trans. Richard Nice (Cambridge: Harvard University Press, 1984).

16. Herbert Gans, *Popular Culture and High Culture: An Analysis and Evaluation of Taste* (New York: Basic Books, 1974), 70.

17. Critics of Bourdieu have attempted to see economic class as only part of a fabric of factors that determines taste culture, and they address some of these other possible marks of difference, such as "ethnicity, gender, religion and life-style." John R. Hall, "The Capital(s) of Cultures: A Nonholistic Approach to Status Situations, Class, Gender and Ethnicity," in *Cultivating Differences: Symbolic Boundaries and the Making of Inequalities,* ed. Michéle Lamont and Marcel Fournier (Chicago: University of Chicago Press, 1992), 259. Jim Lane has begun to expand the view beyond class to examine factors such as age and gender in relation to the status appeals of the Brattle Theatre, an art house in Cambridge, Massachusetts. Jim Lane, "Critical and Cultural Reception of the European Art Film in 1950s America: A Case Study of the Brattle Theatre (Cambridge, Massachusetts)," *Film and History* 24 (1994): 49–64.

18. Bourdieu, *Distinction,* 68.

19. Gans, *Popular Culture and High Culture,* 89.

20. Bourdieu, *Distinction,* 133.

21. Theodor Adorno and Max Horkheimer, *Dialectic of Enlightenment* (New York: Herder and Herder, 1972), 126, 137.

22. Leo Lowenthal, "Historical Perspectives of Popular Culture," in *Mass Culture: The Popular Arts in America,* ed. Bernard Rosenberg and David Manning White (New York: Free Press, 1957), 55.

23. Russell Lynes, "Highbrow, Lowbrow, Middlebrow," *Harper's,* February 1949, 21.

24. Dwight Macdonald, "A Theory of Mass Culture," in *Mass Culture: The Popular Arts in America,* ed. Bernard Rosenberg and David Manning White (New York: Free Press, 1957), 63.

25. It is important to consider the intentions of the cultural critics in their attacks on "midcult" and the middlebrow tendency to incorporate elements of high culture. As Andrew Ross has noted, Dwight Macdonald and other Old Left intellectuals tried to protect their intellectually dominant position within society by elevating formal education as an important mark of distinction between people of culture and people without culture. Andrew Ross, *No Respect: Intellectuals and Popular Culture* (New York: Routledge Press, 1989), 63. Lamenting what he saw as the end of the avant-garde, Macdonald considered the various possible roles for intellectuals within a mass-culture society: "The conservative proposal to save culture by restoring the old class lines has a more solid historical base than the Marxian hope for a new democratic classless culture. . . . The only practical thing along those lines would be to revive the cultural elite which the Avantgarde created." Macdonald, "A Theory of Mass Culture," 70–71.

26. David Riesman with Nathan Glazer and Reuel Denney, *The Lonely Crowd* (New Haven: Yale University Press, 1961), 73. Writing in the late 1950s, coauthor Denney (a less well-known academic than Riesman) critiqued work that portrayed the audience for popular culture as passive. Denney expressed an interest in examining the ways in which audiences take action, such as how "an audience or audience segment chooses among the media leisure alternatives." Reuel Denney, *The Astonished Muse* (Chicago: University of Chicago Press, 1957), 19.

27. See Warren Sussman with Edward Griffin, "Did Success Spoil the United States? Dual Representations in Postwar America," in *Recasting America: Culture and Politics in the Age of Cold War,* ed. Lary May (Chicago: University of Chicago Press, 1989), 19–37.

28. C. Wright Mills, *White Collar* (New York: Oxford University Press, 1956), 257.

29. Ibid., 256.

30. Russell Lynes, "The Tastemakers," *Harper's,* June 1947, 481.

31. Lynes, "Highbrow, Middlebrow, Lowbrow," 19.

32. Ibid., 28.

33. Ibid., 27.

34. Ibid., 25.

35. "High-brow, Low-brow, Middle-brow," *Life,* 11 May 1949, 100–1.

36. Winthrop Sargeant, "In Defense of the High-brow," *Life,* 11 May 1949, 102. For another analysis of the *Harper's* and *Life* articles, see Joan Shelley Rubin's *The Making of Middlebrow Culture,* in which she focused on the tone of the articles, describing them as parodic and flippant. Joan Shelley Rubin, *The Making of Middlebrow Culture* (Chapel Hill: University of North Carolina Press, 1992), xiii–xiv.

37. Riesman with Glazer and Denney, *The Lonely Crowd,* 295.

38. Ibid.

39. Lane, "Critical and Cultural Reception of the European Art Film," 59.

40. Pierre Bourdieu, "The Production of Belief: Contribution to an Economy of Symbolic Goods," *Media, Culture and Society* 2 (1980): 269.

41. Seldes, *The Great Audience,* 15.

42. Andrew Dowdy, *"Movies Are Better Than Ever": Widescreen Memories of the Fifties* (New York: William Morrow and Company, 1973), 1.

43. David Cook, *A History of Narrative Film,* 2nd ed. (New York: W. W. Norton and Co., 1990), 319 n.

44. "Film's B.O. Pitch for 'Over 35s,'" *Variety,* 14 April 1948, 3.

45. William R. Weaver, "Screen Must Be More Mature in Treatment, Says Koster," *Motion Picture Herald,* 8 March 1947, 43.

46. Belton, *Widescreen Cinema,* 183–210.

47. "7 Houses Plug Foreign Policy," *Variety,* 12 March 1947, 31.

48. Richard Stern, interview by author, 8 October 1996, Wilmette, Ill., tape recording.

49. Herman Weinberg, "The European Film in America," *Theatre Arts,* October 1948, 49.

50. "Cincy Lone Key San Foreign Pix as Denver Takes on British," *Variety,* 10 November 1947, 22.

51. *Variety,* 27 July 1949, 13; *Variety,* 26 March 1947, 5; *Variety,* 20 November 1946, 36. This headline indicates not only the box office success of art/foreign films, but also the major industry's growing interest in profiting from this new market.

52. See, for example, "Little Carnegie Ops Stay Five More Years," *Variety,* 17 December 1947, 24.

53. "Foreign Film War Looms Here," *The Hollywood Reporter,* 29 November 1948, 1; "Lopert Expanding Foreign Film Deal to National Chain," *The Hollywood Reporter,* 1 December 1948, 1.

54. "Foreign Film War Looms Here," 1.

55. In 1948 *Variety* reported that more money was being spent on recreation, but "it's being divvied among an increasing number of entertainment facets." "New Shuffle for Showbiz," *Variety,* 15 September 1948, 1.

56. "More Adult Pix Key to Top Coin," *Variety,* 9 March 1949, 1.

57. "Pix Like 'The Search' OK for Distrib—Rodgers," *Variety,* 22 December 1948, 18.

58. "Skouras, Century Circuits Spurt Foreign Films," *Variety,* 24 September 1947, 16.

59. "Ranks' Pix Packages (Include French, Italian) for Arty U.S. Houses," *Variety,* 11 December 1946, 27.

60. Bosley Crowther, review of *The Quiet One, The New York Times,* 14 February 1949, 15.

61. "Herald-Tribune, MPAA Stress 'Quiet's' Value," *The Hollywood Reporter,* 2 March 1949, 4.

62. "B.O. of Foreign Films Depends on the Critics, Reverse of U.S. Pix," *Variety*, 26 November 1947, 4.

63. Weinberg, "The European Film in America," 49.

64. Stephen Farber, "The Power of Movie Critics," *American Scholar*, Summer 1976, 420.

65. Lane, "Critical and Cultural Reception of the European Art Film," 52.

66. Otis Guernsey, Jr., "'Art Movies' Low in Quality but 'Art Theatres' Thrive," *The New York Herald Tribune*, 30 October 1949, "Cinema—Foreign-U.S." clippings file, Billy Rose Theater Collection, Performing Arts Research Library, New York Public Library at Lincoln Center, New York.

67. Charles Teitel, telephone interview by author, 4 August 1996, tape recording.

68. Stern, interview by author.

69. Dallas Smythe, Parker B. Lusk, and Charles A. Lewis, "Portrait of an Art-Theater Audience," *Quarterly of Film, Radio and Television* 8 (Fall 1953): 30. For a summary of research on art house audiences, see Ronald J. Faber, Thomas C. O'Guinn, and Andrew P. Hardy, "Art Films in the Suburbs: A Comparison of Popular and Art Film Audiences," *Current Research in Film: Audiences, Economics and Law*, vol. 4, ed. Bruce A. Austin (Norwood, N. J.: Ablex, 1988), 48. An interesting exception to this image of the art house audience could be found in the Apollo Theatre, part of Harry Brandt's New York circuit. This theater, located on Forty-second Street, played foreign-language films with subtitles at subrun prices. Because of its low prices compared to other art houses, the Apollo became a center of entertainment for deaf people, who appreciated the subtitled films. According to Richard Brandt (Harry Brandt's son), deaf people came from all over New York City to attend the films at the Apollo. Richard Brandt, telephone interview by author, 5 September 1996, tape recording. See also "Subtitles On Foreign Pix Draw Deaf-Mutes," *Variety*, 7 May 1947, 1.

70. "Film B.O. Pitch for 'Over 35s'," 3.

71. Thomas M. Pryor, "Foreign Films Become Big Business," *The New York Times*, 8 February 1948.

72. Ibid.

73. Blumberg, quoted in "Periodic British Pic Booking Urged by PP's Lewis Blumberg," *Variety*, 30 April 1947, 11.

74. Harland Rankin, "What the Picture Did for Me," *Motion Picture Herald*, 1 February 1947, 52.

75. George H. Weeks, "What the Picture Did For Me," *Motion Picture Herald*, 8 February 1947, 56.

76. Elmer Balaban, interview by author, 19 April 1996, Chicago, tape recording. As true today as when Harvey Zorbaugh studied the area in 1929, the Gold Coast area, which runs along a northern portion of Chicago's Lake Shore Drive, is the neighborhood in which members of Chicago's social register live. The Gold Coast has "the greatest concentration of wealth in Chicago. Here live a large number of those who have achieved distinction in industry, science, and the arts." Harvey Warren Zorbaugh, *The Gold Coast and the Slum: A Sociological Study of Chicago's Near North Side* (Chicago: University of Chicago Press, 1929), 47.

77. Bourdieu, *Distinction*, 270.

78. "20,000,000 Foreign-Language Records Tops to Date; It's 7% of RCA Biz Alone," *Variety*, 25 December 1946, 1.

79. "Importers Seek Theatre Outlets," *Motion Picture Herald*, 8 February 1947, 50.

80. Douglas Gomery, *Shared Pleasures: A History of Movie Presentation in the United States* (London: British Film Institute, 1992), 185.

81. "5,000 'Private Clubs' Become Big Outlet for Out-of-the-Way Films," *Variety*, 16 February 1949, 8. It should be noted that it is not clear how *Variety* came up with this rather high number.

82. Mike Budd, "The Moments of *Caligari*," in *The Cabinet of Dr. Caligari: Texts, Contexts, Histories*, ed. Mike Budd (New Brunswick: Rutgers University Press, 1990), 91.

83. Joan Shelley Rubin, *The Making of Middlebrow Culture*, 144.

84. "Foreign Films Movie Club Launched," *The Foreign Films News*, May 1948, 1, "Foreign Films Movie Club" clippings file, Billy Rose Theater Collection, Performing Arts Research Library, New York Public Library at Lincoln Center, New York.

85. Foreign Films Movie Club brochure announcing 1949 season, "Foreign Films Movie Club" clippings file, Billy Rose Theater Collection, Performing Arts Research Library, New York Public Library at Lincoln Center, New York.

86. Ibid.

87. Ibid.

88. Ibid.

89. "Foreign Films Movie Club Launched," 1.

90. *The Foreign Films News*, April–May 1949, "Foreign Films Movie Club" clippings file, Billy Rose Theater Collection, Performing Arts Research Library, New York Public Library at Lincoln Center, New York.

91. Ibid.

92. Foreign Films Movie Club brochure announcing 1949 season.

93. Ibid.

94. Ibid.

95. "5,000 'Private Clubs' Become Big Outlet for Out-of-the-Way Films," 8.

96. Review of *The Room Upstairs*, *The Hollywood Reporter*, 11 November 1948, 3; Review of *Incorrigible*, *The Hollywood Reporter*, 22 March 1949, 3.

97. "Catholic Pickets Force NY Nabes to Pull 2 Pix," *Variety*, 23 June 1948, 18. *Passionelle* was a French film based on Emile Zola's "Pour Une Nuit d'Amour," about which Bosley Crowther wrote in *The New York Times*, "The only perceptible reason . . . for the making of this film is the very much evidenced enchantments of its principal actress, Odette Joyeux." Bosley Crowther, review of *Passionelle*, *The New York Times*, 1 March 1948, 17. *Torment*, a Swedish film with a screenplay by Ingmar Bergman that won the grand prize at the Cannes Film Festival, received an equally negative review from Crowther: "The subject itself is noxious and, as it is being shown here in New York with obvious cuts by the censors, it is more melodramatic than acute." Bosley Crowther, review of *Torment*, *The New York Times*, 22 April 1947, 34.

98. "'Objectionable' Pix on Rise, Most of 'Em Foreign," *Variety*, 23 November 1949, 4.

99. "Foreign Pix Put on Censor Pan; Clean H'wood Bill," *Variety*, 30 June 1948, 11.

100. Ibid.

101. "Franco-Swedish Duo Parlays into OK B.O.," *Variety*, 29 September 1948, 29.

102. "Sexacious Selling Best B.O. Slant for Foreign Language Films in U.S.," *Variety*, 9 June 1948, 2.

103. The article also estimated that the average Hollywood film earned approximately 10 percent of its revenue from New York. Ibid., 2.

5. "Demitasse Intermissions and Lobbies Hung with Paintings"

1. Joseph R. Springer, "'Sick' Theatres Can Be Cured into Profit-Makers Says Vet Operator," *Variety*, 8 January 1947, 74.

2. "Four Kinds of Film Situations," *Variety*, 28 January 1959.

3. Douglas Gomery, *Shared Pleasures: A History of Movie Presentation in the United States* (London: British Film Institute, 1992), 184.

4. "Lopert, Playing Indies Game, Takes Over Plaza Theatre, N.Y.; Importers Need Own Showcase," *Variety*, 4 December 1957.

5. "Stix Still Nix British Pix," *Variety*, 18 June 1947, 16.

6. "7 Out of 10 Sureseaters Click," *Variety*, 27 July 1949, 13.

7. Elmer Balaban, interview by author, 19 April 1996, Chicago, tape recording.

8. Springer, "'Sick' Theatres Can Be Cured," 74; "17 Houses Plug Foreign Policy," *Variety*, 12 March 1947, 31.

9. "Stix Still Nix British Pix," 16.

10. Richard Brandt, telephone interview by author, 5 September 1996, tape recording.

11. Gomery, *Shared Pleasures*, 188. As art houses became popular, however, plans were made for larger theaters. Leon Siritzky, for example, converted the 2,200-seat Ambassador Theatre in Brooklyn into an art house. "Small-Seaters Have Better Chance at Belly Benefits—Cummins," *Variety*, 26 February 1947, 29.

12. "7 Out of 10 Sureseaters Click," 13.

13. "Small-Seaters Have Better Chance at Belly Benefits—Cummins," 29.

14. Ibid.

15. "Sureseaters," *Time*, 17 October 1949, 100.

16. "Chicago Ticket Prices Hit Peak," *Motion Picture Herald*, 22 February 1947, 22.

17. "Average Adult Pic Price: 50 cents," *Variety*, 22 September 1948, 3.

18. "New Paris Theatre Ready to Open," *The New York Times*, 5 September 1948, "Paris" clippings file, Billy Rose Theater Collection, Performing Arts Research Library, New York Public Library at Lincoln Center, New York.

19. Fine Arts Theatre advertisement for *The Red Shoes, The Hollywood Reporter*, 27 December 1948, 5.

20. The decision to four-wall a film had a great deal to do with a recent court decision that forbade distributors from setting minimum prices for exhibitors. Universal, which was part of this ruling, could not tell exhibitors to set the price for *Henry V* and so rented out theaters (four-walled) in order to charge the $2.40 admission price. Eagle-Lion, on the other hand, which distributed *The Red Shoes*, was not part of the court decision and therefore worked with exhibitors to set the admission price at the same $2.40. "U and EL in Direct Opposition, Both with Rank Films," *Variety*, 22 September 1948, 9. Some "prestige," mainstream films, such as *The Best Years of Our Lives*, were also road shown and audiences were charged top prices.

21. Art house attendance also permitted audiences to dress less formally than did these other high-culture pursuits.

22. "Maurer's French Yen," *Variety*, 19 November 1947, 22.

23. Balaban, interview by author.

24. Richard Stern, interview by author, 8 October 1996, Wilmette, Ill., tape recording.

25. "Italian Newsreel in American Market," *Variety*, 11 February 1948, 6.

26. "N.Y. House Keys Pathé's US Chain," *Variety*, 18 February 1948, 6.

27. "Chi Class Nabe, Esquire, a Mecca for Showmen on Deluxe Operation," *Variety*, 25 May 1938, "Esquire" clippings file, Billy Rose Theater Collection, Performing Arts Research Library, New York Public Library at Lincoln Center, New York.

28. "Elmer Balaban—16 mm Ambassador at the 35 mm Court," *Film News*, January 1948, 24.

29. "French-Italian Stage Shows for Foreign Film Theatre on Broadway," *Variety*, 5 June 1946, 25; "Siritzkys Sign Chevalier," *Motion Picture Herald*, 8 June 1946, 40.

30. As Gomery noted, the problems reported with double bills included a concern about eyestrain, the tendency of theaters to pair one "good" film with a "poor" film, and the decrease in exhibition of short films during double-bill programs. Gomery, *Shared Pleasures*, 77-78.

31. Balaban, interview by author.

32. Brandt, interview by author.

33. "Sureseaters Now Surefire B.O.," *Variety*, 26 March 1947, 22.

34. "First 17 months at the Paris: Only 2 Films and Now a 3d.," *The New York Herald Tribune*, 15 January 1950, "Paris" clippings file, Billy Rose Theater Collection, Performing Arts Research Library, New York Public Library at Lincoln Center, New York.

35. Brandt, interview by author. *The Red Shoes* was produced by the Michael Powell and Emeric Pressburger unit for J. Arthur Rank and released in 1948. *Tight Little Island* is discussed in more detail in chapter 1.

36. "100 Weeks Played on B'way in Nabes, 'City' Reopens in First Run," *Variety,* 11 February 1948, 4.

37. Stern, interview by author.

38. Gomery, *Shared Pleasures,* 184.

39. "The Paris," *Theatre Catalog 1948-49,* 96, "Paris" clippings file, Theatre Historical Society, Elmhurst, Ill.

40. Judith Ostberg, "What's Going On?" *The Foreign Films News,* February 1949, "Foreign Films Movie Club" clippings file, Billy Rose Theater Collection, Performing Arts Research Library, New York Public Library at Lincoln Center, New York.

41. "Theatre Planned for 58th Street," *The New York Times,* 30 May 1948, "Paris" clippings file, Billy Rose Theater Collection, Performing Arts Research Library, New York Public Library at Lincoln Center, New York.

42. "New Feathers for Pathé," *Time,* 20 September 1948, 91; "NY House Keys Pathé's US Chain," 6.

43. "Sureseaters Now Surefire B.O.," 22.

44. Stern, interview by author.

45. Gomery, *Shared Pleasures,* 79.

46. Although some art houses continued to serve popcorn, others refused to allow the crunching noise in their theaters.

47. Brandt, interview by author.

48. Christine Grenz, *Trans-Lux: Biography of a Corporation* (Norwalk: Trans-Lux Corporation, 1982), 48.

49. "Film Chain Finds Cure for Box Office Blues," *Business Week,* 22 March 1958, 76.

50. "Manager's Roundtable," *Motion Picture Herald,* 24 May 1947, 55.

51. Mailings are discussed in greater detail later.

52. Balaban, interview by author.

53. Stern, interview by author.

54. Apollo Theatre programs, "Apollo" clippings file, Billy Rose Theater Collection, Performing Arts Research Library, New York Public Library at Lincoln Center, New York.

55. Ambassador Theatre program for *Volpone,* "Ambassador" clippings file, Billy Rose Theater Collection, Performing Arts Research Library, New York Public Library at Lincoln Center, New York.

56. Elysée Theatre program for *Private Life of an Actor,* "Siritzky" clippings file, Billy Rose Theater Collection, Performing Arts Research Library, New York Public Library at Lincoln Center, New York.

57. Fifth Avenue Playhouse program for *Day of Wrath, Blood of a Poet,* and *Zero for Conduct,* 8 December 1949, "Fifth Avenue Playhouse" clippings file, Billy Rose Theater Collection, Performing Arts Research Library, New York Public Library at Lincoln Center, New York.

58. Ibid.

59. *Symphonie Pastorale* was a French-language film directed by Jean Delannoy that was based on a story by the Nobel Prize–winning author André Gide. Pathé produced the film.

60. Paris Theatre program for *Symphonie Pastorale,* 13 September 1948.

61. *Stairway to Heaven* was a British film produced, directed, and written by Michael Powell and Emeric Pressburger for J. Arthur Rank.

62. The subscription policy of the Park Avenue Theatre under the management of Walter Reade is discussed in greater detail in chapter 2.

63. Park Avenue Theatre program for *Stairway to Heaven.*

64. For example, the glitzy film premiere generally associated with the opening of a Hollywood film was rarely imitated for the premiere of an art film. However, there were reports that the Fine Arts Theatre in Los Angeles began its art film policy with a "traditional Hollywood style" premiere of *The Red Shoes.* This premiere, a benefit for a Greek Orthodox Church, was "garnished with search lights, music, film fans and stars." "Fine Arts Will Splash with 'Red

Shoes' Preem," *The Hollywood Reporter,* 27 December 1948, 5. This sort of film opening probably had more to do with the fact that the theater was in Los Angeles than that it was an art house opening.

65. Brandt, interview by author.

66. Some art house operators also advertised on FM radio stations, which at that time ran primarily educational and "highbrow" programming. Stern, interview by author.

67. Charles Teitel, telephone interview by author, 4 August 1996, tape recording.

68. Ibid.

69. There certainly are examples of art films' being promoted through outdoor signs and lobby displays that were not subtle. This practice was probably more common in smaller towns or cities where art film attendance was not quite as strong as in the major urban areas and art houses were working to build up attendance. For example, a photograph in *Motion Picture Herald* showed Dallas's Telenews, which had plastered the front of the theater with posters and photos of its current feature, *The Specter of the Rose. Motion Picture Herald,* 12 April 1947, 49.

70. Gomery, *Shared Pleasures,* 186.

71. Midtown Theatre mailing for *Open City,* 1948, "Open City," clippings file, Billy Rose Theater Collection, Performing Arts Research Library, New York Public Library at Lincoln Center, New York.

72. Ibid.

73. Stern, interview by author.

74. Mary Beth Haralovich, "Motion Picture Advertising: Industrial and Social Forces and Affects, 1930–1948," Ph.D. diss., University of Wisconsin—Madison, 1984, 1.

75. Dallas Smythe, Parker B. Lusk, and Charles A. Lewis, "Portrait of an Art-Theater Audience," *Quarterly of Film, Radio and Television* 8 (Fall 1953): 30. See also Ronald J. Faber, Thomas C. O'Guinn, and Andrew P. Hardy, "Art Films in the Suburbs: A Comparison of Popular and Art Film Audiences," *Current Research in Film: Audiences, Economics, and Law,* vol. 4, ed. Bruce A. Austin (New Jersey: Ablex, 1988), 48.

76. "Sureseaters," 102.

77. Stern, interview by author.

78. Teitel, interview by author.

79. "Exhibs Voice Pressbook Beefs," *Variety,* 21 August 1946, 15.

80. Balaban, interview by author.

81. Brandt, interview by author.

82. "Newspaper Ads Sell Stage Show for Parkhurst," *Motion Picture Herald,* 22 February 1947, 63.

83. Stern, interview by author.

84. Esquire Theatre advertisement for *Champion* and Cinema Theatre advertisement for *Blanche Fury, The Chicago Tribune,* 1 September 1949, part 2, 15.

85. Balaban, interview by author.

86. Ibid.

87. Teitel, interview by author.

88. Ibid.

89. Esquire advertisement for *Never Say Goodbye* and Cinema advertisement for *On Approval, The Chicago Tribune,* 15 March 1947, 14.

90. Balaban, interview by author.

91. John Rehm, *Advertising Agency,* April 1950, 70, quoted in Haralovich, "Motion Picture Advertising," 226.

92. Richard Thruelsen, "Movie-House Manager," *Saturday Evening Post,* 15 November 1947, 90.

93. "Pointing Up Sexy Angles of Femme Star in Ads Spices Nipups on Films," *Variety,* 12 January 1949, 4.

94. The rules added to the voluntary Advertising Code included: "Clothed figures shall not be represented in such manner as to be offensive or contrary to good taste or morals" and "Court actions relating to censoring of pictures ... are not to be capitalized in advertising or publicity." "Purifying the Ads," *Newsweek,* 11 August 1947, 89.

95. RKO Grand Theatre advertisement for *Smash Up, The Chicago Tribune,* 19 March 1947, 27.

96. Esquire Theatre advertisement for *Smash Up, The Chicago Tribune,* 24 June 1947, 18.

97. "Film Chain Finds Cure for Box Office Blues," 75. Interestingly, though it is not clear when this occurred, Sher eventually turned his chain to showing "adult films when Sher discovered that it was the skin that was bringing the audiences in." Eric Schaefer, *"Bold! Daring! Shocking! True!" A History of Exploitation Films, 1919-1959* (Durham: Duke University Press, 1999), 337.

98. Brandt, interview by author.

99. Stern, interview by author.

100. World Playhouse advertisement for *Open City, The Chicago Tribune,* 18 May 1946, 14.

101. World Playhouse advertisement for *Portrait of a Woman, The Chicago Tribune,* 26 October 1946, 15.

102. Surf Theatre advertisement for *Jenny Lamour, The Chicago Tribune,* 18 June 1948, part 2, 9.

103. Arthur Mayer, *Merely Colossal* (New York: Simon and Schuster, 1953), 233.

104. Ibid.

105. Mayer had experience as both a film distributor and an exhibitor. He owned New York's Rialto Theatre, which, until the late 1940s, specialized in grade-B horror films, causing Mayer to become known as the "Merchant of Menace." Mayer, *Merely Colossal,* 170. In the late 1940s, as Mayer considered switching the Rialto to an art house policy, *Variety* reported, "He'd like to latch on to foreign pix which are steeped in a reminiscent flavor of action and sex so that the drop-ins continue to haunt his theatre." "Rialto, Broadway Horror Showcase, May Switch to Class Lingos," *Variety,* 29 October 1947, 5.

106. "Sexacious Selling Best B.O. Slant for Foreign Language Films in U.S.," *Variety,* 9 June 1948, 2.

107. Studio Theatre advertisement for *Waltz Time, The Chicago Tribune,* 20 July 1946, 10.

108. Sheridan Theatre advertisement for *Waltz Time, The Chicago Tribune,* 23 September 1946.

109. Alba Theatre advertisement for *Open City, The Chicago Tribune,* 30 August 1946, 20; Imperial Theatre advertisement for *Open City, The Chicago Tribune,* 13 October 1946, part 6, 19.

110. "Franco-Swedish Duo Parlays into OK BO," *Variety,* 29 September 1948, 29.

111. Harding Theatre advertisement for *Blithe Spirit, The Chicago Tribune,* 29 March 1946, 29; Cinema Theatre advertisement for *Blithe Spirit, The Chicago Tribune,* 20 June 1946, 21.

112. Richard deCordova, "The Rise of the Art Film in Post-War Chicago," paper presented at the College of Art Association Convention, Boston, 1987.

Conclusion

1. Raymond Williams, "Base and Superstructure in Marxist Cultural Theory," *New Left Review* 82 (November/December 1973): 11.

2. Andy Newman, "More than Just a Movie House," *The New York Times,* 12 November 1998, E1.

3. With approximately two hundred members, Cinema 16 began screening films as a private film society in 1948 at the Fifth Avenue Playhouse. Cecile Starr, "Occasion for Cheers," *The Saturday Review,* 9 December 1953, 36. Cinema 16 screened films in art houses at times when the theaters did not have their own commercial screenings scheduled. For more information about Cinema 16, see the special *Wide Angle* issues entitled "Cinema 16: Documents

Toward a History of the Film Society," Parts I and II, *Wide Angle* 19 (January 1997 and April 1997).

4. Starting at $10 in 1948, a Cinema 16 membership cost $16.50 by 1962. "Private," *New Yorker*, 5 May 1962, 36.

5. The membership of celebrities, such as Allen Ginsburg, Leonard Bernstein, Marlon Brando, and Joshua Logan, also added to the prestige of the society. Starr, "Occasion for Cheers," 37; Amos Vogel, "Cinema 16: An Interview with Amos Vogel," interview by Scott MacDonald, *Film Quarterly* 37 (1984): 23.

6. Interestingly, the title of Amos Vogel's book is *Film as a Subversive Art* (New York: Random House, 1964). It is unlikely that many art house operators would have referred to film as subversive.

7. This comparison of Cinema 16 and commercial art houses is meant not to deny any of the real cultural opportunities available through art houses, but only to note the differences in how these two representatives of potential alternative cultures attempted to attract audiences.

8. Television appeared to take the place of motion pictures as the predominant form of family entertainment, thus requiring the film industry to find new ways to attract audiences to movie theaters.

9. Eric Schaefer, "Massacre of Pleasure: Historicizing the Sexploitation Film," paper presented at the 17th Annual Ohio University Film Conference, Athens, Ohio, 1995.

10. Bosley Crowther, "Hollywood Accents the Downbeat," *The New York Times*, 16 March 1952.

11. Bosley Crowther, "The 'Class' Theatre," *The New York Times*, 4 May 1952.

12. Milton Esterow, "Adult Films, New Comfort Revive City's Movie Going," *The New York Times*, 5 May 1958.

13. Arthur Knight, "Art Gallery for the Millions," *Theatre Arts*, January 1953, 74.

14. "Art House Boom," *Newsweek*, 28 May 1962, 102.

15. Ibid.

16. Michael DeAngelis, "Art Cinema Hits the Suburbs: Exhibition Practices of the 1960s and 1970s," paper presented at the Society for Cinema Studies Conference, West Palm Beach, Florida, 1999.

17. Christine Ogan, "The Audience for Foreign Film in the United States," *Journal of Communication* 40 (Autumn 1990): 66; Schaefer, "Massacre of Pleasure," 1995.

18. Ogan, "The Audience for Foreign Film in the United States," 62.

19. Schaefer, "Massacre of Pleasure," 1995.

20. For example, Schaefer noted that Louis Sher, who operated a circuit of art houses through the 1960s (he had fourteen theaters by 1960 and forty-three by 1972) began distributing sexploitation films in 1965. Ibid.

21. David Elliott, "World Playhouse Shuts Down Tonight," *The Chicago Tribune*, 10 February 1972.

22. Paul Gardner, "Foreign Films, Popular in U.S. in '60's, Being Treated Like Foreigners in '70's," *The New York Times*, 4 October 1973.

23. Ibid.

24. Ibid.

25. Justin Wyatt, *High Concept: Movies and Marketing in Hollywood* (Austin: University of Texas Press, 1994), 77.

26. Ibid., 78–79; Beverly Walker and Leonard Klady, "Cinema Sanctuaries," *Film Comment* 22 (May/June 1986): 63.

27. Douglas Gomery, *Shared Pleasures: A History of Movie Presentation in the United States* (London: British Film Institute, 1992), 98.

28. Ibid., 100

29. "Foreign Features Show Potential to Become Videocassette Staple," *Variety,* 13 October 1982, 50.

30. Films like *El Norte* (Gregory Nave, 1983), *The Brother from Another Planet* (John Sayles, 1984), and *Stranger than Paradise* (Jim Jarmusch, 1984) were noted for their success.

31. Ralph Donnelly, "Classics Arms of Majors Boost 'Little' Pic Prices, but Exhibs Enjoy Title Surplus," *Variety,* 11 January 1984, 11.

32. Debra Goldman, "Business for Art's Sake," *American Film,* April 1987, 45.

33. Ibid., 48.

34. Turner Entertainment eventually bought New Line, and New Line became part of Time Warner when Time Warner acquired Turner Entertainment in 1996. For more on New Line, see Justin Wyatt, "The Formation of the 'Major Independent': Miramax, New Line, and the New Hollywood," in *Contemporary Hollywood Cinema,* ed. Steve Neale and Murray Smith (London: Routledge, 1998), 76–78.

35. Amy Taubin, "Walking a Fine, New Line," *The Village Voice,* 19 November 1996, 3.

36. Gomery, *Shared Pleasures,* 195.

37. Charles Teitel, "Abe Teitel Had a Dream," *Variety,* 5 December 1984.

38. Jim Robbins, "USA Plans Natl. Arthouse Circuit Following Boston Ventures Deal," *Variety,* 16 July 1986, 7.

39. Walker and Klady, "Cinema Sanctuaries," 66.

40. "Specialized Theatre Gives N.Y. an Outlet for Smaller Pictures," *Variety,* 10 June 1987, 7.

41. For two articles that discuss this point, see Alexander Cockburn, "Rituals in the Dark," *American Film,* August 1991, 25–27, and David Denby, "The Moviegoers," *The New Yorker,* 6 April 1998, 94–98.

42. Richard Stern, interview by author, 8 October 1996, Wilmette, Ill., tape recording.

43. Ibid.

44. Carolyn Geer, "Coming Soon: An Art Theater Near You," *Forbes,* 6 July 1998, 45.

45. Dave Karger, "Art House Buildup," *Entertainment Weekly,* 6 June 1997, 35.

46. Ibid.

47. Dan Margolis and Monica Roman, "Exhibs Target Stix for Niche Pix," *Variety,* 24 March 1997, 11.

48. Geer, "Coming Soon," 46.

Bibliography

Note: Several years of certain trade journals have been reviewed in full. These years are indicated in the bibliographic entries for the journals, and specific articles from these years have not been listed individually in the bibliography, although full citations are in the notes. Additionally, full citation information was not available for some materials found in archives. In these cases archival information has been provided both in the bibliography and in the notes.

Abbie, Lynn. "Esquire Theatre." *Chicago Art Deco Society,* Spring 1986. "Esquire" clippings file. Theatre Historical Society, Elmhurst, Ill.
Adorno, Theodor, and Max Horkheimer. *Dialectic of Enlightenment.* New York: Herder and Herder, 1972.
Amidei, Sergio. "'Open City' Revisited." *The New York Times,* 16 February 1947.
Aries, Phillipe. "The Family and the City in the Old World and New." In *Changing Images of the Family,* ed. Virginia Tufte and Barbara Myerhoff, 29–41. New Haven: Yale University Press, 1979.
"Art House Boom." *Newsweek,* 28 May 1962, 102.
Auerbach, Erich. *Mimesis: The Representation of Reality in Western Literature.* Trans. Willard R. Trask. Princeton: Princeton University Press, 1953.
Austin, Bruce A. *Immediate Seating: A Look at Movie Audiences.* California: Wadsworth Publishing Co., 1989.
Balaban, Elmer. Interview by author, 19 April 1996, Chicago. Tape recording.
Balio, Tino. "A Mature Oligopoly, 1930–1948." In *The American Film Industry,* rev. ed., ed. Tino Balio, 253–84. Madison: University of Wisconsin Press, 1985.

————. "Retrenchment, Reappraisal, and Reorganization." In *The American Film Industry,* rev. ed., ed. Tino Balio, 401–47. Madison: University of Wisconsin Press, 1985.

"Banned Bicycle." *Newsweek,* 13 March 1950, 78.

Barr, Charles. *Ealing Studios.* London: Cameron and Tayleur Books, 1977.

Bazin, André. "De Sica: Metteur en Scene." In *What is Cinema?* Vol. 2, 61–78. Berkeley: University of California Press, 1971.

Beaver, Frank E. *On Film.* New York: McGraw-Hill, 1983.

Belton, John. *Widescreen Cinema.* Cambridge: Harvard University Press, 1992.

Bordwell, David. "The Art Cinema as a Mode of Film Practice." *Film Criticism* 4 (Fall 1979): 56–64.

————. *Narration in the Fiction Film.* Madison: University of Wisconsin Press, 1985

Bordwell, David, Janet Staiger, and Kristin Thompson. *The Classical Hollywood Cinema: Film Style and Mode of Production to 1960.* New York: Columbia University Press, 1985.

Bourdieu, Pierre. *Distinction: A Theoretical Critique of the Judgment of Taste.* Trans. Richard Nice. Cambridge: Harvard University Press, 1984.

————. "The Production of Belief: Contribution to an Economy of Symbolic Goods." *Media, Culture and Society* 2 (1980): 261–93.

"Box Office Pinch." *Business Week,* 4 October 1947, 62–63.

Brady, Thomas F. "The Hollywood Wire." *The New York Times,* 14 November 1948.

Brandon, Thomas J. "Foreign Film Distribution in the U.S." Interview by Edouard L. de Laurot and Jonas Mekas. *Film Culture* 2 (1956): 15–17.

Brandt, Richard. Telephone interview by author, 5 September 1996. Tape recording.

Brodie, John, and Monica Roman. "H'wood May Be Too Big for Its Niches." *Variety,* 10 June 1996, 1.

Brown, John Mason. Review of *Lost Boundaries.* In *The Saturday Review,* 10 September 1949, 33.

Budd, Mike. "Authorship as a Commodity: The Art Cinema and *The Cabinet of Dr. Caligari.*" *Wide Angle* 6 (1984): 12–19.

————. "The Moments of *Caligari.*" In *The Cabinet of Dr. Caligari: Texts, Contexts, Histories,* ed. Mike Budd, 7–119. New Brunswick: Rutgers University Press, 1990.

————. "The National Board of Review and the Early Art Cinema in New York: *The Cabinet of Dr. Caligari* and Affirmative Culture." *Cinema Journal* 26 (Fall 1986): 3–18.

Burstyn, Joseph. "Talent Surplus in France." *The New York Times,* 27 August 1939. "Joseph Burstyn" clippings file. Billy Rose Theater Collection, Performing Arts Research Library, New York Public Library at Lincoln Center, New York.

The Chicago Tribune, 1945–1952.

"Chi's Class Nabe, Esquire, a Mecca for Showmen on Deluxe Operation." *Variety,* 25 May 1938. "Esquire" clippings file. Billy Rose Theater Collection, Performing Arts Research Library, New York Public Library at Lincoln Center, New York.

Cianfarra, Jane. "Italian Film Industry Is Wary of Americans." *The New York Times,* 2 May 1950.

Cinema 16 Collection. Anthology Film Archives. New York.

"Cinema 16: Documents Toward a History of the Film Society," parts 1 and 2. *Wide Angle* special issues (January 1997 and April 1997).

Cockburn, Alexander. "Rituals in the Dark." *American Film,* August 1991, 25–27.

Cook, David. *A History of Narrative Film,* 2nd ed. New York: W. W. Norton and Co., 1990.

Course, Irwin (acting director of the New York State Department of Education's Motion Picture Division). Letter to Arthur Mayer and Joseph Burstyn, Inc., dated 6 February 1946. File 47909, Box 1209. Motion Picture Records of the New York State Department of Education's Motion Picture Division, New York State Archives, Albany, New York.

Crowther, Bosley. "The 'Class' Theatre." *The New York Times,* 4 May 1952.

————. "Hollywood Accents the Downbeat." *The New York Times,* 16 March 1952.

———. Review of *Lost Boundaries*. In *The New York Times*, 1 July 1949, 14.

———. Review of *Open City*. In *The New York Times*, 26 February 1946, 24.

———. Review of *Passionelle*. In *The New York Times*, 1 March 1948, 17.

———. Review of *The Quiet One*. In *The New York Times*, 14 February 1949, 15.

———. Review of *Torment*. In *The New York Times*, 22 April 1947, 34.

———. "Unkindest Cut." *The New York Times*, 2 May 1950.

DeAngelis, Michael. "Art Cinema Hits the Suburbs: Exhibition Practices of the 1960s and 1970s." Paper presented at the Society for Cinema Studies Conference, West Palm Beach, Florida, 1999.

DeCherney, Peter. "Cult of Attention: An Introduction to Seymour Stern and Harry Alan Potamkin (Contra Kracauer) on the Ideal Movie Theater." *Spectator* 18 (Spring/Summer 1998): 18–25.

DeCordova, Richard. "The Rise of the Art Film in Post-War Chicago." Paper presented at the College Art Association Convention, Boston, 1987.

Denby, David. "The Moviegoers." *The New Yorker*, 6 April 1998, 94–98.

Denney, Reuel. *The Astonished Muse*. Chicago: University of Chicago Press, 1957.

Donnelly, Ralph. "Classics Arms of Majors Boost 'Little' Pic Prices, but Exhibs Enjoy Title Surplus." *Variety*, 11 January 1984, 11.

Dowdy, Andrew. *"Movies Are Better Than Ever": Widescreen Memories of the Fifties*. New York: William Morrow and Company, 1973.

"Dowling, Lopert, Korda Form Distributing Co." *Boxoffice*, 16 December 1950, 37.

Draper, Ellen. "'Controversy Has Probably Destroyed Forever the Context': *The Miracle* and Movie Censorship in America in the Fifties." *Velvet Light Trap* 25 (Spring 1990): 69–79.

Elliott, David. "World Playhouse Shuts Down Tonight." *The Chicago Tribune*, 10 February 1972.

Ellis, Jack C. *A History of Film*, 2nd ed. Englewood Cliffs: Prentice-Hall, 1985.

"Elmer Balaban—16 mm Ambassador at the 35 mm Court." *Film News*, January 1948, 24.

Elsaesser, Thomas. "Putting on a Show: The European Art Movie." *Sight and Sound*, April 1954, 22–26.

Esterow, Milton. "Adult Films, New Comfort Revive City's Movie Going." *The New York Times*, 5 May 1958.

Faber, Ronald J., Thomas C. O'Guinn, and Andrew P. Hardy. "Art Films in the Suburbs: A Comparison of Popular and Art Film Audiences." In *Current Research in Film: Audiences, Economics and Law*, vol. 4, ed. Bruce A. Austin. 45–53. Norwood, N.J.: Ablex, 1988.

Falkenberg, Pamela. "'Hollywood' and the 'Art Cinema' as a Bipolar Modeling System: *A Bout de Souffle* and *Breathless*." *Wide Angle* 7 (1985): 44–53.

Farber, Manny. Review of *Lost Boundaries*. In *The Nation*, 30 July 1949, 114.

———. Review of *Open City*. In *The New Republic*, 15 July 1946, 46.

Farber, Stephen. "The Power of Movie Critics." *American Scholar*, Summer 1976, 419–23.

"Film Chain Finds Cure for Box Office Blues." *Business Week*, 22 March 1958, 72–76.

Film Daily Year Book. New York: J. W. Alicoate, 1940–51, 1964.

"First 17 months at the Paris: Only 2 Films and Now a 3d." *The New York Herald Tribune*, 15 January 1950. "Paris" clippings file. Billy Rose Theater Collection, Performing Arts Research Library, New York Public Library at Lincoln Center, New York.

"Foreign Features Show Potential to Become Videocassette Staple." *Variety*, 13 October 1982, 50.

"Foreign Films Movie Club Launched." *The Foreign Films News*, May 1948, 1. "Foreign Films Movie Club" clippings file. Billy Rose Theater Collection, Performing Arts Research Library, New York Public Library at Lincoln Center, New York.

"Foreign Language Chain Planned by Sidney Pink." *Boxoffice*, 22 March 1947, 35.

"Foreign Showcase." *Newsweek*, 20 September 1948, 98.

Frank, Stanley. "Sure-seaters Discover an Audience." *Nation's Business*, January 1952, 34–36, 69.

Gans, Herbert. *Popular Culture and High Culture: An Analysis and Evaluation of Taste*. New York: Basic Books, 1974.

Gardner, Paul. "Foreign Films, Popular in U.S. in '60's, Being Treated Like Foreigners in '70's." *The New York Times*, 4 October 1973.

Geer, Carolyn. "Coming Soon: An Art Theater Near You." *Forbes*, 6 July 1998, 45–46.

"Global Interest in Aid for Foreign Films." *Christian Science Monitor*, 2 September 1950, 15.

Goldman, Debra. "Business for Art's Sake." *American Film*, April 1987, 44–48.

Gomery, Douglas. *Shared Pleasures: A History of Movie Presentation in the United States*. London: British Film Institute, 1992.

Gorelik, Mordecai. *New Theatres for Old*. 1940; rpt. New York: Octagon Books, 1975.

Grenz, Christine. *Trans-Lux: Biography of a Corporation*. Norwalk: Trans-Lux Corporation, 1982.

Griffith, Richard. "European Films and American Audiences." *Saturday Review of Literature*, 13 January 1951, 52–54, 85–87.

Guback, Thomas H. "Hollywood's International Market." In *The American Film Industry*, rev. ed., ed. Tino Balio, 463–86. Madison: University of Wisconsin Press, 1985.

Guernsey, Otis L., Jr. "'Art Movies' Low in Quality but 'Art Theaters' Thrive." *The New York Herald Tribune*, 30 October 1949. "Cinema—Foreign-U.S." clippings file. Billy Rose Theater Collection, Performing Arts Research Library, New York Public Library at Lincoln Center, New York.

Guzman, Anthony Henry. "The Exhibition and Reception of European Films in the United States during the 1920s." Ph.D. diss., University of California at Los Angeles, 1993.

Hall, John R. "The Capital(s) of Cultures: A Nonholistic Approach to Status Situations, Class, Gender and Ethnicity." In *Cultivating Differences: Symbolic Boundaries and the Making of Inequalities*, ed. Michéle Lamont and Marcel Fournier, 257–85. Chicago: University of Chicago Press, 1992.

Hall, Leonard. *Washington Daily*, 1 April 1927. Quoted in Bettina Gunczy. "The Bloodless Revolt." *National Board of Review Magazine* 2 (May 1927): 1.

Haralovich, Mary Beth. "Motion Picture Advertising: Industrial and Social Forces and Affects, 1930–1948." Ph.D. diss., University of Wisconsin—Madison, 1984.

"High-brow, Low-brow, Middle-brow." *Life*, 11 May 1949, 99–102.

The Hollywood Reporter, 1948–49.

Horak, Jan-Christopher. "The First American Film Avant-Garde, 1919–1945." In *Lovers of Cinema: The First American Film Avant-Garde, 1919–1945*, ed. Jan-Christopher Horak, 14–66. Madison: University of Wisconsin Press, 1995.

"How Do You See the Movies? As Entertainment and Offensive at Times or as Candid Art?" *Newsweek*, 8 August 1955, 50–51.

Huettig, Mae D. "Economic Control of the Motion Picture Industry." In *The American Film Industry*, rev. ed., ed. Tino Balio, 285–310. Madison: University of Wisconsin Press, 1985.

Hutchens, John. "L'Enfant Terrible." *Theatre Arts Monthly*, September 1929. Michael Mindlin Collection, Film Study Center, Museum of Modern Art, New York.

"Ilya Lopert Dies; Film Official, 65." *The New York Times*, 1 March 1971. "Ilya Lopert" clippings file. Billy Rose Theater Collection, Performing Arts Research Library, New York Public Library at Lincoln Center, New York.

"Independent Income." *Time*, 5 November 1945, 84.

"Independents' Day." *Time*, 17 May 1948, 91–92.

Inglis, Ruth A. "Self Regulation in Operation." In *The American Film Industry*, rev. ed., ed. Tino Balio, 377–400. Madison: University of Wisconsin Press, 1985.

"Jean Goldwurm." Press release. "Jean Goldwurm" clippings file. Billy Rose Theater Collection, Performing Arts Research Library, New York Public Library at Lincoln Center, New York.

Johnston, Eric. "The Motion Picture on the Threshold of a Decisive Decade." In *Motion Picture Association of America 24th Annual Report*, 25 March 1946.

Karger, Dave. "Art House Buildup." *Entertainment Weekly*, 6 June 1997, 35.

Kasson, John F. *Amusing the Million: Coney Island at the Turn of the Century.* New York: Hill and Wang, 1978.

Kleinhans, Chuck. "Independent Features: Hopes and Dreams." In *New American Cinema,* ed. Jon Lewis, 307–27. Durham: Duke University Press, 1998.

Knight, Arthur. "Art Gallery for the Millions." *Theatre Arts,* January 1953, 74–77.

Kumlien, Gunnar D. "The Artless Art of Italian Films." *Commonweal,* 22 December 1953, 177–79.

Lane, Jim. "Critical and Cultural Reception of the European Art Film in 1950s America: A Case Study of the Brattle Theatre (Cambridge, Massachusetts)." *Film and History* 24 (1994): 49–64.

Lears, Jackson. "A Matter of Taste: Corporate Cultural Hegemony in a Mass-Consumption Society." In *Recasting America: Culture and Politics in the Age of Cold War,* ed. Lary May, 38–57. Chicago: University of Chicago Press, 1989.

Lefkovits, Harold. "The Little Cinema Marches On." *The New York Times,* 6 February 1938.

Leprohon, Pierre. *The Italian Cinema.* New York: Praeger, 1972.

Lev, Peter. *The Euro-American Cinema.* Austin: University of Texas Press, 1993.

Levine, Lawrence W. *Highbrow/Lowbrow: The Emergence of Cultural Hierarchy in America.* Cambridge: Harvard University Press, 1988.

"Lots of New Foreign Films." *PM New York,* 10 November 1947. "Foreign Films" clippings file. Billy Rose Theater Collection, Performing Arts Research Library, New York Public Library at Lincoln Center, New York.

Lowenthal, Leo. "Historical Perspectives of Popular Culture." In *Mass Culture: The Popular Arts in America,* ed. Bernard Rosenberg and David Manning White, 46–57. New York: Free Press, 1957.

Lynes, Russell. "Highbrow, Lowbrow, Middlebrow." *Harper's,* February 1949, 19–28.

———. "The Tastemakers." *Harper's,* June 1947, 481–91

Macdonald, Dwight. "A Theory of Mass Culture." In *Mass Culture: The Popular Arts in America,* ed. Bernard Rosenberg and David Manning White, 59–73. New York: Free Press, 1957.

MacDonald, Scott. "Amos Vogel and Cinema 16." *Wide Angle* 9 (1987): 38–51.

Margolis, Dan, and Monica Roman. "Exhibs Target Stix for Niche Pix." *Variety,* 24 March 1997, 11.

Matsoukas, Nick John. "The Unconventional Punch and Judy." *Exhibitors Herald-World,* 25 October 1930, 35–36.

Mayer, Arthur. *Merely Colossal.* New York: Simon and Schuster, 1953.

Mayer, Michael. *Foreign Films on American Screens.* New York: Arco, 1965.

McGowan, Roscoe. "Easy Now, Critic'll Keep His Shirt On—Regular One." *The New York Daily News,* 29 October 1926. Michael Mindlin Collection, Film Study Center, Museum of Modern Art, New York.

Mills, C. Wright. *White Collar.* New York: Oxford University Press, 1956.

Mindlin, Michael. "The Little Cinema Movement." *Theatre Arts,* July 1928.

Michael Mindlin Collection, Film Study Center, Museum of Modern Art, New York.

"Miracle on 58th Street." *Harper's,* April 1951, 106–8.

Mitgang, Herbert. "Transatlantic 'Miracle' Man." *Park East,* August 1952, 33–36.

"Moral Breach." *Time,* 30 October 1949, 76.

Motion Picture Herald, 1946–47.

"Movies Worry." *Business Week,* 16 March 1946, 8.

"The National Board of Review." *Film Year Book,* 1927, 477.

Navasky, Victor S. *Naming Names.* New York: Viking Press, 1980.

Neale, Steven. "Art Cinema as Institution." *Screen* 22 (1981): 11–39.

"Nelson in Movies." *Business Week,* 30 June 1945, 22.

"New Feathers for Pathé." *Time,* 20 September 1948, 91–92.

"New Paris Theatre Ready to Open." *The New York Times,* 5 September 1948. "Paris" clippings file. Billy Rose Theater Collection, Performing Arts Research Library, New York Public Library at Lincoln Center, New York.

"New Type of Theatre for Newsreels Opens." *The New York Times,* 16 March 1931.

The New York Times, 22 September 1926. Michael Mindlin Collection, Film Study Center, Museum of Modern Art, New York.

"Newark to Have Unusual Theater." *The Newark News,* 30 October 1929. Michael Mindlin Collection, Film Study Center, Museum of Modern Art, New York.

Newman, Andy. "More than Just a Movie House." *The New York Times,* 12 November 1998, E1.

Nochlin, Linda. *Realism.* London: Penguin Books, 1971.

O'Brien, S. J. Editorial. *Electrical News Letter* 4 (15 February 1927). Michael Mindlin Collection, Film Study Center, Museum of Modern Art, New York.

Ogan, Christine. "The Audience for Foreign Film in the United States." *Journal of Communication* 40 (Autumn 1990): 58–77.

Older, Julia. "I Hate the Movies." *Mayfair,* December 1926. Michael Mindlin Collection, Film Study Center, Museum of Modern Art, New York.

Ostberg, Judith. "What's Going On?" *The Foreign Films News,* February 1949. "Foreign Films Movie Club" clippings file. Billy Rose Theater Collection, Performing Arts Research Library, New York Public Library at Lincoln Center, New York.

"The Paris." *Theatre Catalog 1948–49,* 96. "Paris" clippings file. Theatre Historical Society, Elmhurst, Ill.

Peiss, Kathy. *Cheap Amusements: Working Women and Leisure in Turn-of-the-Century New York.* Philadelphia: Temple University Press, 1986.

Phillips, Lisa. "Architect of Endless Innovation." In *Frederick Kiesler,* ed. Lisa Phillips, 13–35. New York: Whitney Museum of Art, 1989.

"Private." *New Yorker,* 5 May 1962, 35–36.

Pryor, Thomas M. "Boom Market for Yesteryear's Movies." *The New York Times,* 30 January 1944.

———. "Foreign Films Become Big Business." *The New York Times,* 8 February 1948.

———. "Front Runner in Foreign Film Sweepstakes." *The New York Times.* "Joseph Burstyn" clippings file. Billy Rose Theater Collection, Performing Arts Research Library, New York Public Library at Lincoln Center, New York.

———. "Hoeing His Own Row." *The New York Times,* 26 June 1949.

"Purifying the Ads." *Newsweek,* 11 August 1947, 89.

Rabinovitz, Lauren. *Points of Resistance: Women, Power and Politics in the New Avant-Garde Cinema, 1943–71.* Urbana: University of Illinois Press, 1991.

Randall, Richard S. *Censorship of the Movies: The Social and Political Control of a Mass Medium.* Madison: University of Wisconsin Press, 1968.

Ray, Cyril. "These British Movies." *Harper's,* June 1947, 516–23.

"Reissues in Current Year Four Times over 1945–46." *Boxoffice,* 31 May 1947, 9.

Review of *Lost Boundaries.* In *The Exhibitor,* 6 July 1949, 2645.

Review of *Lost Boundaries.* In *Theatre Arts,* October 1949, 96.

Review of *Open City.* In *Life,* 4 March 1946, 111.

Riesman, David, with Nathan Glazer and Reuel Denney. *The Lonely Crowd.* New Haven: Yale University Press, 1961.

Robbins, Jim. "USA Plans Natl. Arthouse Circuit Following Boston Venture Deal." *Variety,* 16 July 1986, 7.

Ross, Andrew. *No Respect: Intellectuals and Popular Culture.* New York: Routledge, 1989.

Rubin, Joan Shelley. *The Making of Middlebrow Culture.* Chapel Hill: University of North Carolina Press, 1992.

Sargeant, Winthrop. "In Defense of the High-brow." *Life,* 11 May 1949, 102.

Schaefer, Eric. "Art and Exploitation: Reconfiguring Foreign Films for American Tastes, 1930–1960." Paper presented at the New England American Studies Association Conference, Providence, Rhode Island, Brown University, 7 May 1994.

———. *"Bold! Daring! Shocking! True!" A History of Exploitation Films, 1919–1959.* Durham: Duke University Press, 1999.

———. "Massacre of Pleasure: Historicizing the Sexploitation Film." Paper presented at the 17th Annual Ohio University Film Conference, Athens, Ohio, 1995.

Schickel, Richard. "Days and Nights in the Arthouse." *Film Comment* 28 (May/June 1992): 32–34.

Seldes, Gilbert. *The Great Audience.* New York: Viking Press, 1950.

Self, Robert. "Systems of Ambiguity in the Art Cinema." *Film Criticism* 4 (Fall 1979): 74–80.

Sherwood, Robert E. "Motion Picture Album." *The New York Evening Post,* 4 December 1946.

Sklar, Robert. *Movie-Made America: A Cultural History of American Movies.* New York: Random House, 1975.

Smythe, Dallas, Parker B. Lusk, and Charles A. Lewis. "Portrait of an Art-Theater Audience." *Quarterly of Film, Radio and Television* 8 (Fall 1953): 28–50.

"Special Theatres Urged for Artistic Pictures." *The New York Times,* 10 October 1926.

"Specialized Theatre Gives N.Y. an Outlet for Smaller Pictures." *Variety,* 10 June 1987, 7.

Spencer, Walter. "Modern Movies: No Kids, No Popcorn." *World Journal Tribune* (New York, N.Y.), 17 October 1966, 13.

Starr, Cecile. "Occasion for Cheers." *The Saturday Review,* 9 December 1953, 36–38.

Stern, Richard. Interview by author, 8 October 1996, Wilmette, Ill. Tape recording.

Stern, Seymour. "An Aesthetic of the Cinema House: A Statement of the Principles Which Constitute the Philosophy and the Format of the Ideal Film Theatre." *The National Board of Review Magazine* 2.5 (May 1927). Rpt. in *Spectator* 18 (Spring/Summer 1998): 26–32.

"Sureseaters." *Time,* 17 October 1949, 100.

Sussman, Warren, with Edward Griffin. "Did Success Spoil the United States? Dual Representations in Postwar America." In *Recasting America: Culture and Politics in the Age of Cold War,* ed. Lary May, 19–37. Chicago: University of Chicago Press, 1989.

"Talk of the Town." *The New Yorker,* 16 November 1946, 23–24.

Taubin, Amy. "Walking a Fine, New Line." *The Village Voice,* 19 November 1996, 3.

Taylor, Nora E. "British Film Goal: Realism." *Christian Science Monitor,* 14 December 1946, 9.

Teitel, Charles. "Abe Teitel Had a Dream." *Variety,* 5 December 1984.

———. Telephone interview by author, 4 August 1996. Tape recording.

"Theatre Planned for 58th Street." *The New York Times,* 30 May 1948. "Paris" clippings file. Billy Rose Theater Collection, Performing Arts Research Library, New York Public Library at Lincoln Center, New York.

Thompson, Kristin. "Dr. Caligari at the Folies-Bergère, or, The Successes of an Early Avant-Garde Film." In *The Cabinet of Dr. Caligari: Texts, Contexts, Histories,* ed. Mike Budd, 121–69. New Brunswick: Rutgers University Press, 1990.

Thruelsen, Richard. "Movie-House Manager." *Saturday Evening Post,* 15 November 1947, 36–37.

Twomey, John. "Some Considerations on the Rise of the Art Film Theater." *Quarterly of Film, Radio and Television* 10 (Spring 1956): 239–47.

"Ultra-Smart Movie House for Hartford." *The Hartford (Conn.) Courant,* December 1926. Michael Mindlin Collection, Film Study Center, Museum of Modern Art, New York.

"U.S. Exports: End of Boom." *Business Week,* 16 August 1947, 103.

Variety, 1945–50.

———, June 1927. Michael Mindlin Collection, Film Study Center, Museum of Modern Art, New York.

Vogel, Amos. "Cinema 16: An Interview with Amos Vogel." Interview by Scott MacDonald. *Film Quarterly* 37 (1984): 19–29.

———. *Film as a Subversive Art.* New York: Random House, 1964.

Wagnleitner, Reinhold. *Coca-Colonization and the Cold War: The Cultural Mission of the United States in Austria after the Second World War.* Trans. Diana M. Wolf. Chapel Hill: University of North Carolina Press, 1994.

Waldman, Walter. "Foreign Film Showings Are on the Upswing." *Boxoffice* 29, November 1947, 18.

Walker, Beverly, and Leonard Klady. "Cinema Sanctuaries." *Film Comment* 22 (May/June 1986): 61–66.

Weinberg, Herman. "The European Film in America." *Theatre Arts,* October 1948, 48–49.

———. "I Title Foreign Films." *Theatre Arts,* April/May 1948, 51.

Willett, Ralph. *The Americanization of Germany, 1945–1949.* London: Routledge, 1989.

Williams, Raymond. "Base and Superstructure in Marxist Cultural Theory." *New Left Review* 82 (November/December 1973): 3–16.

Wohlforth, Robert. "People and Pickets." *The New Republic,* 5 February 1951, 13.

Wolfe, Charles. "The Poetics and Politics of Nonfiction: Documentary Film." In *Grand Design: Hollywood as a Modern Business Enterprise, 1930–1939,* ed. Tino Balio, 351–86. Berkeley: University of California Press, 1993.

"World Pictures." *Business Week,* 8 December 1945, 44.

Wyatt, Justin. "The Formation of the 'Major Independent': Miramax, New Line and the New Hollywood." In *Contemporary Hollywood Cinema,* ed. Steve Neale and Murray Smith, 74–90. London: Routledge.

———. *High Concept: Movies and Marketing in Hollywood.* Austin: University of Texas Press, 1994.

"The Year with One Little Film Group." *The New York Sunday World.* Michael Mindlin Collection, Film Study Center, Museum of Modern Art, New York.

Young, Josh. "Sundown." *The New Republic,* 10 April 1995, 22.

Zorbaugh, Harvey Warren. *The Gold Coast and the Slum: A Sociological Study of Chicago's Near North Side.* Chicago: University of Chicago Press, 1929.

Index

Barbara Wilinsky is assistant professor in the Department of Media Arts at the University of Arizona. Her work has appeared in *Film History, Velvet Light Trap, Quarterly Review of Film and Video, Spectator,* and the anthologies *Mediated Women: Representations in Popular Culture* and *Hollywood Goes Shopping* (Minnesota, 2000).